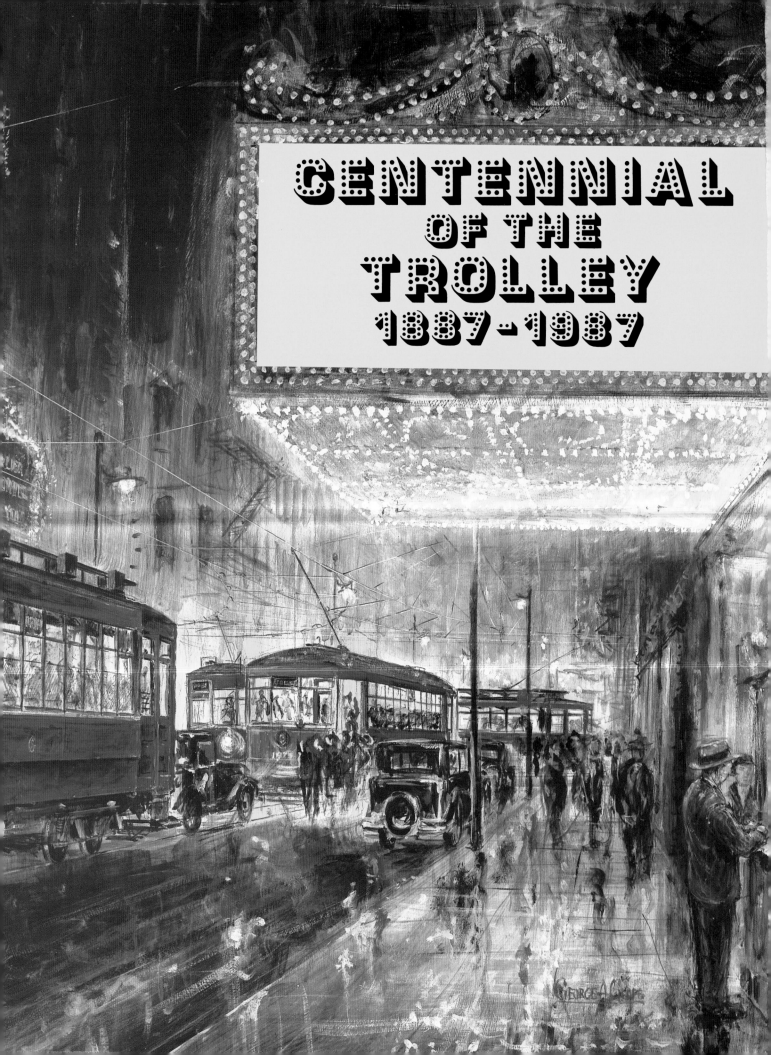

CENTENNIAL
OF THE
TROLLEY
1887-1987

THE TIME
OF THE TROLLEY

The Street Railway from Horsecar
to Light Rail

Volume One

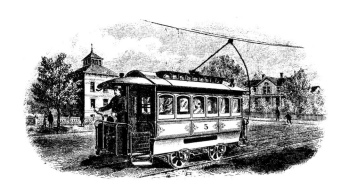

William D. Middleton

1887-1987
CENTENNIAL OF THE TROLLEY

Golden West Books
San Marino, California • 91108-8250

THE TIME OF THE TROLLEY

Volume One
The Street Railway from Horsecar to Light Rail

All Right Reserved

Copyright © 1987 by William D. Middleton
All Rights Reserved
Published by Golden West Books
San Marino, California 91108 U.S.A.

Library of Congress Catalog Card No. 87-21112
I.S.B.N. No. 87095-098-3

Library of Congress Cataloging-in-Publication Data

Middleton, William D., 1928-
  The time of the trolley.

  Bibliography: p.
  Includes index.
  Contents: v. 1. The street railway from horsecar
to light rail.
  1. Street—railroads—United States—History.
2. Electric railroads—cars. I. Title.
TF723.M5 1987   388.4'6'0973   87-21112
ISBN 0-87095-098-3 (v. 1)

Golden West Books
P.O. Box 80250
San Marino, California • 91108-8250

FRANK JULIAN SPRAGUE
(1857-1934)

Widely acclaimed as the "father of the electric railway," Frank Sprague was a Naval officer, engineer and inventor, whose ingenuity and tireless effort, more than those of any other man, made possible the age of electric traction. In addition to his many developments and patents in the field of electric railway transportation, Sprague developed the electric elevator and a host of other electrical inventions in a long and productive career that continued to the very end of his life. During his lifetime Sprague's prodigious achievements were recognized by numerous honorary degrees and memberships, and by such awards as the Gold Medal by the Paris Electrical Exhibition of 1889, and the Grand Prize of the 1905 St. Louis Exhibition, and the prestigious Franklin Medal of the Franklin Institute in 1921.

At the time of his death in 1934 the *New York Herald-Tribune* ranked Sprague with Thomas Edison and Alexander Graham Bell as a "remarkable trio of American inventors who made notable the closing quarter of the last century."

"Perhaps no three men in all human history," said the *Herald-Tribune*, "have done more to change the daily lives of human kind."

Twenty years ago, the first edition of this book was dedicated to Sprague. Today, as we celebrate the 100th anniversary of his extraordinary triumph at Richmond, and as the electric railway that he made a practical reality enjoys a remarkable resurgence, a rededication of this centennial edition of *THE TIME OF THE TROLLEY* to Frank Julian Sprague is more appropriate than ever.

1887-1987
CENTENNIAL OF THE TROLLEY

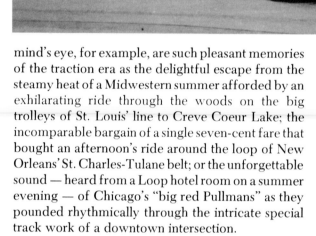

Colorado's Fort Collins Municipal Railway was one of the special delights of the trolley car era. In its final years the system's operations were scheduled so that all three cars in service came together periodically in a glorious flurry of activity at the corner of College and Mountain avenues in downtown Fort Collins. Birney cars Nos. 26, 25 and 20, all built by American Car Company, made the three-way meet in the late 1940's. — *Donald Duke Collection.*

Preface

PROBABLY no industry played a more central role in the development of the American city than did the street railway. When the first horsecar line made its inaugural run down New York's Bowery in 1831, the United States was still a rural nation; scarcely one American in 12 lived in the city, and the nation's largest municipality (New York) had little more than 200,000 inhabitants. By the time the streetcar had for the most part vanished from the American scene more than a century later, close to two-thirds of the nation's populace lived in cities, over a hundred of which by then had passed 100,000 in population.

The street railway impressed itself on the public consciousness to a remarkable degree, unlike such no less necessary, but largely unseen, urban utilities such as the power and telephone companies or the water and sewage works. The trolley car was a visible and noisy part of the urban scene, and during the age of electric traction no place of consequence seemed complete without it. Until the family automobile became commonplace, the streetcar performed a remembered role in the urban existence. Whether for travel to and from work, or for an outing to a theater, a park, or a ball game, riding on the cars was a part of the fabric of daily life.

For the many who knew it, the trolley car is generally remembered with a good deal of nostalgia and affection. In retrospect at least, the time of the trolley seems less hurried and less urgent than the present urban world of high-speed freeways and automobile commuting. Some of my own recollections may perhaps be typical. Still sharp in my

mind's eye, for example, are such pleasant memories of the traction era as the delightful escape from the steamy heat of a Midwestern summer afforded by an exhilarating ride through the woods on the big trolleys of St. Louis' line to Creve Coeur Lake; the incomparable bargain of a single seven-cent fare that bought an afternoon's ride around the loop of New Orleans' St. Charles-Tulane belt; or the unforgettable sound — heard from a Loop hotel room on a summer evening — of Chicago's "big red Pullmans" as they pounded rhythmically through the intricate special track work of a downtown intersection.

When the first edition of this book was completed in 1967, it ended on what must have been thought by many to be an excessively optimistic note, for the trolley continued to operate in scarcely a dozen North Americal cities. But a concept that was then called the "limited tramline" had been responsible for the survival of most of these, and there were those who saw in its technology a likely form for new urban transit systems. Now known as "light rail," the limited tramline concept has since been adopted for new systems either under construction or already operating in nine U.S. and Canadian cities, plans for others are under consideration in at least a dozen more, and almost every one of the surviving systems has been substantially rebuilt and reequipped in accordance with the new light rail technology.

What was originally incorporated into a single volume will now be covered in three separate volumes. This first volume is devoted to a general history of the urban street railway from its horsecar beginnings through modern light rail systems, while

a second volume will include the regional photographic survey titled "America in the Time of the Trolley," updated to the modern light rail era, that was a part of the original single volume. Urban rapid transit systems, covered only briefly in the original book, will become the subject of an entirely new third volume.

I extend my most sincere thanks and appreciation to the many individuals who contributed in some measure to the preparation of this volume. The superb quality and range of the pictorial material has been made possible only through the willing assistance of dozens of collectors, photographers, institutions, and corporations, whose contributions are individually credited. Particular thanks are due Howard E. Johnston, LeRoy O. King, and Stephen D. Maguire, all now deceased, who made available their extensive personal collections; to Suzanne T. Cooper and George H. Menge of the Library of Congress, who helped in locating rare items in the Library's collections; to John H. White, Jr. of the Smithsonian Institution, who assisted with material from the files of that institution; to the late Freeman H. Hubbard, editor of *Railroad* Magazine, who made available valuable material in the magazine's files; and to the *Headlights* editorial staff and the librarian of the Electric Railroaders' Association, who lent a number of choice pictorial items. For assistance with a wide variety of background and regional information, the contributions of Allan H. Berner, Roger Borrup, O.R. Cummings, the late Frank P. Donovan, Jr., Robert W. Gibson, Gene D. Gordon, Wayne C. Olsen, Felix E. Reifschneider, and Eugene Van

Dusen are gratefully acknowledged. And finally, my sincere thanks to Grace Hankinson, who typed the original manuscript, to Diane Brown, who similarly helped with this revised centennial edition, and to the late Stephen D. Maguire, the late E. Harper Charlton, and James W. Walker, Jr., who aided in checking proofs for accuracy.

Much of the historical information that forms the basis for this volume has been drawn from the scores of publications devoted to the history of the street railway era painstakingly prepared by both individuals and the members of the several railway enthusiast groups, usually without profit to their authors. These and other principal sources are summarized in the bibliography.

The original edition of *The Time of the Trolley*, together with *The Interurban Era* and *When the Steam Railroads Electrified*, was published over a 13-year period by Kalmbach Publishing Company to form a "traction trilogy" which surveyed electric rail transportation in America in all its variations. For their constant support and encouragement to that original publication effort, the author remains deeply indebted to the late Al Kalmbach and to David P. Morgan, the longtime editor of *Trains* magazine. He is similarly indebted to Golden West Books publisher Donald Duke for undertaking republication of revised editions of this series.

William D. Middleton

Charlottesville, Virginia
September 1987

Table of Contents

An open "smoking car" rolled down Broadway in New York City on underground-conduit trackage in 1897. — *Library of Congress.*

A two-horse open car clip-clops briskly down New York's Grand Street, which is brilliantly illuminated by newfangled electric street lights, in this woodcut by W. A. Rogers for
an 1889 issue of *Harper's Weekly*. — *Collection of William D. Middleton.*

Before the Trolley

Horse-drawn omnibuses remained a part of the New York scene long after the development of the street railway. This double-deck stage was placed in service on the run up Fifth Avenue to Central Park in 1889. Street railways were never permitted on Fifth Avenue. — *Library of Congress.*

The New York & Harlem Railroad, the first street railway, began operating along the Bowery in 1832 with two of these handsome cars manufactured by John Stephenson. The historic event is depicted in this Clyde O. DeLand painting now owned by the Continental Insurance Companies. — *Library of Congress.*

THERE was a time, not really so many years ago, when the trolley car seemed an indispensable part of urban America. More utilitarian than graceful in appearance, the big electric cars dominated the downtown scene as they moved awkwardly, one after another, through crowded streets at rush hour. By night the trolley car was a cheerful sight as it rumbled noisily through suburban streets, casting a warm yellow glow on the darkened pavement from a brightly lighted interior. Until the noiseless streamliners came along in the declining years of the street railway, the trolley car was an undeniably noisy vehicle; and such characteristic sounds as the dissonant clang of its bell, the *lung-a-lung-a-lung* hammering of its air compressor, the whispering sound of the trolley gliding along the overhead wire, and the rhythmic clash of steel wheels on intricate trackwork echoing in canyonlike streets as a car moved through a downtown intersection were indelibly impressed in the memories of generations of Americans.

In contemplating the few remnants of the street railway era that have survived into the present day or the relatively marginal role played by the trolley car's colorless bus successors in an automobile-oriented midcentury America, it is difficult to imagine the great size and strength enjoyed by the street railway industry less than a half century ago when the trolley car represented an almost universal means of urban transportation — or, indeed, to realize the central and vital role played by the trolley car and its rail-borne predecessors in the development of urban America.

America in the post-Revolutionary War period was a fundamentally different society from the one it is today. In 1790, when the census-takers made the first of their decennial rounds, the United States was an overwhelmingly rural nation. Of the fewer than 4 million Americans then living in the republic, barely 1 in 20, or a little over 200,000 people, lived in the city; Philadelphia, then the nation's largest city, had a population of less than 55,000. But already, as the commerce and industry of the new nation developed, the cities were growing rapidly, and a trend was in motion toward the urbanization of America which has continued without interruption to the present time.

By 1830 more than a million people lived in American cities. The Erie Canal had been completed in 1825, and New York, with an unsurpassed natural harbor, had become the center of American commerce. The population of the thriving city had passed 200,000, a sufficient number to displace Philadelphia as the largest American metropolis.

As long as the cities remained relatively small and compact, urban transportation had presented little difficulty. Those who weren't wealthy enough to own or hire a horse and carriage, or who didn't have access to a horse, simply walked. But as the cities grew, getting around in them became increasingly difficult. Some form of urban public transportation not only became desirable but seemed imperative if the cities were to continue their growth.

What was probably the first regular urban transportation service was opened in Paris in 1819 when a line of horse-drawn stagecoaches began operating in the city. A similar line of what by then had become known as omnibuses began running in London 10 years later. New York City got its first public transportation in 1827 when a man named Abraham Brower inaugurated a regular stagecoach service up and down Broadway at a fixed fare. Four years later a large omnibus built for Brower by John Stephenson, a coachmaker who was destined to become one of the leading street railway carbuilders of the 19th century, began running on Broadway between Bond Street and the Battery at a fare of 12½ cents. Omnibus services quickly became popular; within only a few years hundreds of them were operating in New York and similar services were being operated in Philadelphia and Boston.

At almost the same time, however, the greater efficiency of the then new railway suggested itself as a means of providing a superior urban transportation service; and on April 25, 1831, America's first street railway, the New York & Harlem Railroad Company, was incorporated with John Mason, president of the Chemical Bank of New York City, at its head. Rails were laid along the Bowery from Prince Street to 14th Street, and coachbuilder John Stephenson turned out a pair of handsomely decorated cars, each bearing the name *John Mason* in honor of the railway's president. The cars were fitted with cast-iron wheels and incorporated a number of fea-

JOHN STEPHENSON

John Stephenson (1809-1893), Irish-born New York carriage builder, constructed both the first omnibus and the first streetcar to run on the streets of the city. His firm became the leading street railway carbuilder for most of the 19th century. — *Smithsonian Institution.*

Before horsecar architecture evolved into a style of its own, early streetcars closely resembled their omnibus predecessors. This car operated on Broadway in New York during the 1850's. — *Collection of LeRoy O. King.*

New England's first horsecar line (below) opened between Boston and Cambridge in 1856. Travel aboard the Cambridge cars was a congenial outing if the sketch above is representative. — *Library of Congress (below); New York Public Library (above).*

tures later patented by Stephenson, chief among them an arrangement whereby the center of gravity was lowered by dropping the entrance to each of the three compartments below the tops of the wheels and placing the seats above the wheels. "They resemble an omnibus, or rather several omnibuses attached to each other, padded with fine cloth and with handsome glass windows, each capable of containing outside and inside, fully 40 passengers," stated a contemporary description.

By the afternoon of November 14, 1832, all was in readiness, and a crowd of 60 distinguished guests rode the cars in a gala opening celebration. The *Morning Courier & New York Enquirer* reported:

> Officials of the New York & Harlem Railroad, with Mayor Walter Bowne and others of distinction, left the city hall in carriages to the depot near Union Square where two splendid cars, each with two horses, were in waiting. The company was soon seated and the horses trotted off in handsome style, with great ease, at the rate of about 12 miles, followed by a number of private barouches and horsemen. Groups of spectators greeted the passengers of the cars with shouts and every window in the Bowery was filled.

That evening the event was celebrated with a festive dinner at City Hall, including speeches heralding the dawn of a new era of speed in city transportation. "This event will go down in the history of our country as the greatest achievement of man," declared Mayor Bowne in what might be termed a masterful piece of overstatement.

The new service proved popular, and soon Stephenson constructed three additional cars for the railway — the *Mentor*, the *For-Get-Me-Not*, and the *President*. Two years later New Orleans became the second American city to have a street railway. Horsecars went into service on the Magazine Street branch of the New Orleans & Carrollton Railroad early in January 1835, and a few weeks later a second branch opened on Jackson Street.

After these beginnings, more than 20 years went by before further interest was shown in street railways. But by 1850, when the population of urban America had grown to more than 3½ million and there were no less than a half-dozen cities exceeding 100,000 in population, the need for more adequate urban transportation had become greater than ever. Early in the 1850's further street railway lines were constructed in New York City, and the Brooklyn City Railroad began horsecar operation in 1853.

Boston became the next city to enjoy street railroad service. The first section of the 3-mile Cambridge Railroad was opened between Boston and Cambridge on March 26, 1856, beating a rival line into operation by the purchase of secondhand cars from the Brooklyn City Railroad. In order to popu-

Just the thing for warm weather travel was this two-mule, four-bench Hawaiian Tramways open car shown in front of the Royal Government buildings on Honolulu's King Street in 1888. — *Public Archives, State of Hawaii.*

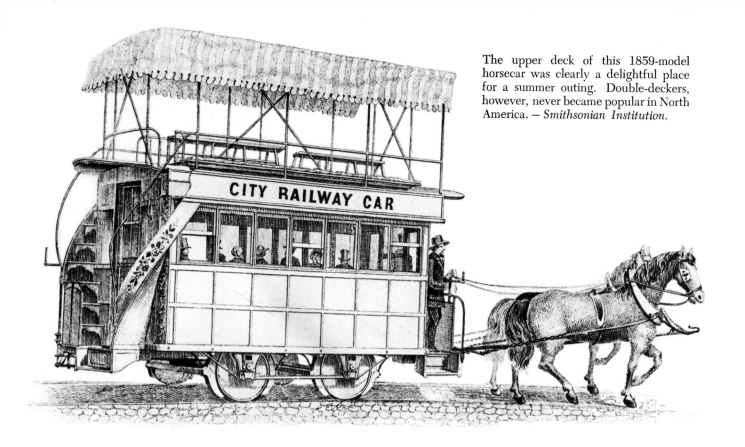

The upper deck of this 1859-model horsecar was clearly a delightful place for a summer outing. Double-deckers, however, never became popular in North America. — *Smithsonian Institution.*

larize its service, the Cambridge line tried the novel idea of letting everyone ride free, and within a week it was transporting more than 2000 passengers a day. After some two months of free transportation, the line's conductors began to ask for fares. The

public was outraged at this imposition. Many demanded that the company's franchises and privileges be revoked, and a few extremists even suggested that the line's officials should be hanged on Boston Common.

Philadelphia's first street railway began operating 2 years later, and by 1859 lines were running in Baltimore, Pittsburgh, Cincinnati, and Chicago as well.

These early street railways were not always received with universal acclaim. Carriage owners asserted that the rails in the streets constituted a serious hazard to the safety of their horses and vehicles, and it was widely believed that the speeding horsecars would take a terrible toll of pedestrian traffic. Said the Philadelphia *Sunday Dispatch* in 1857, when the city's first horsecar line was under construction: "It is perhaps scarcely worthwhile to allude to the fact that in New York City they kill one person each week on city railroads and mangle

Interior appointments of this 1886 Boston car, constructed by the Metropolitan Railroad Company in its own shops, were considerably more luxurious than in most horsecars in order to satisfy the wealthy Beacon Street and Commonwealth Avenue trade on the company's Back Bay line. The ceiling was covered with a "tastefully decorated" painted cotton lining, windows were of a large "parlor-car style," and the seats were stuffed with curled hair and covered with moquette. Oil lanterns provided interior illumination. The cards above the windows marked one of the earliest uses of this type of advertising. — *Street Railway Journal.*

The 19th century horsecar was often a joy to behold. This elaborately decorated specimen operated on the Mount Auburn & Boston line. — *Collection of LeRoy O. King.*

three or four on an average in the same space of time. Human life is really of little value nowadays."

Often the early street railways suffered the ill will of cabmen and carters. Soon after the Montreal City Passenger Railway opened in 1861 it experienced trouble on this score. Cab drivers and carters hooted and yelled at the street railwaymen, stoned the cars, and placed obstacles on the tracks. Stern measures were taken to repress such ruffianism. Reported the Montreal *Gazette* after one such inci-

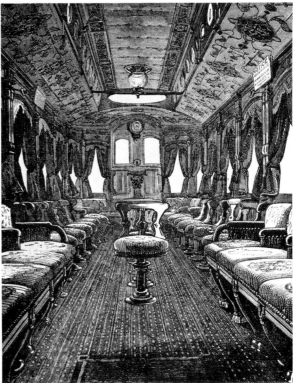

Discriminating travelers on New York's Third Avenue Railroad rode aboard this richly furnished drawing-room car constructed for the horsecar line in 1871 by the Pullman Palace Car Company. The car made four round trips daily except Sunday. — *Courtesy of Pullman Company and Railroad Magazine.*

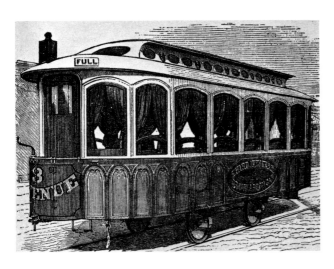

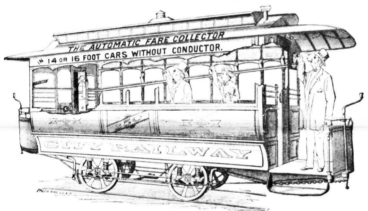

Because of its operating economy the one-horse, one-man "bobtail" car was one of the most popular car types with street railway operators. Passengers, who had to board the cars by the small step at the rear and then push their way to the front of the car to deposit their fare, weren't nearly as fond of it. This bobtail operated on a Washington (D. C.) line. — *Smithsonian Institution.*

Small's automatic fare collector, developed in 1884, permitted passengers on one-man horsecars to deposit their fares without having to reach the fare box beside the driver at the front of the car. — *Street Railway Journal.*

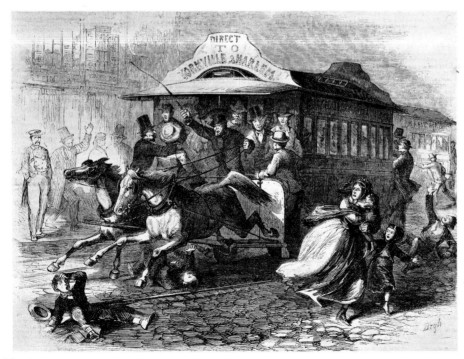

Many regarded the horse-drawn streetcars as a menace to life and limb. This imaginative woodcut, which appeared in an 1865 issue of *Frank Leslie's Illustrated Newspaper*, was part of a more or less continuous editorial campaign carried on by *Leslie's* against reckless horsecar operation. — *Library of Congress.*

Rather than struggle with snow removal, several Canadian cities simply converted their horsecar lines to sleigh operation when heavy snows came. This runner-equipped horsecar was constructed for the Winnipeg Street Railway by the John Stephenson Company of New York City. — *Smithsonian Institution.*

dent, "As a warning to those who have by placing [sic] obstructions in the track and otherwise interfered with the running of the cars, we have to state that Hermidas Racette was yesterday committed to gaol by Mr. Coursol on a charge of felony, the pris-

oner having placed a stone upon the track upon the approach of the cars."

The question of Sunday operation was another hot issue for the early street railways. When the Ridge Avenue & Manayunk Railway Company in

This dramatic drawing by I. P. Pranishnikoff for an 1877 issue of *Harper's Weekly* shows the tracks being cleared by big horse-drawn snow sweepers in New York City. — *New-York Historical Society.*

Two conflicting views of street railway travel are reflected in these drawings from the horsecar era. The idyllic scene above of life on the tramway is from a German publication of 1882. A less favorable view was presented in a drawing (below) which appeared in a New York weekly shortly after a crime aboard one of the cars. — *Both photos, New York Public Library.*

Philadelphia decided to begin Sunday service during the 1860's, the management attempted to mollify the more puritanical element with the diplomatic announcement that "this service will enable persons residing temporarily in the country to attend their usual places of worship in the city." Despite this ploy there was a storm of protest and the mayor finally had to work out a compromise agreement whereby the cars would not begin operating until 1 p.m. and their bells would be removed and the horses walked rather than trotted past the churches. Even at that, some drivers were arrested, and writs of *habeas corpus* obtained. The issue wasn't settled until the Supreme Court of Pennsylvania finally ruled in favor of Sunday operation in 1867.

Winter posed still another problem for early horsecar operators. Before the advent of street railways, cities had made no effort to remove snow from their streets. During the winter months a few streetcar systems in such northern cities as Toronto and Montreal simply converted to the operation of sleighs similar in construction to their regular horsecars, but most lines found it more expedient to remove snow from their tracks to enable continued operation. This usually brought loud protests, since it ruined the sleighing. Some lines favored the use of salt for snow removal, a practice that had to be discontinued in Boston after the chairman of the Board of Health ruled that it was injurious to the public health because it worked as salt does in an

ice cream freezer, lowering temperatures 10 degrees and giving pedestrians violent colds.

Whatever their problems, the horsecar systems developed rapidly to meet the increasing demand for urban transportation. As early as 1855 New York City's horsecar lines were transporting well over 18 million passengers a year, and within the next 30 years their traffic approached 188 million. In 1881 there were in the United States some 415 street railway companies operating 18,000 cars pulled by more than 100,000 horses and mules over 3000 miles of track and doing an annual business in the vicinity of 1¼ billion dollars.

If Americans were quick to make use of street railway service, they were equally quick to find fault with it. Editorializing on the inadequacies of the city's streetcar and omnibus service in 1886, the New York *World* declared: "For filth, dilapidation, and a general appearance of squalor and slovenliness some of the streetcar lines of this city cannot be surpassed in the civilized world. Ladies and gentlemen are compelled to sit down on seats sticky with nastiness, breathe loathsome air, and look out of cracked windows that are splashed with dirt from one end of the year to the other. Some of these cars are washed only by the rain." And so on.

The earliest horsecars were little more than omnibus bodies mounted on flanged cast-iron wheels, but this arrangement gradually evolved into a style of car more suitable for street railway service. The usual arrangement consisted of a closed car with a single passenger compartment provided along each side with longitudinal seats which accommodated anywhere from 20 to 30 people. Perhaps the most widely used type was a small single-end car that could be drawn by one horse. A platform was provided for the driver at the front end and passengers entered from the rear. Sometimes a full platform was installed at the rear, but more often — in what was usually known as a "bobtail" car — only a step, leading to a rear entrance door, was supplied. These smaller cars were usually operated by one man, and passengers had to struggle all the way to the front of the car to deposit fares in a money box next to the driver. In 1884 an inventor named Small came up with an "automatic fare collector" that obviated this difficulty. This was simply an inclined brass channel running forward from the rear of the car into which a passenger deposited his fare; it then rolled forward into the fare box.

Almost as numerous as the one-horse cars, and generally employed on the more heavily trafficked routes, were larger cars drawn by two horses and usually provided with both a driver and a conductor to collect the fares. These larger cars often had full platforms at front and rear and could be quickly reversed at the terminus of the line simply by walk-

For the men who drove the cars from their unprotected front platform, winter could be cruel. This drawing of a driver's misery appeared in a 19th century periodical. — *New York Public Library.*

A New York newsboy's narrow escape from death or disfigurement under grinding car wheels was depicted in a drawing accompanying an article in an 1893 issue of *Once a Week* decrying the street accidents that were a daily occurrence. — *Courtesy of Railroad Magazine.*

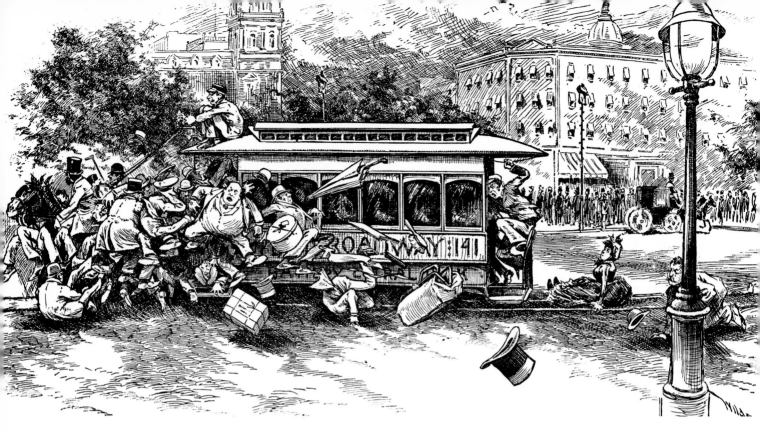

Crowded rush-hour conditions on the Broadway line in 1889 were slightly exaggerated by an artist of the period.

ing the team around to the opposite end of the car.

The closed car was by far the most common type, but many systems also maintained fleets of open cars, fitted with transverse benches running the full width of the car and full-length running boards for boarding. These were operated in summer service. Less widely used was the double-decker, which was tried by a few systems but never attained any degree of popularity.

Horsecars were constructed of wood, the lightest and most easily fabricated material then available. The carbody normally was built upon a heavily framed floor platform, which had to have sufficient strength to support the running gear. In order to avoid excessive weight, sides and roofs were built of lightweight three-ply veneers. Horsecars were almost invariably four-wheel vehicles, with the axle bearings spring-supported in pedestals attached directly to the floor platform.

Interior appointments were generally of a rudimentary sort. Seats were usually of solid wood construction or were made of molded three-ply birch or mahogany veneers. In the more luxurious cars, seats were covered with rattan or carpet — some were even upholstered. At least one line, New York's Third Avenue Railroad, operated a plush extra-fare drawing-room car constructed by the Pullman Palace Car Company.

One of the most vexing problems faced by horsecar operators was that of car ventilation and heating, there being almost as many opinions on this subject as there were passengers. Most lines provided no heat at all, only straw on the floor to help keep their passengers' feet from freezing. Some lines that did supply heat placed a coal-burning heater on the front platform and carried hot air into the car with registers. New York's Second Avenue line used a box furnace mounted under the car and fired from outside. Pipes carried hot air under the seats, an arrangement that occasionally resulted in a car's being set afire.

When the public demanded heat in cars, most horsecar operators regarded it as an unnecessary frill or even downright unhealthy. Complained one official, "If you heat the cars, the next thing they will want is Axminster carpets and satin cushions." Commented President W. H. Hazard of the Brooklyn City Railroad, "The people want it, so we must give it to them whether it is detrimental to health or not." He evidently thought better of it, though, and removed the heaters from his cars in the spring of 1871. To one sarcastic letter writer, who offered to take up a collection to put them back if the company was too poor to do it, Hazard replied, "Keep the money and buy yourself an overcoat!"

If horsecar accommodations frequently left something to be desired, the cars themselves often were a joy to behold. Most lines painted their cars in bright colors and decorated them handsomely with elaborate lettering and striping. Among the most ornate cars were those of Boston's Highland Street Railway, which painted them in the plaid of the Scottish

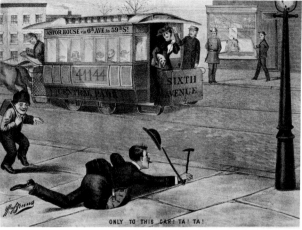

ARE YOU GOING FAR? — NOT FAR.

ONLY TO THIS CAR! TA! TA!

Boy meets girl — humor in the horsecar age as depicted by a colorful pair of 1882 lithographs. — *Library of Congress.*

Highlanders. In the center of each carside was a panel painted with a historical scene or a portrait of the Massachusetts governor for whom the car was named.

Despite the success of horsecars in accommodat-ing the demand for transportation, animal traction as a means of street railway motive power had some serious shortcomings. To begin with, horsecars were not very fast. Most lines managed an average speed of only 5 or 6 mph, and this set a limit to the size of

Overcrowding of the horsecars, as shown in this drawing by Sol Eytinge Jr., was an entirely too frequent happen-ing. Horses were usually good for no more than 3 to 5 years of such service. — *New York Public Library.*

23

urban areas which could effectively be served by street railways. More important, horses were an extremely expensive form of motive power.

Street railway systems had a tremendous investment tied up in their horses and stables. Most companies had to have 5 to 10 horses for each car they operated, and the street railway systems in major cities owned thousands of the animals. As late as 1890, for example, 15,000 horses were engaged in street railway service in New York City alone. A good street railway horse cost around $125, and its keep usually amounted to anywhere from 40 to 60 cents a day.

Street railway work was hard on horses, and most were good for no more than 3 to 5 years of service before they had to be sold for less arduous work. A rather remarkable exception to this rule was "Old Crooked Tail," a five-year-old purchased by the Chicago City Railway in 1863. More than 21 years later Old Crooked Tail was still going strong in daily service, having worked seven days a week without missing a day for 21 years 5 months. During this time the gelding had covered 120,540 miles in 17,090 round trips over the railway. Citing this performance, a letter writer to the *Street Railway Journal* claimed a record length of service for Old Crooked Tail.

Once a car was in motion, it could be moved along by the horses without too much difficulty, and hand brakes on the car saved them much of the strain in stopping the heavy load. Getting the cars started, though, was extremely hard on street railway horses. In the heavy New York City traffic, for example, horses in street railway service were

Caring for the large number of horses required for street railway service was a costly item for horsecar operators. Mechanical devices helped to keep the costs down. An 1884 issue of the *Street Railway Journal* showed the newly invented Pennington's Grooming Machine which had a cylindrical brush driven by a flexible shaft. — *Street Railway Journal.*

often required to start a full car from a dead stop as many as a dozen times in the space of two city blocks. Inventors developed all manner of devices designed to ease the starting of the cars, but no one was able to come up with anything that was really workable in solving the problem. Typical of these was the "car starter" devised by A. R. Witmer of Safe Harbor, Pa., in 1886. It consisted of springs coiled about the car axles and a clutch arrangement whereby the springs were wound up by the momentum of the car in stopping. The spring tension was used to help start the car.

Still another problem for the animal railways was the down-to-earth one of manure. A Dr. Kemp of New York City, after a careful study of the subject, estimated that each street railway horse deposited 10½ pounds of solid matter in the streets daily, creating an obvious sanitation problem along a heavily traveled horsecar line. Disposal of manure from the stables was another problem. Most companies solved this problem by selling it; and earnings from the sale of manure often represented a sizable part of a company's income. One system that reported annual revenues of a little over $400,000 from passengers, earned almost $14,000 from the sale of manure during the same period.

During the Great Epizootic in 1872, horsecar service was maintained in Boston only because drivers and conductors offered to pull the cars by hand. — *Library of Congress.*

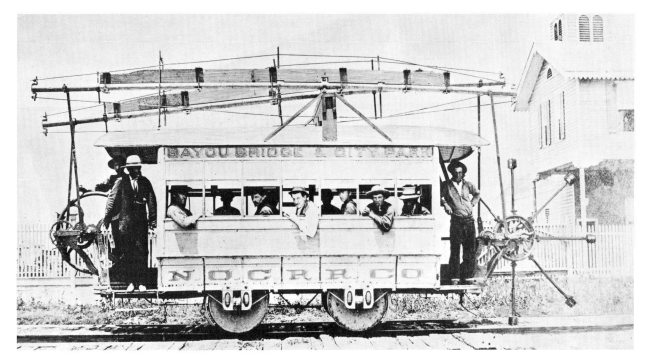

An earlier attempt to apply human power to the street railway was this unique contraption which operated briefly at New Orleans in 1866. The former horsecar was powered by a man who turned the large handwheel on the front platform. Reduction gears and the rooftop "walking beam" arrangement transmitted the power to the paddle-wheel-like device at the rear, which was fitted with eight iron "shoes." Speed was obviously limited. — *Duke-Middleton Collection.*

A typical horsecar of the 1860's is shown here on the Lynn & Boston Railroad. During the 1860's carbuilders began to adopt the "monitor roof," which had a raised deck running the length of the carbody with windows in the sides of the deck for better illumination and ventilation. — *Smithsonian Institution.*

26

Labor disputes were not uncommon on the street railways of the late 19th century, when labor unions were beginning their rise to power. These woodcuts from the February 9, 1889, issue of *Harper's Weekly* illustrate some of the violence in the streets of New York and Brooklyn after the street railway companies attempted to restore service with "scab" labor during a strike of nearly 7000 streetcar men that tied up 26 car lines in the two cities. The principal disagreement stemmed from the companies' refusal to recognize the Knights of Labor, or any other labor organization, as the bargaining agent for the car men. A demand for a wage increase to $2.25 for a 12-hour day was also an issue. — *All drawings, collection of William D. Middleton.*

The fragrant odor of the manure pits brought continuous complaints from residents in the vicinity of horsecar barns, and despite the use of all kinds of favorite disinfectants no one ever came up with a real solution to the problem.

Street railway horses were subject to an almost endless variety of ailments, and the pages of early *Street Railway Journals* were filled with discussions of veterinary problems. Numerous remedies were published for such common horse afflictions as colic, corns, collar gall, shoulder strains, severe coughs, runny noses, and pink eye. Proper shoeing of horses for the rough service on cobblestoned pavements was the subject of continuous debate. Many felt that the horses shouldn't be shod at all, but for those who preferred shoes, a tremendous variety of patented ones were available.

The vulnerability of street railway systems to animal ailments became evident late in 1872 when an epidemic of a horse disease known as Epizootic Apthnae, or the "Great Epizootic," swept through stables in the cities of eastern North America. The disease, previously known in Europe, reached America in 1870, grew to epidemic proportions in Montreal and Toronto 2 years later, then spread swiftly through the principal cities of the eastern United States. Thousands of horses died from it, and many others were disabled. In a large number of cities, street railway service had to be severely curtailed or discontinued altogether; in some, service was maintained only by hiring gangs of the unemployed to draw the cars through the streets.

The devastating effect of the Great Epizootic served only to intensify a search that had already been going on for years to find a suitable means of mechanical traction for street railways. The earliest efforts in this direction had been to apply the steam locomotive to street railway service, but this form of motive power had obvious drawbacks. The smoke, cinders, and noise of steam locomotives

In the aftermath of the great Blizzard of 1888, twice the usual motive power was required to keep this Philadel- phia Traction Company car moving on the 12th and 16th streets line. — *Smithsonian Institution*.

Although cable railway tracks were already laid, an almost endless procession of horsecars along New York's Broadway dominated this 1893 scene at Madison Square. — *Library of Congress.*

A two-mule bobtail car laid over at the end of the Louisville Street Railway's line to the Exposition grounds in 1883. A handy water barrel supplied refreshment for the animals. — *Smithsonian Institution.*

Grossly overloaded, a single horse plodded through Courthouse Square at Santa Rosa, Calif., with a two-car train during the 1880's. The three Santa Rosa horsecar systems offered a family pass. — *Collection of Gilbert H. Kneiss.*

made them unpopular in city streets, and their frightening appearance usually struck terror into horses. The latter shortcoming was overcome somewhat by enclosing small locomotives in carbodies similar in appearance to those of ordinary horse-cars. These were generally called steam dummies.

A few lines attempted the use of single-unit cars powered by steam, but developing a unit of this kind that could be operated economically proved difficult. More often, steam dummy locomotives

The horsecar in the Old West. An Albuquerque streetcar paused in front of the Metropolitan Hotel and Saloon at First and Railroad Avenue (now Central Avenue) in the early 1890's. — *Collection of Gary G. Allen.*

Denver's famous *Cherrelyn* car (left) gave the horse a free downhill ride on the rear platform. Ontario (Calif.) car horses rode a special trailer (below). — *Collection of Joseph Felix (left); Historical Collections, Security First National Bank, Los Angeles (below).*

In small towns and cities the horsecar sometimes lingered long after the adoption of electric traction elsewhere.

The mule-powered *Aileen* was still serving in Washington, Ga., in 1908. — *Library of Congress.*

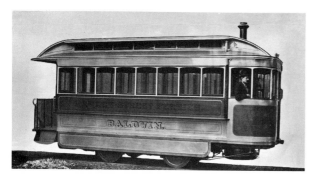

This self-contained steam-powered streetcar, built by the Baldwin Locomotive Works, operated for about four months on the Market Street Railroad at Philadelphia during the 1876 Centennial Exhibition. — *Collection of H. L. Broadbelt.*

hauling several passenger cars were used, an arrangement that proved more adaptable to suburban-type services than it did to the purely urban street railway systems with their frequent-service requirements. Steam dummy lines were constructed in a number of cities, and sometimes they developed into important systems. San Francisco, for one, had an extensive system. The city's first steam dummy line, the Market Street Railroad, began operating down the principal thoroughfare in 1860, but was replaced by horse operation only 7 years later. In subsequent years a number of steam-operated systems of a more or less suburban character were developed in connection with the city's cable railways to carry passengers to such destinations as the Seal

To help promote the sale of lots in his Coronado development, San Diego financier Elisha S. Babcock Jr. constructed the Coronado Beach Railroad. Horses provided the motive power until the Baldwin Locomotive Works delivered steam dummy No. 1 in 1886. The trains operated from a connection with Babcock's steam ferry line across San Diego Bay to the Coronado Strand, where Babcock completed his Hotel del Coronado in 1888. — *Historical Collection, Union Title Office, Title Insurance & Trust Co.*

Stripped of its usual horsecar body design, a typical Baldwin steam dummy looked like this. — *Collection of H. L. Broadbelt.*

During the 1870's the Baldwin Locomotive Works built a number of four-wheel dummies of the type shown here for street railway service. The Ferro-Carril Urbano One-Spot is seen on what was evidently a trial run over a Philadelphia horsecar line. The "apron boards," hung from the carbody to hide the side rods from the view of panicky horses, were a common steam dummy feature. — *Smithsonian Institution*.

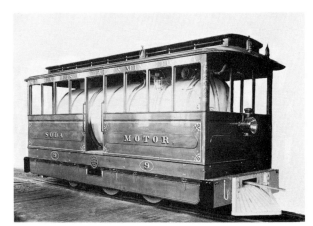

Baldwin turned out this "soda motor" in 1886 for the Minneapolis, Lyndale & Minnetonka, a Minnesota steam dummy line that was getting complaints about the smoke and soot from its regular motive power. The soda motor's oversize boiler and complicated mechanism were concealed beneath a gaily decorated streetcar body. — *Both photos, collection of H. L. Broadbelt*.

The Connelly Motor Company tried this naphtha-powered streetcar at Elizabeth, N. J., in 1889. It was not a success. — *Collection of Howard E. Johnston.*

Rocks, Cliff House, and Adolph Sutro's Baths.

To overcome the objections to steam operation on the grounds of the smoke and cinders, a number of efforts were made to develop a "fireless engine" car. Typical of the attempts was the ammonia car developed by the Standard Fireless Engine Company of New Orleans in 1886. According to the claims of its inventors, it operated with "no fire, no smoke, no steam, and no heat." Ammonia gas was stored under pressure in an iron reservoir under the carbody and was supplied to a reciprocating engine identical to a steam engine. After use, the gas was exhausted into an air-tight water tank under the car which took advantage of the capacity of water to absorb 700 times its volume of ammonia. The gas was later recovered for reuse. At one end of the line, ammonia was pumped into the car at a pressure of 180 to 200 pounds per square inch, and one charge was sufficient to operate the car on a round trip between Canal Street and Carrollton. Fuel consumption was reported to be two gallons of liquid ammonia per car-mile.

A few years later a slight variation of this design appeared in a car which used liquid anhydrous ammonia. The ammonia was contained in a tank surrounded by an outer tank charged with warm water. Heat from the water expanded the ammonia, which passed through a reciprocating engine and was then absorbed by the water in the outer tank. The diluted ammonia was withdrawn, and new charges of warm water and anhydrous ammonia were placed in the tanks at a charging station. One charge was claimed to be good for 30 miles of operation.

Another attempt at a fireless locomotive was the "soda motor." One of these was constructed by the Baldwin Locomotive Works in 1886 for the Min-

neapolis, Lyndale & Minnetonka, a Minnesota steam dummy line. This particular contraption was based upon the discovery by Moritz Honigmann, a German, that a strong solution of caustic soda increases in temperature when water is added. The soda motor employed a large boiler that was charged with soda at a temperature of 329 degrees Fahrenheit at the beginning of a run. Tubes within the boiler contained pure water which evaporated to produce steam for the cylinders. As the steam was exhausted it passed into the soda chamber, where it condensed and reacted with the soda to increase the temperature and produce more steam.

A perennial objective of "fireless engine" inventors of the 19th century was to produce a workable compressed-air car. Most such efforts simply used large storage tanks mounted on the car from which air was released to power a reciprocating engine. The tanks were replenished at a charging station at the end of the line. A rather complicated variation of this basic idea was developed by George A. Clarke of Cincinnati in 1885. Clarke's compressed-air system for street railways employed double metal bottoms on the cars as air chambers; these were charged with air at a pressure of 80 pounds per square inch. A "simple contrivance," unexplained by the inventor, utilized the motion of the car to partially replenish the air supply. To provide additional replenishment, an air line, charged by a 12 h.p. compressor at each end of the line, was laid underground parallel to the track. Every few miles the cars were supposed to stop and tap the line for more air by means of special surface fittings.

Still another attempt to develop a mechanical streetcar was the Connelly gas motor car, powered by a rudimentary internal combustion engine fueled by naphtha gas. This car was tried out in Brooklyn

Compressed air was another often-tried source of streetcar motive power that never worked out. The patented Hughes & Lancaster's low-pressure compressed-air tramcar was tried in Chester, England. — *New York Public Library.*

Based on an early photograph, this drawing from an 1875 *Scientific American* depicts Hallidie's Clay Street cable line shortly after its opening, with Hallidie himself on the front platform of the trailer. — *New York Public Library.*

and Elizabeth, N. J., in the late 1880's. Naphtha and an absorbent material were placed in an inner tank surrounded by a water-filled outer tank. Pipes connected this outer tank with the water jacket of the car's two-cylinder engine, heating the water and evaporating the naphtha. Air drawn through the inner tank produced a combustible mixture of air and naphtha gas; this passed to the cylinders where it was compressed and ignited by an electric spark generated by a small dynamo attached to the machine. The engine ran at a continuous speed, and the speed and direction of the car were controlled by an "ingenious arrangement" of levers. Like almost all such efforts, the Connelly car was not a success.

Of all the inventions and ideas that were brought forth in the effort to mechanize the street railway, only one achieved any degree of success in the years before the electric street railway became a practical system. This was the remarkable cable railway invented by a London-born San Francisco businessman named Andrew S. Hallidie in the 1870's.

Hallidie, a manufacturer of the "wire rope" invented by his father, had noted the extreme difficulty with which horsecars negotiated the city's notori-

Here is a cross-section view of the screw-type grip developed by Hallidie for his pioneer cable railway. — *Collection of Stephen D. Maguire.*

One of the few significant improvements to Hallidie's original cable car design was this lever-type "California Street grip" developed by Henry Root. — *Smithsonian Institution.*

A broken cable immobilized an entire line. Splicing it was always a difficult and tedious task. — *Library of Congress*.

This 1886 cutaway drawing by Poole & Hunt of Baltimore, Md., one of the largest builders of machinery for cable railway power plants, shows the massive steam-powered driving equipment and the intricate construction beneath the street required for cable railway propulsion. — *Smithsonian Institution*.

ANDREW S. HALLIDIE

Andrew S. Hallidie (1836-1900), San Francisco wire-rope manufacturer and cable-car inventor, opened the world's first cable railway on the city's Clay Street hill in 1873. — *Smithsonian Institution.*

An unsuccessful variant of the cable railway idea was the elevated cable system devised by an imaginative San Francisco blacksmith named Henry Casebolt. The cable was carried by overhead poles and the grip was mounted on the ornate structure atop the roof. The experimental car is shown with Casebolt himself at the controls. The system proved less popular than the underground system. — *Smithsonian Institution.*

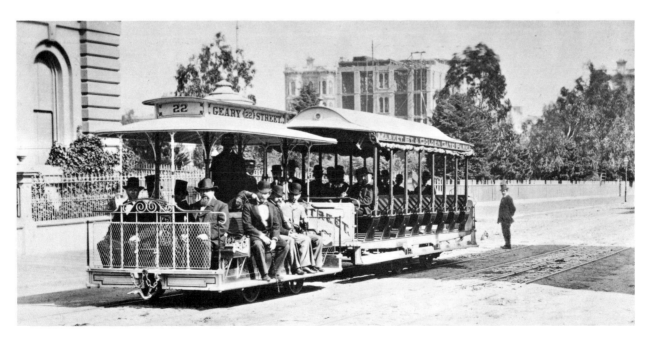

Opened in 1880, San Francisco's Geary Street, Park & Ocean Railroad provided cable car transportation from Market Street to Cemetery stop at Central Avenue, where passengers transferred to steam dummy trains operated by the same company to complete a journey to Golden Gate Park. In the year following the line's opening, the company's ornate grip car No. 22 and an open trailer were photographed at Geary and Powell with a group of impeccably attired San Franciscans aboard. —*Historical Collections, Security First National Bank, Los Angeles.*

Among lesser cable lines in San Francisco was Frederick O. Layman's Telegraph Hill Cable Railroad, which extended from Powell Street up Greenwich Street hill to an ornate resort operated by Gustav Walter. The single-track line was provided with a turnout at midpoint, necessitating simultaneous starts from top and bottom. — *Collection of Roy D. Graves, from LeRoy O. King.*

From the horsecar days of the 1860's until completion of the San Francisco-Oakland Bay Bridge in 1936, the focal point of San Francisco's surface transportation was the Ferry Building at the foot of Market Street where transbay commuter and transcontinental traveler alike arrived aboard the steam ferries of the Southern Pacific Company. Horsecars and cable cars both can be seen in this 1888 scene. — *Southern Pacific Company.*

In the 87 years since this 1880 stereopticon view was taken of the California Street hill, the venerable California Street Railroad has remained an unchanging part of the Nob Hill scene. The line, opened in 1878, has long since succeeded to the title of the world's oldest operating cable railway. — *Historical Collections, Security First National Bank, Los Angeles.*

ous hills. Indeed, some of the hills were so steep that no horsecar could even attempt them. One rainy winter night in 1869 Hallidie had witnessed a cruel horsecar accident of a sort that was all too common. A heavily overloaded car drawn by four horses was struggling up a hill. About halfway up, one of the horses slipped and fell. The driver quickly wound up his hand brake, but the chain which set the brakes snapped and the car, out of control, rolled back down the hill, dragging the unfortunate horses across the cobblestoned pavement and injuring the animals so severely that they had to be destroyed.

The tough steel cable manufactured in Hallidie's San Francisco plant was already being used in such applications as elevators and several long aerial tramways that brought gold and silver ores down from the inaccessible heights of California's Sierra Nevada. Why, he thought, couldn't the same idea be applied to the street railway?

Organized by San Diego alderman John C. Fisher in 1889 to replace an unsuccessful electric street railway project, the San Diego Cable Railway was one of the most ill-starred of cable railway ventures. On opening day, June 7, 1890, cable car No. 2, *El Escondido*, was decorated with palms and the national ensign and carried a brass band. The line, a financial failure, operated under cable power for little more than 2 years. In 1896 it reopened as an electric line. — *Collection of Frederick W. Reif, from Eric Sanders.*

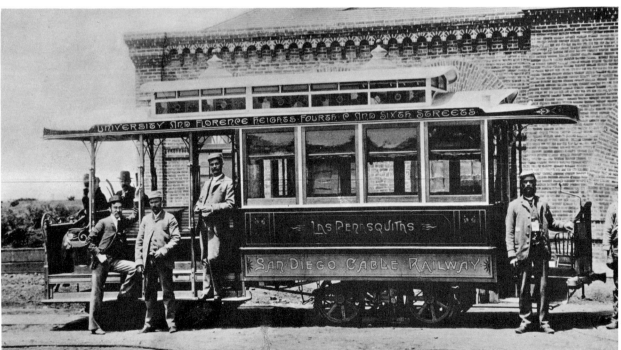

Among the rolling stock of the San Diego Cable Railway were a dozen exceptionally handsome semi-open cars designed by the company's chief engineer, Frank Van Vleck, and constructed by the Stockton Combine, Harvester and Agricultural Works. Interiors of the closed sections were finished in rare woods, stained glass was installed in the transoms, and the windows were richly curtained. Exteriors of the exquisitely lettered cars were finished in maroon and gray. In 1890 the company's car No. 3, *Las Penasquitas*, posed with its proud designer, Van Vleck, standing at left with arm raised. — *Collection of Frederick W. Reif, from Eric Sanders.*

This gala celebration at Downey Avenue and Pritchard Street in Los Angeles on November 2, 1889, marked the extension of cable railway service into East Los Angeles by the Pacific Railway Company. Proclaimed as the largest and most advanced cable railway system in the world, the Pacific Railway actually completed 21 miles of a projected 65 miles of cable railway. Only a few years later, however, the cable system was sold to the rival Los Angeles Consolidated Electric Railway and converted to electric operation. — *Title Insurance & Trust Company, Los Angeles.*

One of the principal engineering features of Los Angeles' Pacific Railway Company was the 1535-foot San Fernando Street viaduct opened in 1889, which carried East Los Angeles cable cars over the Southern Pacific yards at Alameda Street. After cable operation ended, the structure was continued in service as an electric railway bridge by the Los Angeles Consolidated Electric Railway until it was torn down in 1907. — *Historical Collections, Security First National Bank, Los Angeles.*

Seattle joined other major West Coast cities in 1888 when the city's first cable railway began operating on Yesler Way to Lake Washington, returning over Jackson Street. One of the early grip cars is seen at Lake Washington with an ornately embellished trailer of evident animal railway ancestry. A second cable line opened in 1890 on the extreme 17 per cent grade of the city's Queen Anne Hill. Employing a counterbalance arrangement, the line remained in operation until 1939 to haul electric cars up the hill. — *Collection of LeRoy O. King Jr.*

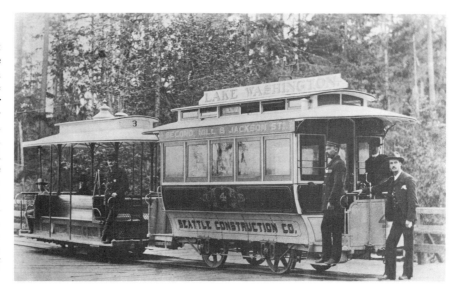

Pacific Railway grip car No. 115 and an open trailer are seen at Broadway and Third in downtown Los Angeles bound for Westlake Park. Opened late in 1889, the route out West Seventh Street to Westlake Park was the last cable line built by the company. — *Historical Collections, Security First National Bank, Los Angeles.*

41

In later years of cable railway operation Seattle adopted double-truck cars of the semi-open pattern in preference to the original grip-car-and-trailer arrangement. No. 52 operated on the Lake Washington line. — *Washington State Historical Society, from Robert S. Wilson.*

Chicago's cable railway mileage was second only to that of San Francisco. The Windy City's first cable line was a route of the Chicago City Railway on State Street between Madison and 21st opened early in 1882. By the time this view of State Street, at Madison, was taken around 1890, the street had become the scene of intense cable car activity. By the early 1890's the Chicago City Railway was operating as many as 300 cable cars simultaneously during rush hours. — *Chicago Historical Society.*

Between 1888 and 1891 the North Chicago Street Railroad converted three of its principal routes between downtown Chicago and the North Side to cable operation. In this view from the early 1890's, a Lincoln Avenue line grip car and trailer are northbound on Dearborn Street at Washington. — *Chicago Historical Society*.

The greatest day's traffic in the history of the Chicago City Railway came on October 9, 1893, when the company hauled some 700,000 passengers — almost all of them on its cable lines — to the Chicago Day celebration at the World's Columbian Exposition in Jackson Park. A virtually endless parade of cable trains, jammed almost beyond belief, accommodated the unprecedented traffic. — *Chicago Historical Society.*

To provide a through service into downtown Chicago, cable trains of the Chicago City Railway's Wabash Avenue and State Street lines picked up trailers from several of the company's horsecar routes. Because the city refused to permit installation of trolley wire in Loop streets, the arrangement was continued even after electrification of the connecting horsecar lines. In this 1905 view a State Street train is seen northbound at Adams Street with an Archer Avenue trolley car in tow. — *Chicago Historical Society.*

In order to avoid the frequent drawbridge delays occasioned by water traffic on the Chicago River, cable trains of the North Chicago Street Railroad used the La Salle Street tunnel, which had been built in 1871 to provide an uninterrupted crossing for vehicular traffic to and from the North Side. In a 1906 view at the south end, a southbound train from the Wells Street line is emerging from the tunnel, while a northbound Clark Street train is entering. To supply illumination for the cars while in the tunnel, the company installed an overhead trolley wire and placed trolley poles on its grip cars. A metal "pan" at each portal automatically raised and lowered the poles. Cable operation ended less than a year after photo was taken. — *Chicago Historical Society.*

Hallidie's scheme was simplicity itself. An endless wire rope, powered by a steam engine at a central power plant, could be pulled through a trough placed between the rails and below the street. Streetcars attached to the cable would be drawn through the streets, using the almost limitless energy of the central power plant to surmount the steepest of hills. A special contrivance with which the operator could grip the cable or release it at will would permit the car to be stopped at any point.

Joined by three close friends, Hallidie organized a cable railway company in 1872 and obtained a franchise to construct a line on the Clay Street hill, a route which included grades of more than 12 per cent. Development of the various mechanical devices required for the system proved difficult; con-struction of the line itself proceeded at a slow and laborious pace; and not until the final day for expiration of the franchise, August 1, 1873, was all in readiness for the trial run. At five o'clock on that historic morning the first car, with Hallidie himself at the controls, successfully made its way down the Clay Street hill and back up again. Later in the day, the Clay Street line's first revenue run — attended by such San Francisco notables as Mayor William Alvord, Fire Chief David Scannell, and the city's beloved eccentric, Emperor Norton I — was made to fulfill the franchise requirements.

Placed in regular service a short time later, Hallidie's cable railway proved to be a sensational success. In 1877 a second cable line was opened on Sutter Street, and the next year a splendid new

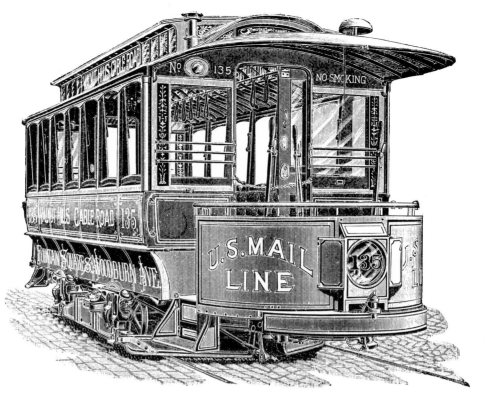

This ornate grip car for Cincinnati's Walnut Hills Cable Road was constructed by car-builder John Stephenson. — *Smithsonian Institution.*

Pulling what was undoubtedly a former horsecar, a grip car of the Baltimore City Passenger Railway Company's North Charles Street line rattled past Calvert Station about 1893. — *Collection of LeRoy O. King.*

Soon after Congressional legislation of the late 1880's hurried the departure of horsecars from the streets of the nation's capital, cable cars were clanging down principal Washington thoroughfares. In this mid-1890's view from the steps of the Treasury Building, cable cars of the Capital Traction Company share the broad expanse of Pennsylvania Avenue with a leisurely pedestrian, bicycle, and horse traffic which characterized that unhurried time.

Cable railway operation on the Avenue ended abruptly on the night of September 30, 1897, when fire destroyed the company's power plant at 14th and Pennsylvania, immobilizing 15 miles of cable lines. By that time electric traction had long since proved itself, and the company's directors decided to electrify their lines rather than re-equip the road for cable operation. — *Collection of Le-Roy O. King.*

In the place of its birth the cable railway survived to become a unique symbol and a durable San Francisco institution. This young group rides a car on the California Street line, now in its second century of service. — *San Francisco Convention & Visitors Bureau.*

cable railroad costing nearly a half million dollars was constructed on California Street by a group of powerful San Francisco capitalists that included Mark Hopkins and Charles Crocker, two of the original "Big Four" who had built the Central Pacific Railroad. The California Street Railroad was opened to service on April 10, 1878, amid civic festivities that included an address by Gov. Leland Stanford, and achieved no less a success than that of the pioneer Clay Street line. Other systems soon followed, and by the late 1880's San Francisco was served by an extensive network of cable lines comprising some 112 miles of track operated by eight separate major companies.

Other cities were quick to follow San Francisco's example. Even without hills to conquer, cable railways afforded numerous advantages over animal railways. Their average speed of around 9 or 10 mph was almost double that of a typical horsecar line. Despite the high cost of cable railway construction — many lines came to well over $100,000 a mile to build — the elimination of the many expenses associated with animal traction made cable lines much more profitable than horsecars had ever been. Cable cars were clean and quiet, and proved

immensely popular with the public. Real estate values increased rapidly along cable lines. In Chicago it was found that property values increased 50 per cent to 200 per cent in a single year following the construction of cable railways.

Chicago was the second city to adopt Hallidie's invention. Officials of the Chicago City Railway, searching for something more effective than horse traction for their large network of street railway lines serving Chicago's South Side, traveled to San Francisco in 1880 to study the several cable lines already in operation there. Plans were quickly formulated for conversion of the company's lines on State Street and Wabash Avenue. Construction started the following summer, and by January 1882 the first line, extending along State Street from Madison to 21st, was ready for operation. Appropriate ceremonies marked the opening of the line on January 28. A special train made up of two grip cars and seven trailers was assembled at Madison Street. The Lyon and Healy band climbed aboard the first grip car, a group of street railway officials boarded the second grip, and the seven trailers were filled by assorted civic dignitaries. With the band playing, the inaugural run proceeded proudly down State Street to the company's powerhouse at 21st Street, where a brief ceremony was held.

During the next 10 years the Chicago City Railway extended its cable lines far out into the South Side, and the West Chicago and North Chicago street railway companies constructed an extensive network of lines serving the West and North sides. By 1893 Chicago's street railway companies had invested an estimated 25 million dollars in a cable railway system totaling 82 miles, over which some 710 grip cars were operated. Next to that of San Francisco, it was the largest cable railway system in North America.

Philadelphia got its first cable line in 1883, and during the same year cable-powered cars began operating over the Brooklyn Bridge. Conversion of horsecar lines in the nation's capital was hurried by 1888 Congressional legislation requiring that some form of mechanical propulsion be substituted for horse power; and by 1894 the major lines of the city's principal street railway companies had been converted to cable operation. St. Louis, with 55 miles of cable line, had one of the largest systems. Denver, with 44 miles, was not far behind.

Cable railway construction in the latter city was enlivened by a rivalry between two companies, and at one point this reached an intensity reminiscent of the competition that on occasion had characterized steam railroad construction in Colorado. In 1889 the two rivals, the Denver Tramway Company and the Denver City Cable Railway Company, became embroiled in a dispute over which one would construct cable track on Lawrence Street between 15th and 19th streets. The Tramway Company dramatically settled the argument on the night of December 18, 1889, when it marshaled a force of 1600 men; brought in the necessary ties, rails, and cable equipment; and by dawn had laid down four blocks of cable railway. Ironically, the company's cable cars never did use the track!

By the early 1890's cable railways were serving some 28 American cities, and cable systems constructed under American supervision were functioning in cities in the British Isles, France, Australia, and New Zealand. By 1894 cable railway mileage in the United States had reached a peak of 662 miles, nearly 5000 cable cars were in operation, and cable railway traffic was in the vicinity of 400 million passengers a year.

Throughout the era of cable railways the mechanical details of their operation changed but little from those contrived by Hallidie for his original Clay Street line in 1873. To provide a conduit for the cable, the rails were supported by a series of cast-iron yokes, usually firmly set in concrete. The cable ran through the opening formed by the yoke and was supported at intervals by rollers or sheaves attached to the yokes. The yokes curved inward to cover the top of the conduit and supported continuous steel members that formed a narrow slot in the pavement.

One of the most intricate parts of the cable-car mechanism was the grip with which the car was attached to the cable. Hallidie's original line used a screw-operated grip mechanism operated by a handwheel. A considerably improved grip mechanism was created a few years later by Henry Root, the engineer in charge of construction for the California Street Railroad. Root's device was operated by a long grip lever on a quadrant arrangement, resembling a brake handle. This "California Street grip," or a similar design, was used on a majority of cable railways, and constituted the principal deviation from Hallidie's original system. Any number of inventors applied themselves, without any degree of success, to improving the grip mechanism. In 1882 the *Street Railway Journal* was said to have on hand copies of over 1000 patents for cable railway systems. In each of them the grip mechanism was the important feature.

The cable itself was a wire rope of anywhere from 1½ inches to 1¾ inches in diameter, ordinarily consisting of six strands made up of 16 to 19 steel wires each. It was lubricated with linseed oil, and a hemp center provided flexibility. The cable was guided around curves by arrangements of sheaves or pulleys, and reversed its direction at the end of a line by means of a huge horizontal sheave under the street. The cable entered a powerhouse at right

Halfway up the steep grade between Market Street and the top of Nob Hill, cable cars of the California Street line intersect the Grand Street "main drag" of San Francisco's Chinatown, a hallmark of the city only slightly less noted than the cables. — *William D. Middleton.*

angles to the track and was wound several times around a huge driving wheel 10 to 25 feet in diameter powered by a reciprocating steam engine. Before leaving the powerhouse the cable passed around a large-diameter vertical sheave mounted on a movable carriage. A counterweight attached to the carriage served to maintain a constant tension on the cable and helped to compensate for changes in its length brought about by variations in temperature and load or the age of the cable.

Usually several cables, each serving a particular line or section of line, were operated from a single power plant. Sometimes the individual cables reached extraordinary lengths. Probably the largest single cable railway power plant was that constructed in 1889 at Lawrence and 18th streets in Denver by the Denver City Cable Railway Company. All of the company's cable lines were powered from this single plant by means of five separate cables totaling almost 30 miles in length. The longest of them was approximately 7 miles long.

The life of a street railway cable varied considerably, depending upon the traffic and the amount of curvature on a line. On some heavily traveled Chicago lines a cable lasted less than three months; on other lines a cable might last for more than a year.

In construction and appearance, cable cars were little different from the horsecars they replaced. Most cable systems used small four-wheel "grip cars," equipped with the grip mechanism, to haul one or more trailers through the streets. Quite often, these trailers were no more than former horsecars. In later years a number of lines developed large double-truck cars for cable service. In order to provide the gripman adequate visibility from his location near the center of the car, the early grip cars almost invariably were built as open cars. When double-truck cars were introduced they most often were built to the "semi-open" pattern, in which one end of the car was closed and the other, where the gripman was located, was open.

In several larger cities the Post Office Department found the speedy cable cars useful in providing more rapid mail distribution to branch post offices. New York was one of the earliest cities to get cable-car mail service when a Railway Post Office was inaugurated on the Third Avenue Railway on October 1, 1895. Ten special trailer cars, painted white and bearing the legend UNITED STATES MAIL RAILWAY POST OFFICE in blue, were constructed for this duty. The cars were loaded on a special siding on Mail Street at the General Post Office and were drawn by horses to the running tracks of the Third Avenue line; there they were picked up by cable trains. Mail was sorted in the Railway Post Office cars en route to the branch post offices. This particular route lasted only until 1897, when it was replaced with a pneumatic tube system. A similar service was started on the Cottage Grove-Wabash line of the Chicago City Railway in 1896. San Francisco and Cincinnati were among other cities with cable-car mail service.

Whatever its advantages over the horsecar, the cable railway had more than a few inherent shortcomings of its own. Because of the great weight of the cables, a disproportionate share of the energy delivered by a powerhouse was absorbed just by the moving parts of the system. A study made in San Francisco in 1888 estimated that 57 per cent of the power generated was devoted to moving the cable itself, 39 per cent to moving the cars, and only 4 per cent to moving passengers.

Cable systems were vulnerable to a wide variety of breakdowns and mishaps, most of them involving either the cable or the grip mechanism. One of the most spectacular mishaps would occur when a broken strand from the cable became entangled with the grip, making it impossible for the gripman to release the cable. As the car sped unchecked through the streets, bell clanging furiously, the passengers usually "joined the birds" while the conductor ran for the nearest telephone to call the power-house and have the cable stopped. To avoid an inevitable collision, cars ahead of the runaway would join the dash through the streets, and sometimes five or six cars, all clanging noisily, could be seen racing along pursued by the runaway. New York's Metropolitan Railway had special boxes set in the pavement at intervals which a conductor could open to pull a wire that would stop the cable. San Francisco cars were equipped with a "slot brake," a steel wedge that could be driven into the cable slot to bring a car to a halt when all else failed.

Gripmen had to be alert to release the cable at junctions or wherever it passed through a series of sheaves or pulleys, such as at curves and similar locations. Failure to do so was a cardinal sin for a gripman and almost always resulted in wrecking a grip and "cutting the rope." When this happened a line would be immobilized for 2 to 6 hours while the cable ends were located, pulled together with horse-drawn grips, and spliced.

The moving cable was often irresistible to small boys, who learned how to fish for it with a wire or string. A box or wagon could then be attached and dragged through the streets to the peril of pedestrians and other street traffic.

Sunday afternoon finds the Aquatic Park terminal tranquil as a car of the Powell & Hyde streets line is swung on the turntable by its crew in preparation for the return trip to Powell and Market. — *William D. Middleton.*

50

Inbound to Market Street, a Powell & Hyde car surmounts the harrowing Hyde Street hill against a spectacular backdrop of San Francisco Bay, Alcatraz, and the Marin County hills. At this same point in the fall of 1964 a car bound up the hill broke loose from the cable and rolled backward down the hill out of control. Tragedy was averted only by use of the last-resort slot brake. — *William D. Middleton.*

Cable systems were relatively indifferent to the hazards of winter weather, since they gave no trouble from slipping wheels regardless of the condition of the tracks. When all other means of transportation were tied up by heavy snow, the cable cars could often be found operating as usual. The greatest hazard of winter to cable systems was the problem of snow and ice accumulating in the cable tube. Chicago understandably had a great deal of trouble from this source and installed steam pipes at many points to melt the accumulation of ice. A horse-drawn steam boiler was brought to the site of the obstruction to fill the steam pipes.

Even as the cable railways began to displace ani-mal traction on major street railways throughout the United States, a host of inventors and tinkerers were coming closer and closer to success in their effort to perfect a rival means of power that would supplant horsecars and cable railways alike. As early as 1883, when the cable car boom had hardly begun, President H. H. Littell of the American Street Railway Association proclaimed in an address at Chicago, "I see in the recent subjugation of the subtle and hitherto elusive force of electricity to the needs of man boundless possibilities for the world's three great requisites of advancement: heat, light, and motion." But even Littell had little idea of how swift or complete would be the triumph of electric traction.

A Time of
Trial and Triumph

Opening of one of the pioneer electric lines of the 1880's was invariably the occasion for a gala civic celebration. This dignified Los Angeles crowd attended the January 4, 1887, opening of the first electric road on the West Coast, a Daft system line built on Pico Street by the Los Angeles Electric Railway Company. Like most of the Southern California trolleys that followed it, the Pico Street line was built to promote a real estate venture, the "Electric Railway Homestead Association Tract." Within three days of the opening the tract was sold out. — *Historical Collections, Security First National Bank, Los Angeles.*

EVEN as the first horse-drawn streetcars began their historic journey along New York's Bowery in 1832, the first of the long series of inventors and tinkerers had begun the half century of experimentation that was eventually to lead to the overwhelming triumph of electric traction.

What might be described as the first step on the long road to development of electric transportation was the work of the distinguished English physicist, Michael Faraday, who in 1821 discovered that electricity could be made to produce mechanical motion. Faraday's principle of electromagnetic rotation, as it was called, was fundamental to the later development of the electric motor.

By far the most important of the early electric railway experimenters was a young Brandon (Vt.) blacksmith named Thomas Davenport. His accomplishments were all the more remarkable in the light of his limited education. Davenport was born at Williamstown, Vt., in 1802 and at the age of 14 was apprenticed to the village blacksmith. In 1833 he began the study of electromagnetism and in 1835 exhibited at the Rensselaer Institute in Troy, N. Y., and the Franklin Institute in Philadelphia a battery-powered rotary engine driven by electricity. Later the same year Davenport constructed a small circular railway driven by his electromagnetic motor. During the next few years he built over a hundred different motors of various types; one of them he used to power the world's first electric printing press on which he published a newspaper, *The Electro-Magnet.* In 1846 Davenport started work on the application of electric current to the strings of musical instruments and was preparing a patent application for what might have been the first electric guitar when he was stricken with a fatal illness and died in 1851.

The next important step in electric traction development was taken by Robert Davidson of Aberdeen, Scotland, who about 1838 constructed a 7-ton electric locomotive powered by a 40-cell iron-zinc sulphuric acid battery. Davidson's locomotive made several successful trips on the Edinburgh-Glasgow Railway, but then was wrecked by steam locomotive engineers and firemen who were fearful of the rival means of propulsion.

In 1847 Prof. Moses G. Farmer of Dover, N. H., operated a small experimental electric locomotive that pulled a car capable of carrying two people around an 18-inch-wide track. A 48-cell Grove nitric acid battery provided the power. Three years later Farmer, aided by Thomas Hall, exhibited a small electric railway at Boston — the first known use of the rails to carry the power supply to the car from a stationary source.

In 1851 Prof. Charles G. Page of the Smithsonian Institution, with $30,000 appropriated by Congress, constructed a battery-powered electromagnetic locomotive propelled by a 16 h.p. reciprocating electric motor of his own design. By reversing the polarity, a hollow solenoid and core produced a reciprocating motion which was applied to the flywheel by a crankshaft, much like a steam engine. Page's locomotive reached speeds as high as 19 mph on a 39-minute 5-mile trip between Washington and nearby Bladensburg, Md., over the Washington

THOMAS DAVENPORT

Thomas Davenport (1802-1851), a Brandon (Vt.) blacksmith, inventor, and classic example of the resourceful Yankee mechanic, built a model electric railway that was an important early step toward practical electric transportation. — *Smithsonian Institution.*

Davenport's circular electric railway of 1835, now on display at the Smithsonian Institution, was driven by a rotating electromagnetic motor. A crude battery provided the power. — *Smithsonian Institution.*

Professor Farmer's battery-powered electric train was a remarkably sophisticated-appearing machine for its time. "My father used the apparatus in 1847 when lecturing on electricity," his daughter later recalled. "He laid the rails around the hall and ran his car carrying four children." — *Smithsonian Institution.*

little further progress was made in the advancement of electric traction.

One of the first attempts to operate an electric car with generated power was made by Professor Farmer in 1867 utilizing a crude dynamo, but the first person to successfully operate an electric locomotive with power drawn from a dynamo was a German named Ernst Werner Siemens. Siemens, who was born at Lenthe in Hanover in 1816, had made

MOSES G. FARMER

Prof. Moses G. Farmer of Dover, N. H., built an electric train in 1847 that could actually carry two adults. Twenty years later, Farmer was one of the first to operate an electric car with power obtained from a dynamo. — *Smithsonian Institution.*

& Baltimore Railroad. The trip was not a complete success, for Page's pottery battery cells cracked at the slightest jolt, and by the time the return trip was completed the battery had been entirely destroyed.

If the early experimentation proved anything, it was that batteries were an unsatisfactory and uneconomical source of electricity for an electric railway. Consequently, until the development of a satisfactory dynamo, or generator, between 1860-1870

CHARLES GRAFTON PAGE

Prof. Charles Grafton Page (1812-1868) of the Smithsonian Institution operated an experimental car which attained 19 mph on a round trip between Washington and Bladensburg, Md., on April 29, 1851. A 100-cell battery provided the power. Congress put up the money for the venture. — *Smithsonian Institution.*

55

ERNST WERNER VON SIEMENS

Dr. Ernst Werner von Siemens (1816-1892), German electrician and inventor, built the first successful generator-powered electric railway in 1879 and the first commercial electric line in 1881.—*Siemens Archive, Munich.*

A year after his Lichterfelde line opened, Siemens electrified the horse railroad between Spandauer Bock and Charlottenburg. This early drawing shows the two-wire overhead system and four-wheel troller favored by Siemens after the use of running rails for power supply proved inadvisable. — *Smithsonian Institution.*

a number of important electrical discoveries and inventions, and, with J. G. Halske in 1847, had founded the Siemens & Halske electrical firm at Berlin. Even today the firm represents one of the foremost electrical undertakings in the world. At the Berlin Industrial Exhibition in 1879, Siemens & Halske constructed a small electric railway operating around an oval track about ⅛ mile long. A

locomotive which drew its power from a third rail between the running rails was capable of hauling three trailers accommodating 18 passengers at a speed of about 8 mph.

In May 1881 Siemens opened the world's first commercial electric railway at Lichterfelde, near Berlin. A car capable of carrying 26 passengers and of operating at a speed of about 30 mph was operated over the 1½-mile line. A single motor mounted beneath the carbody and connected to the axles by wire cables powered the car. Initially, 100-volt power was drawn from the running rails, an

Siemens' pioneer dynamo-powered electric railway at the 1879 Berlin Industrial Exhibition whisked passengers around an oval track at 8 mph. Some 80,000 passengers were transported. — *Siemens Archive, Munich.*

arrangement that was later changed to an overhead system after some rude experiences by horses and pedestrians. A year later Siemens electrified a horse railroad between the Berlin suburbs of Charlottenburg and Spandauer Bock.

At the Paris Exposition in 1881 Siemens displayed an electric car equipped with one of the earliest attempts at an overhead trolley system. Two years later, under the direction of Dr. Werner Siemens' brother, Sir William (a naturalized Briton who managed the company's branch in England), the Siemens firm installed at Portrush, Ireland, a 6-mile electric line notable for the first use of a hydroelectric power supply.

In the decade following the Siemens success at the Berlin Exhibition, increasingly rapid progress was made in electric railway development in both Europe and the United States. About 1879 Stephen D. Field, a son of Cyrus Field, promoter of the first successful transatlantic cable, developed plans for an electric railway taking its power from a third rail mounted in a slotted conduit. During 1880-1881 Field constructed and operated an experimental electric locomotive at Stockbridge, Mass. At about the same time, Thomas A. Edison began experimenting with electric traction, and in 1880 Field, Edison, and Siemens all applied for similar patents within three months of each other.

Edison's electric railway experimentation began in the spring of 1880 when a short loop of narrow-gauge track was installed at the inventor's Menlo Park (N. J.) laboratories. One of Edison's electric

lighting dynamos was used as a motor for a small locomotive which drew its power from the running rails. Initially, the motor was connected to the wheels through a system of friction pulleys. When this proved impractical, a belt drive was installed.

With financial backing from Henry Villard, president of the Northern Pacific Railroad, Edison constructed an improved locomotive the following year. Villard had plans for electrifying some of the Northern Pacific's branch lines in the wheat regions of the northwest, but the Northern Pacific's bankruptcy a short time later brought an end to the work. Other railroadmen expressed little interest in electrification, and Edison soon turned his energies to other projects.

In 1883 Edison's interests were joined with those of Field to form the Electric Railway Company of the United States. Edison himself took little part in the work of the new company, which was managed by Field. By June 1883 the Edison-Field firm had completed an experimental 3-ton locomotive, *The Judge*. This engine pulled a passenger car along ⅓ mile of narrow-gauge track laid in the gallery of the main building at the 1883 Exposition of Railway Appliances at Chicago. It reached speeds as high as 12 mph and carried approximately 27,000 passengers.

About this time several important new inventors entered the electric railway field. Late in 1883 a British-born inventor named Leo Daft, who had been experimenting with electric traction since 1881, constructed the *Ampère*, a 2-ton electric loco-

Dr. Siemens' one-car mile-and-a-half line opened at Lichterfelde in 1881 and provided the world's first regular fare-paying electric railway service. These two views depict the line before a double-wire overhead system re-placed the original method of current distribution through the running rails some 12 years after the line opened. — *State Historical Society of Wisconsin (right); Siemens Archive, Munich (left).*

Thomas A. Edison's Menlo Park electric railway of 1880 (left) zipped around the track at speeds as high as 40 mph, and the inventor delighted in carrying visitors on high-speed joy rides over the line. On at least one occasion a party of dignitaries was hurled into a ditch when the little locomotive derailed on a curve. A larger, improved model (right) constructed the following year with financial backing from the Northern Pacific was equipped with a huge cowcatcher, headlight, and cab, giving it a remarkable resemblance to a steam locomotive. — *Smithsonian Institution (left); Duke-Middleton Collection (right)*.

Steam locomotive architecture obviously influenced the builders of the experimental Edison-Field locomotive, *The Judge*, built for the Exposition of Railway Appliances at Chicago in 1883. Power was obtained from a center third rail. — *Smithsonian Institution*.

motive that was successful in hauling a standard railroad coach carrying 75 people up a grade of almost 2 per cent on the Saratoga, Mt. McGregor & Lake George Railroad. After installing several successful exhibition lines, Daft was engaged in 1885 by Thomas C. Robbins, general manager of the Baltimore Union Passenger Railway, to electrify the company's 2-mile suburban line to Hampden. The conditions for a trial of the Daft system could hardly have been worse. Grades on the line were as steep as 6.6 per cent, and curves had a radius of as little as 40 feet.

Skeptical directors of the company specified that payment would be made for the installation only after it had been in satisfactory operation for a year; and even at that, they almost backed out of the deal when an "eminent scientist" called in to look over the line declared, "The man who undertakes to operate this section by electricity in the present state of the art is either a knave or a fool." Only General Manager Robbins' threat to resign deterred the directors from canceling the contract then and there.

Daft installed a powerhouse and a third-rail distribution system, and by August 10, 1885, the line

LEO DAFT

Leo Daft (1843-1922), British-born inventor who constructed several successful exhibition lines in the early 1880's, electrified at Baltimore in 1885 America's first commercial electric railway to operate for any appreciable length of time. — *Smithsonian Institution.*

Two of these little four-wheel electric "tractors," as inventor Daft called them, pulled former horsecars over Baltimore's 2-mile Hampden line. Each of the 12½-foot locomotives was powered by a single 8 h.p. motor. — *Smithsonian Institution.*

After several unfortunate encounters between street traffic and the third-rail system on his Baltimore installation, inventor Daft was forced to erect an overhead power arrangement wherever the line crossed major streets. Here, with its crude pole raised to the gas pipe overhead, is electric dummy *Faraday.* — *Smithsonian Institution.*

was ready for regular operation. Standard 16-foot horsecars were pulled by two four-wheel dummy-type locomotives, the *Morse* and the *Faraday*, both capable of a speed of 10 mph with two trailers. The company soon reported that power costs for the line were only $7 a day, even with twice the former traffic; previously it had cost $18 a day to maintain the line's mules. After a year of reasonably satisfactory operation, the equipment was formally accepted; Daft was paid in full; and two more locomotives, the *Ohm* and the *J. L. Keck*, were ordered. Ultimately, however, the line reverted to horse power.

A Daft system line opened on Pico Street in Los Angeles in 1887 by the Los Angeles Electric Railway Company was powered by electric dummy locomotives almost identical to those used on Daft's historic Baltimore electrification 2 years before. The Pico Street line was equipped with a two-wire overhead system and troller current collection instead of the third-rail system used on the Baltimore installation. Dummy operation continued until a June 1888 boiler explosion at the powerhouse and subsequent bankruptcy put the company out of business. Pico Street electric operation was resumed in 1891 by a new company and continued until early 1963. — *Title Insurance & Trust Company, Los Angeles.*

Inventor John C. Henry of Kansas City, Mo., supplied electrical equipment for San Diego's Electric Rapid Transit Street Railroad Company, which opened for business late in 1887. Despite glowing initial accounts of the performance of the Henry equipment, the Electric Rapid Transit, like most of the early electric car ventures, was less than a complete success and operation ended by mid-1889. — *Herbert R. Fitch, from Eric Sanders.*

During the next few years Daft constructed several other small electric lines, none of them particularly successful. After repeated difficulties with third-rail current collection, Daft switched to a two-wire overhead system. Current was collected by a little four-wheeled carriage that rode on the wires and was connected to the car by a flexible cable. The device was called a "troller" after the manner in which it was towed behind the car; and from this the term, "trolley" eventually evolved. One reported disadvantage of the troller was its tendency occasionally to jump the wires and come crashing through the roof of the car, an occurrence that must have done little to promote feelings of ease or confidence among Daft line passengers.

Probably the most successful of the early Daft installations was the Sea Shore Electric Railway at Asbury Park, N. J., which opened with eight cars on September 19, 1887, and ran continuously until abandonment in 1931. The Daft "troller" system originally installed, however, was replaced only a year later with pole trolleys.

The earliest use of overhead current collection in the United States had been made by Prof. John C. Henry, a former Kansas City telegraph operator, who built an experimental line in 1884 that employed a two-wire overhead system using a troller for current collection similar to that later adopted by Daft. Henry, as a matter of fact, charged that the Daft overhead system was an infringement of his patents.

In 1885 Henry moved his experiments to the tracks of the Fort Scott & Gulf Railway, and during the following winter arranged to electrify a mile of track for the East Street Railway Company, a Kansas City horsecar line. Four motor cars were each equipped with a 25 h.p. motor which projected through the floor of the car so that all working parts were in full view of the motorman. The cars were noisy but the inventor was able to glibly explain this failing. "The buzzing of the motors is easily overcome," wrote one newspaper reporter, "but at present Mr. Henry prefers to have the noise as a notice to people on the streets."

Although Henry's Kansas City line operated reasonably well, it was not a commercial success and went bankrupt after a short time.

In 1887 a group of promoters in San Diego, Calif., who had organized the Electric Rapid Transit Street Railroad Company to construct what was proposed to be the largest electric street railway in the country, engaged Henry to install his system of electrification on their new line. Cars for the new venture were constructed locally, and the Henry Electric Railway Company supplied motors and other electrical equipment. Instead of using the two-wire system employed in his Kansas City experiments, Henry set up a single overhead wire and utilized the rails for the return circuit. Power was transmitted from the motor to the wheels of the cars through a friction clutch and differential gears.

The first line of the new company was placed in operation late in 1887 over a 4-mile former steam dummy line between San Diego and Old Town, and San Diegans marveled at the new electric cars. "The San Diego Electric Rapid Transit Railway is a success," proclaimed the San Diego *Union* a few days later. "The rapidity of motion is entirely under control. It surmounts almost incredible grades. It starts, stops, and moves promptly and smoothly." Stated another contemporary account, "The only noticeable noise was that caused by the electricity as it passed around the wheels."

Only a few weeks later, though, the San Diego *Sun* was reporting on "the baleful effect of the current on watches by the dynamos." "The finer classes of watches are injured," proclaimed the *Sun*. "A watch that has fallen under the electric influence may not show the effects right away, but it is liable to stop at any time and prove unreliable. A respected citizen says the company should never be permitted to run the electric motors without a car attached. It would be well for persons having fine watches to keep off the motors when riding over the electric road." For a short time a lively business was done by enterprising merchants who offered to demagnetize watches, but a few weeks later the company announced that Dr. Gochenauer (one of the promoters) had perfected a new motor "properly enclosed in glass" that would not injure watches.

Hardly had the company opened when it was in trouble. After a falling out with the Old Town steam dummy line over which the electric cars operated, the company discontinued service and dismantled the electric overhead less than a month

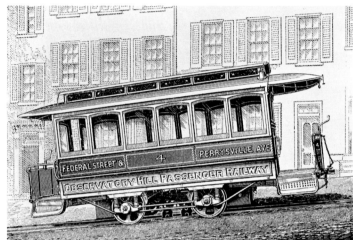

The Observatory Hill Passenger Railway at Allegheny City, Pa., was opened on January 1, 1888, the second in a series of unsuccessful attempts by the Bentley-Knight Company to perfect the underground conduit system of current collection. The underground system was installed on about a mile of the line, while a two-wire side-mounted troller system powered the remainder. Ultimately, a conventional system of overhead trolley wire was installed. Four cars, each powered by two 15 h.p. motors, operated over the line, which included grades of almost 10 per cent. — *Library of Congress.*

61

The first important Van Depoele installation, a mile-long line powered from an underground conduit, was built at the Toronto Industrial Exposition in 1884. For a bigger and better installation the following year, Van Depoele devised a crude pivoted beam arrangement (above) to take power from an overhead wire. It was probably the first use ever made of the underrunning trolley pole. — *Both photos, Toronto Transit Commission.*

CHARLES J. VAN DEPOELE

Charles J. Van Depoele (1846-1892), the son of a master mechanic for Belgium's East Flanders Railway System, gave up a successful art furniture business in Detroit to devote his time to electrical experimentation. He installed the world's first completely electrified street railway system in Montgomery, Ala., in 1886. — *Smithsonian Institution.*

by an equally ill-fated cable railway venture {see page 39}.

Another approach to the problem of current collection was taken by Edward M. Bentley and Walter H. Knight, who electrified 2 miles of track on the East Cleveland Horse Railway Company in 1884. The Bentley-Knight line drew its power from underground conductors placed in a slotted wooden conduit between the rails. A "plow" placed on the cars was used for current collection. Although the line was not particularly successful, it operated until the fall of 1885.

In 1888 the Bentley-Knight Company electrified the Observatory Hill Passenger Railway at Allegheny City, Pa. About a mile of the 4-mile line was equipped with the conduit system, while the remainder used a side-mounted two-wire overhead

Among the early Van Depoele installations was this electrification opened on New Year's Eve 1885 to carry trains of the Minneapolis, Lyndale & Minnetonka, a steam dummy line, into downtown Minneapolis. Installed in response to protests against steam operation through city streets, the electrification lasted only a short time. A year later the line was experimenting with the soda motor {see page 33}. — *Street Railway Journal.*

after service was started. Grandiose plans were announced for other routes, and on New Year's Day 1888 a new line was opened on Fourth Street in San Diego. Operation continued for a year and a half, but the Henry equipment proved to have numerous weaknesses and the line was frequently shut down for mechanical difficulties. By June 1889 the company was losing $20 a day, and the Electric Rapid Transit quietly went out of business, to be replaced

Wheeling, W. Va., was among the earliest U. S. cities to receive electric traction service when a Van Depoele installation opened in 1887. After developing the first crude trolley pole in 1885, Van Depoele returned to the use of two-wire overhead systems and trollers dragged behind cars on a flexible cable for most of his subsequent installations. Clearly visible on *Evangeline*'s front platform is the platform-mounted motor and chain drive Van Depoele favored, an arrangement that was to give endless trouble. — *Collection of LeRoy O. King.*

Proud citizens of Montgomery, Ala., flocked downtown to see the cars of the world's first all-electric street railway system. The 15-mile Van Depoele-equipped system, opened in 1886, brought the electric railway close to the point of commercial success. Reassuring the citizenry, the Montgomery *Advertiser* said, "There is more real danger . . . in a Texas mule's heels than in all the electric motor system." — *Smithsonian Institution.*

system. A conventional overhead trolley system was installed later.

During 1888-1889 the firm made a final attempt to perfect the underground conduit system in an installation on Boston's West End Street Railway Company. After six months of almost daily failures and troubles, the conduit system was abandoned and soon afterward the Bentley-Knight firm disappeared from the field.

Still another of the electric traction pioneers of the 1880's was Sidney H. Short, a professor of physics at the University of Denver. About 1885 Short conducted experiments, using an underground conduit system, with a small electric car operating over a loop of track installed on the university campus. The success of this trial installation led to the formation of the United States Electric Company, which constructed about 4 miles of electric railway in North Denver for the Denver Electric & Cable Company. Operation began in 1885 and continued until late 1887, when horsecars replaced the electric service.

The principal difficulties encountered in the Denver installation were created by the unusual "series" system of current collection devised by Short. In the Short system the power feed was installed in a conduit between the rails, with two iron plates forming a 1½-inch slot in the pavement. A series of contactors, or "circuit breakers," was installed in the conduit at a spacing of 17 feet. On arms projecting to the front and to the rear of the cars were metal shoes which slid along the slot. Suspended on hangers from the shoes was an 18-foot "brush" — a hickory slat on which were mounted brass strips wired to the motor. The arrangement was such that as the brass strips came in contact with the contactors in the conduit, a series circuit was completed through the motor. A switching coil box permitted the speed of the motor to be varied, and a means was provided for bypassing a stopped car. Otherwise, as with bulbs on a Christmas tree, if one car stopped, all of them would have had to do the same. The wide pavement slot permitted all manner of debris to fall into the conduit, aggravating the already formidable problem of maintaining the hundreds of circuit breakers installed under the pavement. In case of wet weather or malfunctions the iron plates forming the slot frequently became "hot" — creating a serious shock hazard to horses and pedestrians — since Short's series system required a much higher voltage than more conventional systems.

Foremost among the inventors who developed the electric railway to the edge of practicality during the mid-1880's was an immigrant Belgian cabinetmaker named Charles J. Van Depoele. After arriving in the U. S. in 1871 at the age of 25, Van Depoele continued the electrical experiments he had long pursued, and in 1881 his electrical manufacturing company began lighting the streets of Chicago utilizing a dynamo of his own invention. About this time Van Depoele became interested in electric railways. In the winter of 1882-1883 he constructed an experimental line at Chicago using an overhead system of current collection, and during the fall of 1883 he exhibited at the Industrial Exposition in Chicago a car which drew its power from an overhead wire.

The following year Van Depoele installed a 1-mile electric railway between a local horsecar line and the grounds of the Toronto Industrial Exposition. Drawing its power from an underground conduit, the little train that operated over the line could carry as many as 200 passengers a trip and was able to reach a speed of 30 mph. In the fall of 1885 Van Depoele was back at the Toronto Exposition with a bigger and better train. This time a motor car and a train of three cars were operated. The most important difference in the line from the previous year was the installation of an overhead wire power system. To draw current from the wire, Van Depoele devised a contact wheel, carried on a pivoted beam, that was held against the underside of the wire by spring tension. This was probably the first use of the trolley pole in substantially its permanent form. The train operated from 8 a.m. to 10:30 p.m. daily throughout the Exposition, carrying as many as 225 to 250 passengers a trip and over 10,000 people a day.

The second year of operation at the Toronto Exposition was a huge success, and Van Depoele soon found himself swamped with contracts for new installations. By November 14, 1885, a 1¼-mile Van Depoele installation was ready for operation at South Bend, Ind., and the line's four electric cars each carried 70 to 100 passengers during trial runs. Abandoning the trolley pole current collection developed for his Toronto line, Van Depoele used a carriage traveling on the overhead wires and connected to the car by means of a flexible cable, an arrangement more or less similar to the trollers employed by Daft and Henry.

Only a month after the South Bend line was completed, the Van Depoele forces opened a mile-long line, much like that operated a few months previous at Toronto, on the New Orleans Exposition grounds. Still another Van Depoele line opened on New Year's Eve 1885, when the Minneapolis, Lyndale & Minnetonka Railway, a steam dummy line, completed electrification of its route into downtown Minneapolis. By early 1886 other Van Depoele lines were under construction in Detroit, Mich., Appleton, Wis., and Montgomery, Ala.

By far the most ambitious electric railway installation up to that time was the Van Depoele electrification of the Capital City Street Railway Company at Montgomery. Construction work began early in 1886, and the first car operated over the line with the inventor himself at the controls in a secret test between midnight and 1 a.m. on March 25, 1886. Regular operation with two converted horsecars began on the company's Court Street line on April 15.

Initially, Van Depoele used a troller system for current collection on his Montgomery installation, but after experiencing repeated difficulties with it he switched to the trolley pole system he had developed the year before at Toronto. As on most of his earlier installations, Van Depoele mounted the electric motor on one platform of the car and used a chain drive to deliver the power to the wheels, an arrangement that proved the source of endless trouble.

If the Montgomery installation was still far short

After a winter storm draped the Richmond trolley wire with sleet and icicles, Pat O'Shaughnessy, Sprague's Irish mechanic, climbed atop the first car out of the barn and wielded a broom to clear the wire as the car moved through the streets. The event was depicted for *The Century Magazine* by Jay Hambidge. — *Virginia State Library*.

of perfection, it did operate reasonably well over grades as steep as 7.5 per cent, and the electrification was gradually extended until some 18 cars were being operated over 15 miles of track, giving Montgomery the first completely electrified street railway system in the world. Except for a temporary return to mule power in 1888 after a fire leveled the company's powerhouse, the Montgomery system was at least successful enough to achieve permanent operation, something that no other line had yet been able to do.

Years of painstaking trial and error were finally bringing results, and by the late 1880's electric traction was showing real promise. At the start of 1888 there were 21 electric railway companies operating some 172 electric cars over a grand total of 86 miles of track. It was still a small beginning, representing scarcely 1 per cent of the total U. S. street railway mileage; but before the year was over, the dazzling

Atrocious trackwork and grades as steep as 10 per cent complicated Sprague's work in the Richmond electrification. This view, dating from about 1887, shows the long Franklin Street hill. — *Virginia State Library*.

65

Frank J. Sprague

Frank J. Sprague (1857-1934), Naval Academy graduate and electrical inventor, applied a scientific approach to electric traction development. His electrification of the Richmond Union Passenger Railway Company in 1887-1888 was the first wholly successful installation of any consequence and set in motion a wholesale conversion of America's street railway systems to electric power. In later years he turned his talents to such notable developments as high-speed electric elevators and the multiple unit system of train control. — *Virginia State Library.*

triumph of a young former Naval officer and inventor named Frank Julian Sprague at Richmond, Va., was to set in motion a remarkable electric railway boom that would make electric traction supreme in the street railway industry in less than a decade.

Sprague brought to electric railway development a considerably more scientific approach than that of the majority of the inventors and experimenters then active in the field. Sprague was born at Milford, Conn., in 1857, and entered the United States Naval Academy in 1874. Even as an Annapolis undergraduate, Sprague had an intense interest in electricity. Following his graduation in 1878 he continued his electrical experimentation during off-duty hours.

During a Far Eastern cruise aboard the flagship U.S.S. *Richmond,* Sprague produced nearly 60 inventions covering a wide range of subjects. While assigned to the training ship *Minnesota,* the ambitious young ensign developed a scheme for installing incandescent light aboard the ship, utilizing an Edison dynamo and a disconnected single-cylinder boiler pump. When he failed to obtain the loan of a dynamo, Sprague had to call the project off.

In the spring of 1881 the *Minnesota* was ordered to Newport, R. I., where Sprague built a novel type of dynamo and tested it for Prof. Moses G. Farmer, then a government electrician at the Newport Torpedo Station.

After terminating his experiments at the Torpedo

Station, Sprague sought orders to attend the 1880-1881 Paris Electrical Exhibition. He was unsuccessful in this, but obtained a temporary assignment to the U.S.S. *Lancaster* — then going out as flagship of the European Squadron — with a three-month leave at his own expense on arrival. It was too late for Sprague to attend the Paris Exhibition, and he was ordered instead to the 1882 British Electrical Exhibition being held at the Crystal Palace in London. There he was made secretary of the jury testing dynamos and gas engines. Although he overstayed his leave by several months, Sprague regained the good graces of the Navy Department by submitting a voluminous report on the test results.

During his stay in London Sprague often rode on the city's pioneer steam-operated underground railway opened in 1863. For the first time he began to think seriously of the application of electric operation to railways and conceived the idea of an overhead power system using a type of underrunning electric railway operation. The method of mounting electric motors had been the source of endless trouble to the early electric railway pioneers. Edison, Field, Daft, Van Depoele, and others all had placed the motors inside the car or on the platform and had connected them to the axles by means of belts, chains, or other flexible couplings rather than by some means of positive gearing. Bentley and Knight, in their 1884 installation at Cleveland, had placed the motors under the carbody — a considerable improvement — but had connected them to the axles with wire cables. Sprague developed a method of mounting that permitted the motor to be geared directly to the axle. In the Sprague arrangement, sometimes called a "wheelbarrow" mounting one side of the motor was hung from the truck frame on a spring mounting, the other was supported directly by the axle. Bearings in the axle side of the mounting permitted the motor to rotate slightly about the axle, thus maintaining perfect

An improved truck was developed by Sprague in 1888 for the pioneer Richmond system. Sprague's wheelbarrow electric motor mounting became almost universal on electric railways. Double reduction gears made it possible for the two 7½ h.p. motors to propel the cars up Richmond's 10 per cent grades. — *Virginia State Library*.

trolley. Charles Van Depoele was working on similar ideas at about the same time, and the two were later to become involved in a patent controversy over the matter.

Sprague returned to the United States in the spring of 1883. He resigned from the Navy and went to work as an assistant to Thomas Edison in connection with the latter's electric light business. Edison was uninterested in electric traction, and a year later Sprague resigned to form his own company and take up the development of his electric railway ideas. His first efforts were in the direction of elevated railway electrification, and in 1885 he devised a method of motor mounting and gearing which was to be almost universally adopted for alignment between the gearing on the motor shaft and the axle, no matter how irregular the track or the motion of the axle.

In a paper presented to the Society of Arts in Boston in December 1885, Sprague outlined a detailed plan for the electric operation of the Manhattan Railway, and he devoted most of the next year to a series of experiments on a section of elevated track in New York. Among witnesses to one of the early tests were Jay Gould and members of the Field family — the principal owners of the elevated. Attempting an impressive demonstration of the experimental car's capabilities, Sprague opened the controller too abruptly, causing a fuse to blow out with a violent flash. Gould, who was standing

Derailments were a frequent occurrence during the early days of operation in Richmond. Artist Jay Hambidge pictured one of them for *The Century Magazine.* — *Virginia State Library.*

next to the fuse, was so startled by the report that he had to be restrained from jumping off the car. After this unnerving experience the financier abandoned all interest in electric traction. The stockholders and directors of the elevated company also took no further notice of Sprague's work, despite a number of highly successful experiments in subsequent months.

After he failed to develop any interest in his ideas for elevated railway electrification, Sprague turned his attention to the problems of electric operation of street railways. He seems for a time to have favored storage batteries rather than a central generating plant and an overhead distribution system as a source of power for street railways, and some of his first efforts, beginning in the spring of 1887, were a series of experiments with battery-powered streetcars at Boston, New York, and Philadelphia.

Commented the New York *Sun* after one such experiment:

They tried an electric car on Fourth Avenue yesterday. It created an amount of surprise and consternation from Thirty-Second Street to 117th Street that was something like that caused by the first steamboat on the Hudson. Small boys yelled "dynamite" and "rats" and made similar appreciative remarks until they were hoarse. Newly appointed policemen debated arresting it, but went no further. The car horses which were met on the other track kicked without exception, as was natural, over an invention which threatened to relegate them to a sausage factory.

Despite the excitement they caused, Sprague's battery car experiments seem to have been inconclusive in their results. Batteries still were not the answer to the problem of street railway power supply. But even as the battery car experiments were being carried out, the Sprague Electric Railway & Motor Company was obtaining contracts for the electrification of street railways with an overhead power system in St. Joseph, Mo., and Richmond, Va.

The St. Joseph installation was to be a modest one, but the Richmond contract called for what was by far the most important street railway electrification ever undertaken. Backed by speculative New York investors, the Richmond Union Passenger Railway Company had obtained a franchise early in 1887 for construction of an entirely new system of street railways in competition with an already existing horsecar system. Conveniently, the franchise allowed operation by horse or mule power, "or such other motive power as may be hereafter allowed by the Council." A few months later the promoters quietly obtained permission to use electric power at about the same time they completed their contract with Sprague.

The contract was one, as Sprague himself observed later, "a prudent businessman would not ordinarily assume." It obligated the Sprague firm to equip a 375 h.p. central station power plant; to install a complete overhead power system on 12 miles of track, much of which had not yet definitely been located and none built; and to provide the motors and electrical appurtenances for 40 cars, each to be powered by two motors. As Sprague was fond of pointing out in later reminiscences, this was almost as many motors as were in use on all the cars throughout the rest of the world. The installation had to be capable of operating 30 cars at one time on a system with grades as steep as 8 per cent. All of this had to be completed within 90 days. Sprague was to receive a total payment of $110,000, provided the installation was satisfactory to the railway company.

From the viewpoint of actual experience, the Sprague firm had little more to its credit than the New York elevated experiments and a few battery car trials, and must have seemed ill-prepared indeed for a task of such magnitude. But Frank Sprague had an abiding faith in the rightness of his ideas and an almost reckless confidence in the abil-

Frank Sprague's Richmond trolleys represented the last word in 1887 municipal transportation. "All are modeled on the Broadway style and are gems of symmetry, finish, and convenience," proclaimed a Richmond *Dispatch* story, which went on to describe their electric lighting and heating systems and electric signal bell. Closed car No. 13 (above) and open car No. 6 (below) are shown not long after the system opened for regular operation in 1888. — *Both photos, New England Electric Railway Historical Society.*

Brilliantly lit by incandescent lamps, the new trolleys delighted Richmonders. This drawing by Jay Hambidge shows a lineup of cars surrounded by an admiring after-theater crowd. — *Virginia State Library.*

ity of his firm to successfully carry out the project. Before the contract was completed the Sprague firm had lost fully $75,000 on the job, but in its success had gained a reputation that was to prove almost priceless.

Things went wrong from the beginning. Hardly was the ink dry on the contract when Sprague was stricken with typhoid fever, removing him from active participation in the work for over two months. During Sprague's long convalescence, two energetic but inexperienced young assistants, both of whom had resigned from military service to join him in the promising electrical field, were left in charge of the work. Lt. Oscar T. Crosby, a West Pointer, did the overseeing at the firm's New York factory where the electrical equipment was being manufactured. The installation work at Richmond, where track construction had started late in May, was in the charge of Ens. S. Dana Greene, who, like Sprague, was an Annapolis man.

Upon returning to Richmond in early autumn to resume general charge of the work, Sprague found an almost appalling situation. The track installed by the promoters was, as Sprague himself described it, "execrable." Obviously none too strong financially, the line's promoters had built with an eye to economy rather than permanence. The rails were a flat 27-pound tram rail of antiquated pattern, poorly jointed, unevenly laid and insecurely tied,

and installed on an unpaved foundation of red clay. Curves were laid with a radius of as little as 27 feet and were provided with only one guard rail, thus permitting the rails to spread easily. The track was laid on grades as steep as 10 per cent, instead of the maximum 8 per cent for which Sprague had bargained. The longest grade was fully a mile long with a slope varying from 4 to 10 per cent.

As an article in the Richmond *Times* some years later put it, the combination of grades and curves was considered "insuperable," and "the average expert electrician of that day laughed in his sleeve as the work progressed." Fearful that the two 7½ h.p. motors he was installing in each car were inadequate for the task now demanded of them, even if a self-propelled car could maintain adhesion at all on such unprecedented grades, Sprague himself began to lose confidence; he set to work designing an electric motor-driven cable system to be installed in pits sunk beneath the track to haul the cars up the steepest hills.

But perhaps a car could climb the hills unaided after all, suggested Sprague's partner, Edward H. Johnson, at a conference called to consider the new crisis. There was only one way to find out, and late one evening in November, Sprague, Greene, and a picked crew, joined by Superintendent George A. Burt of the street railway company, took a car out of the Church Hill carshed at 29th and D streets to give it the acid test. With Sprague himself at the controls the car made its way up one hill and then another, easily swung through a sharp curve on a 6 per cent grade, and finally climbed steadily to the top of the long Franklin Street hill, where it came to rest amid an enthusiastic after-theater crowd.

It was a sort of Pyrrhic victory. Sprague knew the motors had been severely overheated, and a peculiar bucking movement when he attempted to restart the car told him that a motor had been disabled with a short-circuited armature, a difficulty that was to become all too familiar to Sprague before the Richmond project was completed. Announcing loudly that there was some slight trouble with the circuits, Sprague sent Greene for some instruments so that it could be located, turned out the car lights, and lay down on a seat to wait while the crowd dispersed. Finally, Greene returned with the "instruments" — a team of four sturdy mules — and the car was ignominiously dragged back to the shed from which its journey had begun a few hours earlier.

Having proven that it was at least possible to climb hills of 10 per cent or more, Sprague rushed back to his New York plant to try to come up with a solution to the remaining mechanical problem of getting a car up such severe grades without burning up its motors. Sprague's answer was an intermedi-

This old photograph depicts what was evidently a restaging of the historic lineup of 22 cars with which Sprague convinced President Whitney of Boston's West End Street Railway Company of the ability of his electric system to simultaneously start a large number of closely grouped cars. — *New England Electric Railway Historical Society.*

ate gear permitting a double rather than a single reduction between motor and axle. Tools and jigs were hastily made, new gears cast, and the cars altered.

During the next few months the cars ventured out on the line more and more frequently, but one difficulty after another plagued the installation. The motors were modified again and again as the severe strains of operation over the rough track revealed one weakness after another. Switches in the overhead work were giving trouble. No less than 40 designs for an underrunning trolley were tried before one of Sprague's draftsmen, Eugene Pommer, came up with one that worked reasonably well.

The company's promoters pressed Sprague relentlessly to begin regular operation, but when the 90-day limit expired Sprague still wasn't satisfied with his installation and had to agree to a reduced payment of $90,000 — half of it in the form of the company's bonds — in order to obtain a time extension. By January 7, 1888, the company was able to operate nine cars throughout the day, and several thousand delighted Richmonders were allowed to ride the cars free of charge. According to a report of the event in the Richmond *Whig*, no difficulties of any consequence were encountered, except for that presented by small boys who placed rocks on the curves. At one point three cars were brought to a halt for this reason. "It is hoped that some boy may be caught in the act and severely dealt with," commented the *Whig*, "for not only does it discommode the working of the line and endanger the property of the company, but also jeopardizes the lives and limbs of the passengers."

Two days later the company attempted to begin revenue operation with six cars. Motorman P. N. Grant and Conductor Walter Eubank took the first car, No. 28, out of the 29th and P streets carshed at 6 a.m., and a Church Hill resident, William A. Boswell, presented the first revenue nickel to Conductor Eubank. In order to avoid trouble from the inferior trackwork, a man was stationed at each curve with a brush, broom, and other appliances to keep the track clear. Operation continued sporadically throughout the day, but once again mechanical difficulties interfered and the cars were soon on their way back to the carshed for still more modification work.

A few cars continued to operate intermittently during the next several weeks, and by the end of

Bumping over one of the hose jumpers used to maintain streetcar service, one of the early Sprague cars passed a steam pumper of the Richmond fire department. — *New England Electric Railway Historical Society.*

A rare snowfall that cloaked the Virginia capital in white produced these views of the pioneer Richmond trolleys in the late 1880's. — *Both photos, New England Electric Railway Historical Society.*

January the company was ready to try regular operation once again — this time with about 10 cars. Crowds of children were carried without difficulty throughout the day on February 1, and the following day the line was again opened for regular service. Sprague's new gearing developed a disconcerting tendency to lock, and car after car suddenly stopped dead in the street. The crew would get off, remove the offending gear, and limp on with only one motor, if they could. Otherwise, the disabled car was simply hauled off the track so others could pass.

Sprague was convinced that the castings were faulty or the gears improperly cut, but one of his employees, an Irish mechanic named Pat O'Shaughnessy who had what Sprague himself termed "a most happy mechanical judgment," insisted the trouble was simply due to want of adequate lubrication. More oil was applied and the problem was soon remedied.

Motor difficulties continued to plague the line. Brushes on the motors were one of the most persistent trouble sources. Armatures were continually being grounded or short circuited, and commutators burned owing to arcing. Brushes made of copper, bronze, and brass in a wide variety of shapes and types were tried, but none seemed to work. As Sprague later described it, "The track soon looked like a golden path, for the rough commutator bars acted like a milling cutter, and shearing off the ends of the contact bars would send a shower of shimmering scales over machines and roadway."

At this point Sprague was using about $9 worth of brass daily just for brushes, and a car was unable to complete even half a trip without a stop for inspection and generally a change of brushes. The problem was finally solved by the adoption of carbon brushes, a proposal of Charles Van Depoele.

Armatures were disabled so regularly that replacements often had to be shipped from New York by express in order to keep the cars going. At times equipment was maintained in service only by borrowing parts from other cars. "Greene, this is hell," commented Sprague at about this point.

Despite all, the cars were kept moving, and gradually the difficulties lessened, even if new ones continued to present themselves. Little by little the number of cars in service was increased from 10 to 20. By the first week in May the number had been increased to 30, and for the first time the company was able to provide service over its entire system. Soon afterward, Sprague was able to operate 40 cars at one time, 10 more than he had contracted for. "It is almost needless to say that on that day we felt that we owned the street and the city as well," recalled Sprague in later years. "Fatigue and worry were all forgotten in what was to us a supreme moment."

But Sprague's finest moment at Richmond was yet to come. The West End Street Railway Company of Boston, then the world's largest street railway system, with a stable of some 8000 horses, was contemplating a change in motive power. The company had all but decided to adopt the then-popular cable system; but President Henry M. Whitney of the West End line, together with a party of directors and his general manager, was persuaded to visit Sprague's Richmond installation, stopping en route to visit the Bentley-Knight line at Allegheny City. Whitney was impressed with the Richmond line, but his general manager, Daniel F. Longstreet,

remained a firm advocate of the cable railway. Longstreet was pessimistic about the ability of the electric system to start a large group of cars that had become bunched within a short stretch of track, something that occurred frequently on a big city street railway.

Sprague decided to resolve the question with a dramatic display of electric traction's overload capacity. Late one night, after regular operation had ended, 22 cars were lined up platform to platform at the Church Hill carshed on a section of line designed for the operation of only four well-distributed cars at a time. The engineer at the power plant was instructed to load the feeder fuses, raise the voltage from the customary 450 volts to 500, and to hold on "no matter what."

Whitney and his party were roused from their hotel and taken to the carhouse to witness the test. At the wave of a lantern the cars started up, one after another, as soon as there was room. The line voltage dropped to barely 200 volts, and the car lights dimmed until they were hardly visible, but the cars kept moving. Gradually the voltage began to rise, the lights brightened again, and soon all 22 cars were merrily trundling out of sight.

Whitney was convinced, and promptly went before the Boston Board of Aldermen to obtain permission to electrify his system. Part of it was to be an underground conduit system; the remainder was to have overhead construction. Sprague motors were to be used on all cars.

The electric railway at long last had arrived. After Frank Sprague's "incredible adventure in Richmond," as one writer later termed it, the horsecar was an anachronism, and the cable railway boom would sputter to a halt in only a few more years. By the end of 1889 there were no less than 154 electric street railway systems in the United States, and within 2 years of the opening of the Richmond system the number had increased to more than 200 — well over half of them equipped by the Sprague firm.

The time of the trolley had come.

The coming of the trolley car was the cause for merrymaking and rejoicing. This gala affair marked the opening of the Superior (Wis.) Rapid Transit Railway's line out Tower Avenue to South Superior on September 14, 1892. Following the arrival of the opening-day trolley caravan from downtown Superior, passengers and interested bystanders joined together in a big celebration and barbeque. Rarely has such excitement visited South Superior in the 95 years since. — *Collection of Wayne C. Olsen.*

The Time of the Trolley

WELL BEFORE the end of the 19th century, the trolley car had become an integral part of the urban American scene. Clanging noisily, ornately decorated electric cars rumbled through the city streets carrying Americans to and from their daily work. Balmy summer days brought out the breezy open cars, which hurried the cities' millions to beaches, parks, and other pleasure spots. Leather-lunged guides bellowed their spiels through megaphones as gawking tourists viewed the city from special trolley sight-seeing cars. Sparkling white-and-gold post office cars hurried through the streets, speeding the distribution of the U. S. Mail in America's great urban centers. Clad in dignified black, streetcar hearses rolled solemnly through the city to suburban cemeteries. In the golden age of electric traction the electric cars served almost every urban transportation need.

Rarely has America experienced anything quite equal to the great electric railway boom that fol-

A ceremonial first run was an indispensable feature of the opening of a new trolley line. Here two carloads of dignitaries have just completed an opening-day run over the Knoxville (Tenn.) Street Railroad Company's Lake Ottosee line on May 1, 1890. A similar affair marking the beginning of the Abilene (Tex.) Street Railway in 1908 wasn't quite as successful. The inaugural car derailed and landed in a ditch. — *Collection of Allan H. Berner.*

With Motorman Charles Sawyer and Conductor S. R. Nutbrown in charge, nine-bench open car No. 57 opened the Manchester (N. H.) Street Railway's Massabesic Lake line on August 3, 1895. The resort proved so popular that on the second day of operation each car carried an average of 100 passengers. — *Collection of O. R. Cummings.*

lowed on the heels of Frank Sprague's triumph at Richmond. In 1890, when the Department of Commerce and Labor first made a census of the street railway industry, only some 1262 miles of track were electrically operated. By the time the next census was taken in 1902, the mileage of electric lines had grown almost twentyfold to a total of nearly 22,000 miles.

Much of the growth of electric railways during the early years, of course, simply represented the conversion of horse and cable railways to electric power, but the industry itself was growing at a phenomenal rate too. By almost any index, the total size of the industry more than doubled in the dozen years from 1890 to 1902. Total track mileage increased to almost 3 times the 1890 level. The number of passenger cars and employees doubled. Investment in street railway systems leaped from less than 400 million dollars in 1890 to more than 2 billion dollars in 1902. In 1890 street railways carried slightly over 2 billion passengers. By 1902 they were carrying approximately 5 billion — more than 7 times the total number carried on the nation's steam railroads.

Practical electric transportation had arrived at an auspicious time. During the last few decades of the 19th century and the first few decades of the current century, the U. S. population was increasing at a rate of 10 to 15 million persons every decade; and the trend toward urbanization of the American populace was increasing rapidly. In 1880 less than 30 per cent of the population lived in urban areas; by the start of World War I fully half of the American population would be living in cities. Cities were becoming larger, too. In 1880 there were only 20 U. S. cities that exceeded a population of 100,000; by 1910 there were 50.

Except in those cities that had steam railroad commuter service to suburban areas, the extent of urban development was governed almost entirely by the practical radius of operation of the street railway companies. The horsecar had pushed the limits of residence out to about 4 miles, but its low speed made the animal railway impractical for much more. The faster cable car expanded the limits of urban growth considerably, but its exceedingly high construction costs limited the extent of its adoption. The electric railway, faster than either horse or cable railway and relatively cheap to construct and operate, changed the whole character of the American city.

Filling what a 1902 census report called "an imperative social need," the electric cars permitted the distribution of the burgeoning urban population over a much wider area than would otherwise have been possible. More than any other single development, the electric railways contributed to the growth

Few houses were in sight as the San Diego (Calif.) Electric Railway pushed this new line out University Avenue in 1907. — *Historical Collection, Union Title Office, Title Insurance & Trust Company, San Diego.*

of the metropolitan suburbs. Population growth followed the car lines, and a new trolley line extension invariably increased land values. Not infrequently, real estate syndicates built electric railways just to promote their developments.

In the early years, at least, electric railways were generally an enormously profitable venture. By roughly doubling the radius of practical street railway commuting, the electric cars generated a tremendous amount of new traffic; and the more attractive service provided by trolleys induced still further traffic growth in the form of pleasure travel. Between 1890 and 1902 the average number of streetcar rides per urban inhabitant increased from a little more than 100 a year to 177, and by 1917 had grown to some 260 rides a year.

In comparison with horsecar systems, electric lines were considerably cheaper to operate. The experience of the Lynn & Boston Railroad Company was fairly typical. In 1891, when the system was operated entirely with horses, the company's oper-

This specially decorated California car and the inevitable crowd of local dignitaries heralded the opening of a new suburban line at Fresno, Calif., on May 2, 1923. — *Collection of Allan H. Berner.*

Railways Company which represented the amalgamation of some 114 underlying properties.

Municipalities customarily required some form of franchise for street railways. Understandably, the cities usually endeavored to extract the most favorable possible terms from the traction companies. All too frequently the traction men, in their eagerness to obtain the coveted franchise, paid too little attention to the fine print, or agreed to terms which were ultimately to prove almost ruinous.

In a minority of cases franchises were awarded which placed no particular requirements on the traction companies and entailed no compensation to the municipality. Popular opinion, however, held that the streets belonged to the people, and that a franchise for their use by a private corporation should be

ating expenses per car-mile averaged about 25 cents. In 1897, by which time the system was entirely electrically operated, expenses were averaging less than 15 cents per car-mile. During the same period, while gross earnings increased by not quite 1½ times, net earnings increased to almost 6 times the 1891 level.

In a 1907 census of street railways, 939 companies reported a total net income of over 40 million dollars on gross earnings of not quite 430 million, a profitable state of affairs that held true, more or less, until the beginning of World War I. Some of the greatest American fortunes of the turn-of-the-century period were made in street railway securities, sometimes under circumstances that would be considered highly questionable today. Perhaps the greatest street railway fortune of all was that assembled by Peter Widener, William Whitney, Thomas Ryan, and their associates, who in only 9 years between 1893 and 1902 netted a fortune of an estimated 100 million dollars through the systematic plunder of New York's Metropolitan Street Railway.

Street railway properties were such lucrative investments that scores of eager promoters rushed to construct new lines. In the early years of electric traction it was not uncommon for the larger cities to be served by a number of separate companies, frequently operating rival lines no more than a block or two apart. Even as early as the 1890's, however, an almost inevitable process of consolidation began, with the result that well before World War I street railway properties in most cities had been unified into a single system. What is probably some sort of record in this respect was set by the Pittsburgh

Street railways were built largely with manual labor and animal power. This track gang laid a new line at Piedmont and Fifth streets on the Duluth (Minn.) Street Railway in 1910. — *Collection of Wayne C. Olsen.*

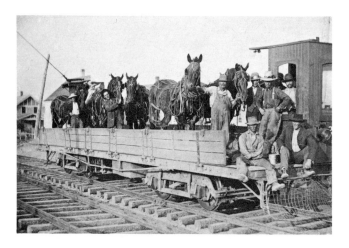

Horses used to build Duluth's East Ninth Street line rode to work in ease. — *Collection of Wayne C. Olsen.*

Street railway trackwork at major intersections was bewilderingly complicated. This 1897 view shows construction work at First and Broad streets on the Richmond (Va.) Traction Company. —*Valentine Museum, Richmond.*

awarded only for limited periods and with provision for compensation to the city. This prevailing viewpoint was expressed by the Mayor of Mansfield, O., who wrote in 1907: "The fact of the matter is that our city council has been too free in granting franchises for the occupancy of its streets by street railways. There are three streetcar lines now operating in our city, and not one cent has been paid, or asked of them, for a franchise, which to my notion is not what it should be."

Most often a franchise called for some form of payment to the municipality. Sometimes a lump sum was required at the time the franchise was awarded; but more often an annual payment, either a fixed amount or a percentage of the gross revenues, was required. Often franchises placed other requirements on the traction companies, such as street paving and cleaning, or snow removal. Some companies accepted "perpetual" franchises in which a fixed rate of fare — usually five cents — was established. Later on, as operating costs rose or municipal boundaries were extended, the companies found it impossible to operate profitably with a nickel fare and usually met with difficulty in attempting to obtain modification of the franchise terms.

Many cities and states required competitive bidding for franchises in order to obtain the most favorable possible terms. Sometimes the results were downright ridiculous. In New York, where the Cantor Act of 1886 required competitive bidding, the franchise for a new territory in the Bronx was awarded to The Peoples Traction Company after the company had agreed to pay to the city 95 per cent of its gross receipts, in addition to the 3 per cent required by the state. It perhaps goes without saying that no lines were ever built or operated under this particular franchise.

Because of the enriching effect on real estate values, the construction of street railways was almost universally regarded with favor by property owners along the route of a new line. One electric railway construction engineer, though, told of a case where property owners took strong exception to installation of a trolley line along their residential street. One lady adamantly refused to allow the erection of a pole in front of her house. When construction men went ahead and dug a 5-foot hole for the pole, the lady jumped into it and refused to get out. The workers dug a new hole beside the first, installed the pole, and then gallantly hauled the lady out.

Sometimes, too, it was feared that the arrival of cheap electric transportation threatened the exclusive nature of a community. Such sentiment led to a bitter conflict in Montclair, N. J., in the early 1890's when an application for a trolley line franchise was filed. At a heated town meeting on April 5, 1892, one anti-trolley speaker declared that he "did not propose to make Montclair a dumping ground for Dutch picnics and sick baby excursions." Anti-trolley sentiment prevailed at this particular engagement, but eventually Montclair got its trolley line anyway. Even so, when a franchise was finally

79

Although details of this early Lexington (Ky.) photo are unknown, it may well represent the opening of the city's street railway system during the 1890's. Street paving was yet to come. — *Collection of William D. Middleton.*

granted in 1898 the cautious authorizing ordinance contained no fewer than 28 pages of regulations.

There were other, more serious, conflicts encountered by the trolley men. Ordinarily the purely urban trolley lines offered no competitive threat to the steam roads, but when the electric cars ventured into suburban territory they began to compete directly with the steam lines for suburban passenger traffic. In 1900, for example, the Pennsylvania Railroad announced that it was giving up its entire Chicago suburban service as a result of the competition offered by new trolley lines.

Occasionally the steam road men attempted to meet the trolley competition with rather forceful measures. A favorite tactic was to refuse the electric roads permission to construct grade crossings with the steam lines. One such attempt at Chicago in 1900 ended in a pitched battle between streetcar and steam railroad workers. The Western Indiana Railroad had obtained an injunction preventing the General Electric Railway from building a line across WI's tracks at 15th and Dearborn streets. After successfully appealing to the Supreme Court of Illinois, which dissolved the lower court injunction,

the electric line moved in a force of 500 men to seize the crossing and lay track. The steam line countered with a force of almost equal size, and 12 men were seriously injured in the battle for possession of the crossing. Superior numbers carried the day for the electric men, who gained control and proceeded to lay the crossing and begin running cars.

An even more violent fracas of this type was the celebrated North Abington (Mass.) riot of 1893, caused by the intractable opposition of the New York, New Haven & Hartford Railroad to construction of a crossing with its line at North Avenue in North Abington by the Rockland & Abington Street Railway. Initially, the New Haven moved to block the crossing by legal means. After a request for an

This is where the power for the cars came from. The generator in the Duluth (Minn.) Street Railway's 11th Avenue West powerhouse was driven by this massive Allis cross-compound condensing Corliss engine, which boasted a 96-ton, 28-foot diameter flywheel. — *Collection of Wayne C. Olsen.*

Street railway track required exceptionally heavy construction to successfully withstand the rigors of both trolley and street traffic. This Monongahela-West Penn Public Service Company line of Marietta, O., used heavy girder rail laid on wood ties, followed by a concrete slab and brick paving. — *Marietta College Library.*

injunction against the work was denied by the courts, the steam road men prepared to take other measures, resulting in what one historian described as the boldest attempt in the history of the Massachusetts Commonwealth of a corporation to defy the laws of the Commonwealth, the power of the state courts, the rights of the community, and the rights of another corporation.

Pending the outcome of the court litigation, Rockland & Abington construction forces had laid rails to within a few feet of the New Haven tracks on either side. Following denial of the steam line's request for an injunction, Maj. Edward P. Reed, president of the street railway company, announced his intention to install the crossing. New Haven Division Superintendent John C. Sanborn, backed by a force of 100 laborers, announced that he would resist the construction.

A temporary truce maintained the peace over a weekend, but on the following Monday morning the trolley men made their move. While the street railway forces laid their rails to within a foot of the New Haven tracks, Superintendent Sanborn and his force, now increased to a strength of 150 men, stood by watchfully.

On Tuesday morning the trolley men arrived at the scene to find that the trolley wire had been cut during the night. Repairs were made, but almost immediately a New Haven car was pulled over the crossing while an employee reached up to again cut the wire. The situation became increasingly tense

Sketch of 1893 North Abington (Mass.) riot. — *Courtesy* Transportation Bulletin, *Conn. Valley Chapter, NRHS.*

as three additional carloads of New Haven laborers arrived to swell Sanborn's "army" to 300 men. A crowd of some 1500 people was drawn to the scene by news of the prospective clash.

Affairs reached a climax on Wednesday, August 16. Seventy New Haven laborers, armed with shovels, patrolled both sides of the tracks. The 300 steam road men on the scene were backed by additional reserves held in nearby Weymouth. North Abington authorities deputized eight special officers to aid the four regular police officers, two special

Bound for a summer outing at Cape Porpoise, excursionists set out from Sanford, Me., over the Atlantic Shore Line Railway. — *Collection of O. R. Cummings.*

This party of trolley car tourists had just debarked from an open car of the Massachusetts Northeastern Street Railway for a visit to John Greenleaf Whittier's birthplace at Haverhill. — *Collection of LeRoy O. King.*

An outing at Fox River Park in Aurora, Ill., about 1915 brought this lineup of Aurora open cars on North Broad-way, where excursionists transferred from interurbans of the Aurora, Elgin & Chicago.—*Aurora Historical Museum*.

officers, and Road Commissioner Augustus H. Wright already on the scene; and an attorney was sent to Boston in an attempt to obtain a restraining injunction against the New Haven.

By noon a crowd of 2000 people had gathered at the scene, including a number of public officials and prominent citizens who repaired to the veranda of the nearby Culver House to watch developments in relative comfort.

At 1:15 p.m. the steam road men received word from New Haven headquarters in Boston to tear up the street railway tracks, and Superintendent Sanborn's crew, headed by blacksmith Angus Frazer swinging his shovel in pinwheel fashion, began the attack. Road Commissioner Wright and a deputy sheriff were manhandled in an unsuccessful attempt to halt the destruction, but two New Haven officials were arrested and hauled off to the local jail.

Commissioner Wright, who also doubled as the local fire chief, retaliated by calling out Hose Company 2 to play two fire hoses on the New Haven forces. At this point the combatants began hurling paving stones, driving the dignitaries on the Culver House veranda to cover and smashing windows in the post office and a nearby store. Many storekeepers in the vicinity had prudently boarded up their windows when the situation had begun to get ugly during the morning.

After about 45 minutes of pitched battle the North Abington forces had pretty well stopped the attack with their fire hoses; but then the New Haven men rallied, cut the hoses, removed the nozzles, and

Riflemen ride a car of the Northampton Traction Company at Easton, Pa. — *Collection of Howard E. Johnston*.

soon finished the job of tearing out the trolley rails.

About 4:30 p.m. Major Reed and Judge Kelley arrived with an injunction prohibiting the New Haven from interfering with the work. Both sides then met at Standish Hall for a peace conference and by six o'clock that evening the trolley rails had been relaid.

In the aftermath of the disturbance five New Haven officials were sentenced to terms of as much as four months in the House of Correction, and the railroad paid $15,000 in damages for injuries and property loss. As a final act of retribution, the New Haven erected a handsome new granite station building in North Abington.

On at least one recorded occasion a similar dispute occurred between two rival trolley companies. In Detroit, Mich., where there had long been antagonism toward the privately owned Detroit United Railway and agitation for municipal ownership, the city in 1920 established a street railway commission to build lines of its own and, ultimately, to buy out the Detroit United system. Early in 1921 the two rival trolley lines clashed head-on when the city set out to build a crossing with the DUR's Mack Avenue line for the first municipally owned trolley route.

When city forces made ready to install the crossing, DUR officials massed heavy equipment at the scene, including a snowplow, a wrecking train, and a number of trucks, in order to block the work. With the full resources of the city behind it, the street railway commission had a force of 200 policemen on hand to prevent any trouble.

As soon as work was started by city crews, a DUR man drove a heavy truck through the gang of workmen and abandoned it where it would obstruct traffic. DUR Assistant General Manager E. J. Burdick, who had been attempting to serve a restraining order issued by the courts to prevent the crossing, was promptly arrested by the city police when he appeared to be preparing to bring other equipment into action. While Burdick was taken to nearby Belle Island by policemen and detained there by the raising of the drawbridge to the mainland, the street railway commission men completed the disputed crossing.

Still another variety of dispute which ended in violence was represented by a 1913 conflict between the Borough of Sunbury, Pa., and the Sunbury & Susquehanna Railway Company. Frustrated in its efforts to get permission for a track extension from a hostile borough council, the street railway company decided to go ahead with the desired work regardless.

Moving in with a force of 15 men early on the morning of April 15, the streetcar men proceeded to tear up paving brick preparatory to laying the new track. Unable to obtain an injunction to stop the work because of the absence of the local judge who was on a fishing trip, Sunbury Chief Burgess S. H. McKinney took matters into his own hands. More than 60 bystanders and local citizens were deputized to act under orders of the Chief Burgess. Several fire companies were called out and their hoses were turned on the trolley men. A crowd of hundreds was quickly drawn to the scene.

Several fistfights broke out between trolley men and police, one trolley man cut a fire hose with an ax, and at several points the dispute threatened to develop into a full-fledged riot. The borough forces hauled ashes to the scene, which were dumped in the street in an effort to hinder the work of the trolley men, and later the borough's large road roller was brought into play in a further effort to disrupt the work.

Finally, tempers cooled and the trolley company withdrew to await a settlement in the courts. To ensure that the trolley men would refrain from further work, a Sunbury attorney made a dash by automobile to locate the judicial fishing party and obtain an injunction restraining the work. Eventually the matter was more or less amicably settled in the local courts, but the extraordinary affair managed to keep tongues wagging in Sunbury for days afterward.

A more celebrated dispute between a municipality and a street railway company was an event that

A unique trolley car outing around the turn of the century was a trip to "tent city" on the Coronado "Silver Strand" across the Bay from San Diego, Calif. Several hundred tents and palm-leaf-covered cottages were set up, a variety of recreation features were installed, and an old ferry boat was converted into a floating casino. An extension of the Coronado Railroad's Orange Avenue line delivered passengers from the Coronado ferry landing direct to the resort.—*Historical Collection, Union Title Office, Title Insurance & Trust Company, San Diego.*

Among the many trolley lines which derived a major portion of their traffic from pleasure travel was the Exeter, Hampton & Amesbury Street Railway of New Hampshire and Massachusetts. The line's principal attraction was Hampton Beach, N. H., where the company installed a large casino offering vaudeville and band concerts. One of the company's smart open cars pauses in front of the casino (above). In this later scene below, automobiles seem to be bringing most of the crowds, but Hampton Beach is obviously still an immensely popular resort. — *Collection of LeRoy O. King (above); Collection of F. W. Schneider III (below).*

Dressed up in their best bowlers and straw hats for a company picnic, employees of the Plainfield (N. J.) Street Railway posed at the Fourth Street carbarn in 1895. — *Collection of Howard E. Johnston.*

Portland (Me.) Railroad's 12-bench open car No. 125 waited for passengers at the company's Riverton Park casino, where facilities included private dining rooms and a dance hall. Other attractions were an open-air theater with vaudeville performances, a deer enclosure "for the edification of the public," and boating in the Presumpscot River. — *Collection of O. R. Cummings.*

took place at Toledo, O., in 1919. For more than 5 years following expiration of the Toledo Railways & Light Company's franchise in 1914 the city and the trolley company had unsuccessfully attempted to negotiate the terms of a new franchise. In the meantime the company had continued to operate without one. The dispute finally came to a head on November 8, 1919, when the city council passed an ordinance ousting the trolley company from the city streets. The trolley men promptly complied and by midnight had run all of the company's cars over an affiliated interurban line into Michigan, where they were safely beyond the reach of any injunction the city might obtain. For almost

a month, while the trolley cars languished in Michigan, Toledo struggled to get along with the stopgap transportation provided by a hastily assembled fleet of 2500 jitneys. Local business suffered severely and increasing pressure was brought to obtain a settlement. Federal Judge John M. Killits finally worked out a temporary agreement, and on December 5 the cars returned to Toledo. The judge himself, attired in a motorman's uniform for the occasion, ceremoniously piloted the first car back into the city.

During the golden age of the electric railway in the years before World War I, the trolleys represented far more than just a utilitarian means of home-to-work transportation. Among the many benefits brought about by electrification was a tremendous growth in pleasure travel, a trend which was quickly noted and assiduously promoted by the street railwaymen.

Whether for a family picnic, a church or social group excursion, a trip to a park, or other entertainment, the trolleys afforded an enormously popular outing. Even if people had no place in particular to go, they boarded the cars for the sheer pleasure of trolley riding. Huge fleets of open-air cars supplied respite from the hot summer weather, and as one early writer noted, "Trolley cars travel fast enough to produce a feeling of mental exhilaration, which is absent from, or scarcely felt by, passengers in horsecars." A ride on the cars was a cheap and popular way to court a young lady. Recalled a nostalgic Yakima (Wash.) newspaperman years later, "Marriages based on streetcar courtships seemed to stick."

There were many who claimed that trolley riding even had definite health benefits. In 1900 a prominent Louisville (Ky.) physician announced "after careful investigation" that streetcar riding was the best possible cure for insomnia. Advocating a 2-hour ride before bedtime, preferably on the front seat of an open car, the good doctor claimed, "An hour's streetcar riding scarcely ever fails to bring on a feeling of drowsiness, and it has actually been able to bring sleep to the most nerve-wracked of insomniacs by this simple device."

One of the most popular and successful implements of pleasure-travel promotion was a resort or park operated by a street railway company. At the time of the 1907 electric railway census there were some 467 parks or pleasure resorts operated by street railway companies, with an annual patronage well in excess of 50 million visitors. Since the streetcar parks were almost invariably located so as to require a trip on the cars to get there, it is reasonable to assume that more than 100 million trolley fares a year were collected from visitors to the "electric parks."

For many smaller lines, traffic to and from com-

Pleasure-seekers arrived at the popular Canobie Lake Park at Salem, N. H., aboard the open cars of the Massachusetts Northeastern Street Railway. — *Collection of LeRoy O. King.*

Open cars of the Concord (N. H.) Street Railway's Clinton Street line gathered outside the Concord State Fairgrounds in 1902 for the homeward rush. — *Collection of Carl L. Smith.*

pany-operated pleasure resorts represented a substantial portion of their total business. For example, in 1902 the Bridgeton & Millville Traction Company, a small New Jersey line, had 350,000 visitors to its summer park, and their travel to and from the park represented well over a third of the line's annual traffic of some 1.7 million passengers.

The streetcar parks offered an almost endless variety of diversions, and the pages of *Street Railway Journal* and other trade publications were frequently given over to detailed descriptions of the more successful parks or the latest fads in amusement devices.

The attractions afforded by Kennywood Park, operated by the Monongahela Street Railway Company, may be considered typical of trolley parks. Opened in 1899, Kennywood was located on an attractive site about 12 miles from Pittsburgh. Boating was available on a lake, and there were tennis courts, croquet grounds, bowling alleys, a general sports field, and a baseball diamond. Amusement devices included a merry-go-round and a three-way figure-8 toboggan slide. For musical entertainment

Pleasure-bent Philadelphians flocked to popular Willow Grove Park on the cars of the Philadelphia Rapid Transit Company. — *Collection of Howard E. Johnston.*

Rustic Otsego Park, on the banks of Otsego Creek not far from Oneonta, N. Y., was a big revenue builder for the Oneonta, Cooperstown & Richfield Springs Railway.

The splendid new amphitheater at Glen Echo Park, a trolley park near Washington, D. C., was ready for the opening of an 1892 chautauqua. — *Collection of LeRoy O. King.*

The handsome Wabash River steamer *Tecumseh* loaded Lafayette (Ind.) excursionists at the foot of Columbia Street around 1906. Naturally, everyone arrived aboard the local streetcars. — *Collection of Ed Hitze.*

In these two delightful drawings, artist F. Cresson Schell has captured the gaiety and excitement of a trolley excursion aboard Philadelphia's brilliantly illuminated "party" cars. — *Both prints, Library of Congress.*

there was a bandstand and an outdoor concert pavilion large enough to accommodate 200 musicians. A dancing pavilion was among the most popular features. Kennywood Park was extremely well-liked and drew a half million visitors in just its first season.

Regular vaudeville performances were frequently offered in outdoor theaters at the trolley parks. In New England, where street railway parks and resorts were probably more numerous than anywhere else, a number of street railways would frequently join together to form a vaudeville "circuit," permitting a different performance to be offered at each company's park every night.

Making the best of bad luck, one New England park, Norumbega at Auburndale, Mass., even managed to convert a disaster to an advantage. Shortly after a 1909 fire destroyed the park's theater, dasher signs of the parent company's streetcars were inviting the public out to the park to view the ruins; and when the company elected to rebuild the theater in record time, a new set of dasher signs proclaimed "Come watch us build new theater in eight days."

Some of the most spectacular trolley park attractions were among those offered by the street railways of Chicago. The principal fascination at Ferris Wheel Park, operated by the North Chicago division of the Union Traction system, was the 250-foot-diameter Ferris wheel originally constructed for the 1893 World's Columbian Exposition. Passengers

The ornate trolley parlor car *Merrymeeting* of the Lewiston, Augusta & Waterville Street Railway in Maine seated 35 in plush upholstered wicker armchairs. The interior was finished in mahogany and the floor was covered with heavy green carpeting. Ornamental ironwork enclosed two observation platforms. The Briggs Carriage Company of Amesbury, Mass., built the car in 1899. — *Collection of O. R. Cummings.*

The Manchester (N. H.) Street Railway's parlor car *City of Manchester* was a vest-pocket version of the *Merrymeeting*. The interior appointments were equally luxurious, and the exterior was finished in royal blue and cream with intricate gold leaf ornamentation. An early account indicates that the car was originally equipped with a nickel-plated truck. Only $5 a day chartered the elegant vehicle. — *Collection of O. R. Cummings.*

were able to view the entire city from the top of the huge wheel, and on a clear day were even able to see the opposite shore of Lake Michigan, 50 miles away.

Sans Souci Park, operated by the Chicago City Railway Company, boasted the largest electric fountain of its kind in the world. The fountain, played twice each evening, was equipped with powerful electric pumps which discharged water at a rate of 150,000 gallons an hour through 2000 nozzles, reaching a height of as much as 150 feet, while 19 10,000-candlepower lamps produced a variety of colored lighting effects.

Daring Chicagoans flocked to ride the feature attraction at Chutes Park, operated on Kedzie Avenue by the Chicago Union Traction Company. Small boats were hauled to the top of the 90-foot-high chutes by an endless chain, then released to slide down a stream of water on a 325-foot runway, reaching a speed of 55 mph before splashing into the lake at the bottom.

Skating rinks were another favorite electric park feature. Duquesne Garden, a former carhouse converted into what was claimed to be the largest artificial ice skating rink in the world, was a popular attraction on the Pittsburgh Railways Company.

The Northampton Traction Company at Easton, Pa., and the Virginia Passenger & Power Company at Richmond, Va., were among a number of companies operating roller skating rinks.

An unusual difficulty experienced by the latter company at its roller rink in City Reservoir Park in Richmond was that of finding a band that could be heard above the continual thumping of falling be-

This trolley sight-seeing party toured Spokane, Wash., in a semi-convertible car of the Washington Water Power Company. — *Collection of LeRoy O. King Jr.*

These photos span a half century of trolley sight-seeing in Washington, D. C. In 1903 "Seeing Washington" cars operated 3 times daily at a fee of 50 cents (above). The *Silver Sightseer* introduced in 1957 (below) featured air conditioning, foam-rubber seats, and a uniformed hostess. The fare was 40 cents. — *Collection of William D. Middleton (above); Joseph P. Saitta (below).*

ginners. "A fife and drum corps were finally used with some success," reported the company's general manager, who noted that a 10-piece Italian band also seemed to work reasonably well.

Almost every trolley line derived extra income by offering its equipment to special parties at charter rates. Many systems operated de luxe parlor cars for the use of company brass and these were also made available for charter service. The luxuriously appointed trolley parlor cars were usually fitted with comfortable wicker or upholstered lounge chairs, heavy plush carpeting, plate glass windows, and draperies. Interiors were customarily finished in wood paneling and carvings, and the cars sometimes had brass-rail-enclosed observation platforms. Facilities for serving light meals and refreshments were frequently provided; and one such car, the *Bramhall*, operated by the Portland (Me.) Railroad, even boasted a special built-in ice-cooled wine closet.

Perhaps the ultimate in luxury trolley travel was proposed in 1900 by two Chicago men, who organized a special buffet car company. Their equipment was to be operated as trailers over the city's street and elevated railway systems under an arrangement comparable to that between the Pullman Company and the steam railroads. Each car was to be staffed with a porter in charge of a complete kitchen; and the service, it was assured, "will be conducted as well as any transcontinental dining car." Buffet car service, which was to be available for only a five-cent extra fare, would be just the thing, claimed the promoters, for someone who wanted to take guests or customers to luncheon while showing them the sights of the city, or for en-

Only a month after its completion by the Montreal Street Railway's Hochelaga shops, the first of the city's famous open-air sight-seeing cars posed at Mount Royal and Park avenues in June 1905 with proud company brass occupy-

ing the varnished observation seats. The car was finished in yellow and gold and generously supplied with ornamental brasswork. Two arches carried beaver emblems. — *Montreal Transportation Commission.*

Rebuilt from an old passenger car, the striped *Scout* of the Kansas City Public Service Company gave Kansas City sight-seers of the 1930's unrestricted visibility. — *Collection of Charles Goethe.*

joying a smoke and a late supper after the theater.

Sight-seeing by trolley was an attraction in almost every large city. Sometimes the trolley lines published guides for tourists making use of regular car services, but more often special sight-seeing services were offered. De luxe "party" cars were frequently used in this kind of service. In Detroit, for instance, the Detroit Citizens Street Railway operated its handsome party car *Yolande* in a regular "tallyho" service. Five times daily the car made a 2-hour sight-seeing excursion over principal lines of the Detroit system. A crack motorman and conductor were assigned to the crew, and a colored attendant looked after the wants of the passengers. Sight-seers paid only 25 cents for the de luxe tour.

A number of cities operated specially constructed sight-seeing cars. Several U. S. lines had roofless open cars — usually rebuilt from older equipment — for summer sight-seeing excursions. Surprisingly, this particular type of equipment enjoyed its greatest popularity in Canada, where special open cars with seats installed in a tiered arrangement were run in Montreal, Quebec, Calgary, and Vancouver.

In its golden age the trolley car played a part in almost every aspect of urban life. Before the automobile hearse usurped its place after World War I, the trolley funeral car was considered not only an acceptable but even a preferred means of transportation to one's final resting place.

Street railway funeral cars probably originated in Mexico City, where the horsecar system was operating 26 of them as early as 1886. The idea began to catch on in U. S. cities during the late 1890's, and almost every major city had one or more special cars operating to on-line cemeteries. The typical trolley funeral car was painted in suitably somber shades. Black was preferred in most cities, but St. Louis used chocolate brown and Buffalo a dark green.

The funeral service operated by the Baltimore & Northern Electric Railway, later the United Railways, was typical of that afforded by street railways. The company's luxurious funeral car *Dolores*, rebuilt in 1901 from an ordinary passenger car, was finished in black and silver, and fitted with enameled trucks. The coffin was loaded into a special zinc-lined vault through a large plate glass door. This gave onlookers a chance to view the costliness and detail of the coffin. A rack was placed above the casket for the display of floral pieces, which could be viewed through two elongated windows. Seats for members of the immediate family, arranged like two Pullman sections, were placed opposite the coffin and were separated from the rest of the car by a partition of carved mahogany and frosted glass. The main compartment was fitted with leather seats and folding chairs for the remainder of the funeral party. Window tops were etched with frosted drapes, and black shades and curtains could be drawn for privacy. Call bells summoned a conductor with ice water from a built-in cooler.

A trolley car funeral cost only $20, with an extra charge if it was outside the city limits. To avoid delaying regular cars, the *Dolores*, carefully waxed and attended by a company official arrayed in a silk topper, was scheduled to arrive at the street corner nearest the home of the deceased at an appointed

San Francisco's Market Street Railway served Mount Olivet cemetery, south of Daly City on the company's San Mateo line. Funeral car *Mount Olivet*, shown here at the cemetery office, was painted white instead of the usual black. — *Collection of Alfred E. Barker.*

time. The coffin was carefully lifted into its compartment, the mourners filed into the car, and the solemn cortege rolled through the streets to the cemetery. For large funerals, the *Dolores* was followed by one or more of the company's parlor cars, *Lord Baltimore, Maryland,* or *Chesapeake.* The greatest trolley funeral cortege ever assembled by the railway was that for Gen. John Mifflin Hood,

a former president of the Western Maryland Railway and chief executive of the street railway company at the time of his death in 1919. On this occasion the *Dolores* was accompanied by all three of the company's parlor cars.

Trolley car wedding parties were much less common than trolley funerals, but at least a few are on record. One such event took place at Minneapolis in 1944 when Frank P. Donovan Jr., a well-known Midwestern railway historian, writer, and trolley enthusiast, chartered a Twin City Rapid Transit streetcar for his wedding with Janice Goerner. Accompanied by 70 University of Minnesota students,

the wedding party rode through downtown Minneapolis singing folk songs and "The Trolley Song" to guitar and accordion accompaniment before being delivered to the First Friends Church for the Quaker ceremonies.

In addition to their primary role of passenger transportation, street railways often furnished a variety of other municipal services. One of the most common was street sprinkling or flushing. In many cities the electric lines were required to provide the service as partial compensation for franchise privileges. In a few cities this was done voluntarily; in

the service. Special gondola cars were operated over the street railways for ash removal or similar purposes in a number of cities. At Regina, Sask., the trolley company's work train hauled the city's garbage from a central collection depot adjacent to the carbarns to a disposal plant located 3½ miles west of the city.

The City of Duluth, Minn., operated a trolley car outfitted as a fire engine, and the Springfield (Mass.) Street Railway had a specially designed trailer for hauling the city's horse-drawn fire-fighting equipment. The Edmonton (Alta.) Radial Railway once

Baltimore's Loudon Park Cemetery had its own mile-long trolley line to transport mourners and visitors from a nearby line of United Electric Railway. Painted black with gold trim, the two former Baltimore city cars, *Linden* and *Loudon*, were used to operate the free service. — *Collection of Stephen D. Maguire.*

Trolley car weddings were rare. This one took place in Hamburg, Germany, in 1962 when tramcar enthusiast Reiner Zimmerman married Fraulein Helgard Voss. Two historic trams conveyed the newly-weds from the church to the reception. — *Conti-Press, from J. H. Price.*

converted a former passenger car for use as a mobile public library. Among other Canadian oddities were the two prison cars operated over the Montreal Tramways. Sheathed in steel and painted jet black, the cars bore the crest of the City of Montreal and the legend "Prison." With the nicest sense of the proprieties, the cars were divided into two compartments, separating accused from convicted prisoners. Twice a day during court sessions Montreal's trolley paddy wagons could be seen rumbling along St. Lawrence Boulevard on their route between the Champ de Mars courthouse and the city's Bordeaux Prison, a forbidding stone structure 7 miles from town.

In almost every major American city trolley car post offices sped the transportation of the U. S. Mail. The earliest use of the electric cars for mail service occurred around 1890, when closed-pouch mail was first handled by trolley on lines between St. Paul and Minneapolis and on New York's Dunkirk & Fredonia Railway. In 1891 Maj. James B. Harlowe, the postmaster at St. Louis, introduced a series of experiments with street railway mail handling, and late in the same year the first trolley Railway Post Office car was placed in operation on a suburban line between St. Louis and Florissant. Within a few years a network of 47 streetcar R.P.O. and closed-pouch routes was providing St. Louis with what one observer called "the best mail-collecting system in the world." A similar service was started in Brook-

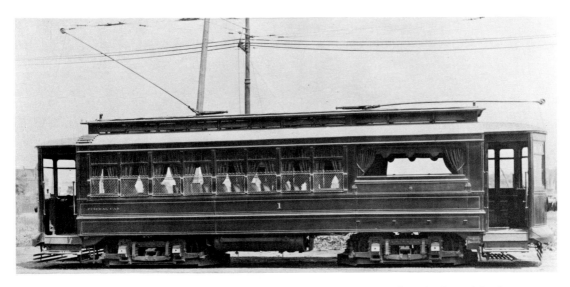

Typical of trolley funeral cars was Chicago's No. 1. A special door facilitated loading and unloading of the coffin, and black curtains afforded privacy. — *Smithsonian Institution.*

lyn in 1894, and by 1908 trolley mail service was being operated in 14 major cities.

Trolley R.P.O. cars performed a number of postal tasks. Mail was carried between the main post office, substations, and steam railroad terminals. Mail was delivered to carriers along the route, and was picked up from substations, carriers, other R.P.O. cars, and letter boxes. The cars were fitted with a work table, pouch racks, and letter cases; and Railway Mail Service clerks canceled and sorted the mail as the car rolled along its route.

The trolley mail cars, often converted from old passenger equipment, were painted white and generally lettered and trimmed in gold. Sometimes a handsome spread eagle seal was applied to each side of the cars as well as the usual "United States

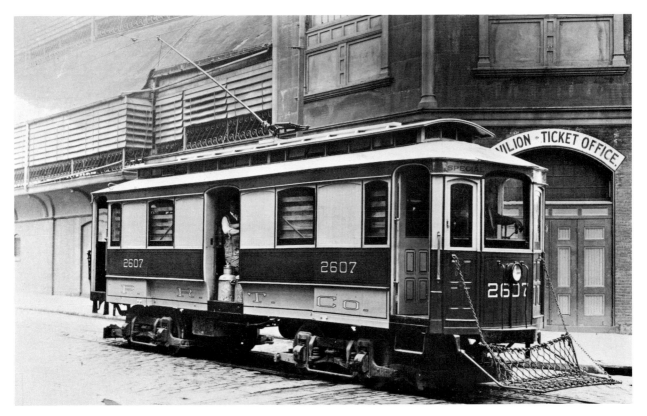

Trolleys even carried the milk in Philadelphia. This Philadelphia Rapid Transit Company car was operated every morning from suburban Doylestown to a terminal at 15th and Huntingdon streets. — *Collection of Charles Goethe.*

Mail Railway Post Office" title. The white mail cars could be easily distinguished from regular passenger equipment, and ordinarily were allowed to run unmolested during street railway strikes. One Chicago line, suffering from labor troubles, attempted to paint all of its passenger equipment white in an effort to avoid interference from strikers. Postal authorities quickly put a stop to the practice.

In Canada, where both Ottawa and Quebec had trolley mail car service, the cars bore the proud "Royal Mail" title. Under Canadian law, any vehicle thus lettered had the right of way over all other traffic, and the Ottawa system is said to have taken advantage of its contract by applying "Royal Mail" to all sorts of equipment.

For the convenience of last-minute letter mailers, the trolley R.P.O.'s were customarily equipped with letter drops on each side. Several cities placed letter boxes on regular passenger cars, permitting people to mail their letters on the first passing streetcar. Arrangements were usually made for a postal employee to collect mail from each car as it passed the point nearest to the main post office.

Trolley mail cars permitted a tremendous improvement in urban postal service over that afforded by the horse-drawn mail wagons previously used. The R.P.O. cars followed regular schedules, which were arranged so that cars from different routes would meet in the downtown area to exchange pouches destined for other parts of the city or the main post office. To further speed mail service, many cities had special trolley R.P.O. night circuits.

Trolley mail service proved to be an early victim of the motor vehicle. Increasing traffic congestion slowed the mail cars, and most post office departments soon found that trucks provided a more advantageous means of urban mail transportation. Despite rising costs, the Post Office Department proved reluctant to increase its three-cents-per-mile rate for the use of the trolley R.P.O.'s, so the traction companies found little financial incentive to continue the service. By 1915 trolley mail cars had ceased to operate in all but three cities. Baltimore, the last city to operate streetcar mail service, gave

This unique Duluth (Minn.) trolley fire car was installed in 1907 to provide fire protection on Park Point — a narrow strip of land separating the Duluth-Superior harbor from Lake Superior — whose only means of transportation was its street railway line. The trolley company furnished a special barn and a motorman for the fire car. The operation ended in 1930 when the city's famous Aerial Bridge, which joined the Point with Duluth, was remodeled to accommodate vehicular traffic. — *Collection of Wayne C. Olsen.*

In Cincinnati the mails went through aboard trolley mail car No. 215. White was the standard color for the street-car post offices. — *Collection of Barney Neuberger.*

Handsomely trimmed and lettered in gold, and bearing an official seal on each side, Chicago City Railway's trolley post office car No. 6 could not be mistaken as it rolled through Windy City streets on its important missions. The car was photographed in 1956 and now is part of a historic collection maintained by the Chicago Transit Authority. — *Stephen D. Maguire.*

Canceling and sorting mail en route helped trolley post offices speed mail service. — *Smithsonian Institution.*

up its trolley Railway Post Office operation in 1929.

Trolley cars almost always participated in holiday celebrations, parades, and similar affairs. An annual event in many cities was the appearance of a specially decorated Christmas trolley that trundled through the streets during the holiday season. Perhaps one of the most bizarre such cars was the "Santa Claus" trolley that took to the streets in Ottawa, Canada, the day before Christmas in 1896. The car was covered with imitation snow and icicles; replicas of reindeer, a sleigh, and Santa Claus were mounted on the roof; and both the sleigh and the trolley were filled with toys. The motorman and conductor were dressed as Icelanders, and an Eskimo stood beside the motorman and played a cornet throughout the trip. Huge crowds lined the Christmas trolley's route, and oranges were thrown to children along the way.

For New Orleans' celebrated Mardi Gras carnival in 1899, 20 special trolley car floats, all brilliantly illuminated by electric lights, were constructed for the big parade down Canal Street. A year later, 20 similar trolley floats were operated for a carnival in Milwaukee. Among the most spectacular floats at this particular affair were a reproduction of the battleship *Wisconsin* and a replica of a whale mounted on a 50-foot flat car and illuminated by 900 lights.

For the 1896 presidential campaign of William McKinley against William Jennings Bryan, the boys at the Fitchburg (Mass.) carbarn converted a 37-foot trolley flat car into the fearsome armored trolley cruiser *McKinley*, said to be patterned after the battleship *Brooklyn*, then the most powerful unit of the Great White Fleet. Two 6-pounders protruded from sponson mounts at each side of the *McKinley*'s massive ram bow, and a big 18-pounder was mounted on deck. A force of 22 soldiers, sailors, and marines in dress uniforms rode the decks of the armored trolley as it rumbled through the streets of

Street sprinkling and flushing was a service often provided by street railways. This trolley sprinkler operated on Cleveland Railways. More often than not the service was required by franchises. — *Collection of Charles Goethe.*

A more elaborate trolley sprinkler was this enclosed model built by the American Car Sprinkler Company of Worcester, Mass. It is shown during a demonstration at Worcester City Hall in 1919. — *Collection of Stephen D. Maguire.*

In the 1890's elaborate holiday street-car decorations were a popular Los Angeles custom, with cash prizes awarded for best trimmings. This Pico Heights car was all done up for the 1894 Independence Day celebration. Beneath all the finery was California car No. 106 of the Los Angeles Consolidated Electric Railway. — *Historical Collections, Security First National Bank, Los Angeles.*

Patriotically decorated open car No. 13 of the Oneonta, Cooperstown & Richfield Springs Railway rolled through the streets of Cooperstown with a capacity crowd. The occasion seems to be a Fourth of July celebration.

Fitchburg in support of the McKinley campaign.

The trolley car's participation in the everyday life of urban America was reflected by its place in the literature and entertainment of the period. Several early "business" novels of the pre-World War I era were set in the street railway industry. Meredith Nicholson's *The Main Chance* of 1903 involved a purely fictitious city and traction enterprise, but Theodore Dreiser's *The Titan*, one of the most celebrated novels of its time, was another matter. Dreis-

er's protagonist, Frank Cowperwood, was taken almost directly from the life of Charles Tyson Yerkes, the great "robber baron" of Chicago traction at the turn of the century. In fact, the library of the Peoples Gas Company in Chicago is said to have contained until recent years a copy of *The Titan* in which real names had been penciled in in place of fictitious names, and some of Dreiser's minor factual errors had been corrected. In a lighter vein, a more recent mystery novel, Ellery Queen's

Specially adorned Christmas trolleys were an institution in many cities. This one toured Seattle, Wash., streets in the 1930's. — *Courtesy of Railroad Magazine*.

The Tragedy of X, published in 1932, used a crowded 42nd Street Crosstown trolley in New York as the setting for a baffling murder.

The electric cars were frequent participants in films of the great era of silent screen comedy. The Keystone Kops, Laurel and Hardy, Harold Lloyd, and Buster Keaton were among the great comedians of the movies' early years who made frequent use of the cars as comedy props. What is perhaps the

William McKinley's successful campaign for the presidency in 1896 was aided by this gaily decorated trolley train which rolled through the streets of San Diego, Calif., shortly before election day. The significance of the Japanese lanterns was not explained. — *Collection of Frederick W. Reif, from Eric Sanders*.

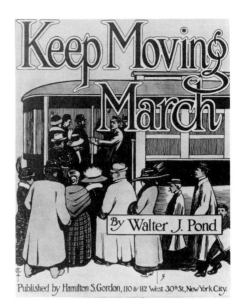

The trolley car inspired many obscure musical efforts, one of which is represented by this sheet music cover. Only one, "The Trolley Song," achieved popular success. — *New-York Historical Society*.

most spectacular trolley car sequence ever recorded on film, however, was a chase scene in an obscure and long forgotten film of 1916 called *The Prince of India*. The plot of this early potboiler, produced by a Utica (N. Y.) motion picture firm, had the villain steal a precious jewel from the prince and make his getaway in a stolen trolley. The prince, pursuing by automobile, leaped to the rear platform of the speeding car and the customary hero-villain struggle followed. The villain, knocked unconscious, fell across

This Birmingham (Ala.) trolley promoted a Wallace Reid movie around 1928. As early as 1900 a few lines sold space on the exteriors of their cars for such advertising as patent medicine signs. The use of streetcars for advertising displays was relatively infrequent, however, for municipal authorities usually discouraged such efforts to de-velop extra revenues. Only in the trolley's declining years did the ad men have much success in getting their messages on the cars. On the other hand, the ubiquitous interior advertising car cards were an inescapable feature of streetcar riding from horsecar days onward. — *Collection of Stephen D. Maguire.*

the controls and front dash as the car ran out of control on a steep downgrade. At the last possible moment the hero prince jumped to safety as the car derailed and plunged off a bridge at high speed. To film the sequence, the moviemakers purchased a retired Ithaca trolley, staged the derailment on a high trestle of the Ithaca Traction Corporation, and actually sent the ill-fated streetcar on a 300-foot plunge into the ravine below.

Throughout the years before World War I the traction industry grew steadily in size and power. By 1917, when street railway systems reached the peak of their physical expansion, electric traction had become a giant industry. There were well over 60,000 streetcars in operation on some 26,000 miles of street railway trackage, and the electric railway industry, exclusive of rapid transit systems or interurbans, represented an investment in excess of 4 billion dollars. Street railway traffic was close to 11 billion passengers a year, and annual operating revenues were in the vicinity of 600 million dollars.

Virtually every city of any size or consequence had an electric railway — altogether there were well over 1000 companies in the U. S. and its possessions — and the trolley car had become an indispensable and universal part of the urban American scene. Throughout the land the trolley was supreme.

Los Angeles' "Flying Tiger" trolley recruited World War II "trolley pilots." — *Stephen D. Maguire.*

Despite a Knights Templar parade, the cars kept right
on rolling on Elm Street in Manchester, N. H., around
1910. — *Collection of O. R. Cummings.*

In pre-automobile days the trolley dominated the urban
scene. This view of heavy streetcar traffic was recorded
at a downtown Indianapolis intersection about 1912. —
Collection of George Krambles.

Although flivver traffic was beginning to get a little heavy in Washington, D. C., conduit-powered streetcars still had the upper hand in this scene at 15th and G streets, N. W., after World War I.—*Library of Congress.*

An extensive street railway network made possible the growth of suburban communities along the east shore of San Francisco Bay. Streetcars of the San Francisco-Oakland Terminal Railways rolled in procession down Oakland's Broadway in 1919.—*Collection of Erle C. Hanson.*

The Wonderful Trolley Car

IN the early years of electric traction the trolley car was little more than a horsecar adapted for electric operation, an arrangement that quickly proved to have serious deficiencies. Horsecar bodies were designed for the lightest possible weight, and axle bearings were generally carried in pedestals attached directly to the body sills, a combination that proved unable to withstand the heavy weight and strains imposed by electrical equipment. On some early cars the electric motors were mounted on the platforms or suspended directly from the carbody, and they quickly managed to shake the entire car structure apart.

One of the first inventors to recognize the insufficiency of horsecar design for electric operation was Frank Sprague, who devised a separate metal truck which supported the carbody and upon which the heavy electrical equipment was carried. Quickly adopted by carbuilders, the independent truck became almost universal in electric car construction.

Apart from the use of separate trucks and the adoption of generally heavier construction, the design of electric cars largely followed the practices that had been standard in horsecar manufacture. Until well after the turn of the century wood continued to be used almost exclusively for carbody

Electric cars of the late 19th century were ornate to a fault, but this Van Depoele car of the late 1880's outdid even most. Operating over the Lynn & Boston Railroad's Highland Circuit, the car was decorated in a Highland plaid. Open platforms left the motorman to the mercy of the weather.—*Smithsonian Institution*.

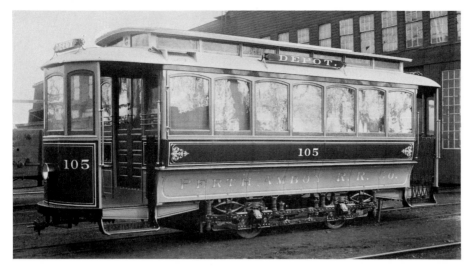

Outshopped during the 1890's by the Delaware Car Works of the Jackson & Sharp Company at Wilmington, Del., for the Perth Amboy Railroad Company of New Jersey, this handsome little four-wheeler was more or less typical of the early electric cars. The ornate striping, scrollwork, and gold leaf lettering required the highest order of paint-shop craftsmanship. — *Collection of Howard E. Johnston.*

fabrication. Seats were nearly always placed longitudinally and were finished in plain wood or in such easily cleaned materials as rattan, leather, or carpeting.

The exterior finish and ornamentation of the early electric cars was often lavish in the extreme. For a high quality finish as many as 15 hand-rubbed coats of paint and varnish were applied to a new car, followed by fancy scrollwork and lettering in colored paints or gilding. For even an ordinary finish a new car spent at least two weeks in the paint shop. The time was one in which individual pride of craftsmanship was at a height, and as an early treatise on car manufacture observed, the appearance of the finished product was largely dependent upon the skill and taste of the head painter.

The Robinson Radial Truck, developed during the 1890's, was a none-too-successful attempt to permit the construction of longer single-truck cars. The carbody was mounted on swiveling bolsters at each of the two end axles, which were connected by a linkage to a center axle that was free to move laterally according to the vagaries of the trackwork. The truck is shown on a car of the Rock Creek Railway at Washington, D. C. — *Collection of LeRoy O. King.*

Interior decoration was, if anything, even more elaborate. Such woods as cherry, maple, white ash, poplar, white oak, bird's-eye maple, red birch, and mahogany were usually chosen for interior finishes. Opalescent and colored glasses were widely used for decorative work. Ceilings were often ornamented with fancy stencilwork or stucco designs, or were decorated with such hand-painted designs as landscapes, figures of men and animals, wreaths

Interior accommodations of the early cars were usually rudimentary. The longitudinal benches and wooden slatted floor of this car, built by the American Car Company in 1893 for the Superior (Wis.) Rapid Transit Company, were typical. The rigorous winters of northern Wisconsin necessitated the bulky heating stove. Passengers either froze or roasted, depending upon their location in the car. — *Collection of Wayne C. Olsen.*

of autumn foliage, or spring blossoms and vines.

Lavish streetcar ornamentation was even considered to advance the public good. Pointed out one 1892 author in advocating fancy interior finishes, "Not only should a reasonable amount of decoration be provided in cars which are patronized wholly by a cultivated class of people, but in all cars, for by this means the comforts and solaces of fine art will be brought to a large number of lives and hearts that

cannot afford to provide them in their own homes."

Initially, electric cars were no larger than their horse-drawn predecessors, which were limited by the pulling capacity of the animals to a length of not much more than 16 feet. The greater power available with electric operation, together with the demand for greater passenger capacity, soon led to a considerably larger car. So long as the single truck was retained, however, its inherent limitations restricted the maximum size of cars. Because of the sharp curves typical in street railway operation, the wheelbase of a single-truck car was limited to about 8 or 9 feet, and over-all car length was restricted by the tendency of carbodies with an excessive overhang to pitch or gallop. This had a devastating effect on even the most substantially constructed track. As a result, the single-truck car was confined to a maximum length of about 30 feet and a total weight of approximately 20,000 pounds.

Several attempts were made to develop a four- or six-wheel single truck with radiating axles which would overcome the length limitations inherent in a truck with axles fixed in a parallel position, but none was sufficiently satisfactory to win wide acceptance. Instead, the demand for an increasingly larger-capacity car led to the widespread adoption of double-truck equipment, thus permitting a substantial increase in the size of carbodies. Although the single-truck car remained in general use well into the current century, double-truck cars had become common even before the end of the 1890's.

Typically, the trolley car of the 1890's was a double-end vehicle with open platforms at each end and only a waist-high dash to protect the motorman from the elements. But by the end of the century an enclosed vestibule for the protection of the operator was becoming more and more common. In many cases its provision was hastened by state or local laws requiring vestibuling. In 1900 the president and the general manager of the St. Louis Transit Company were even ordered to stand trial for failing to equip their cars with vestibules.

The open trolley, a car type that had originated during horsecar days, became an immensely popular vehicle for summer joy riding, particularly in New England and the Eastern states. At the height of its popularity, shortly after the turn of the century, there were nearly 25,000 open cars in service on U. S. street railways.

The typical open car had a roof supported by posts, and canvas side curtains that could be lowered in case of rain. Longitudinal running boards permitted boarding at any point, and transverse benches the full width of the car afforded it a tremendous seating capacity.

Despite their great popularity, open cars had some serious disadvantages. The running board

This otherwise ordinary single-truck car of the Eckington & Soldiers' Home line in Washington, D. C., was notable for the use of an unusual surface contact system of current collection. The long metal "skates" under the car picked up current from contact plates mounted in the street, which were supposed to be energized by the action of magnets mounted on the car. Unfortunately, the contact plates weren't always dead when they should have been, and complaints from owners of electrocuted horses soon ended the experiment.—*Collection of LeRoy O. King.*

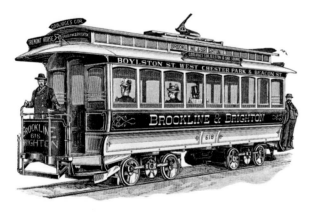

One attempt to solve the problem of obtaining the greatest possible traction from a single-motor truck was the Eickemeyer-Field truck, here applied to a double-truck car of Boston's West End Street Railway. Power was transmitted from the motor to both axles by a side rod arrangement reminiscent of that of a steam locomotive. A similar truck was available for single-truck cars. The design disappeared from the market soon after its debut in the early 1890's. — *Collection of O. R. Cummings.*

arrangement was the source of frequent boarding and alighting accidents. Some traction companies solved this problem by screening in the lower part of the sides and installing a conventional arrangement of vestibules and a center aisle. Still another problem was presented when the tight hobble skirt became fashionable, and women found it almost impossible to board the ordinary single-step open car. J. G. Brill, one of the leading carbuilders, came to the rescue with its patented two-step "Narragansett" open car.

The greatest drawback of the open car, though, was the enormous investment represented by a duplicate set of equipment that was used only during the summer season, and traction companies early set out to develop a summer car that could be used the year round. One approach to this problem was the combination or "semi-open" car which was divided between open and closed sections. This design was favored chiefly in California, where weath-

Double-truck electric cars began to appear during the early 1890's. This model was constructed for the Chester, Darby & Philadelphia Railway Company around 1893 by J. G. Brill and featured Brill's famous "maximum traction" truck. The truck, developed in 1891, provided greater traction with a two-motor car. By means of an offset cen- ter bearing, as much as three-quarters of the weight was placed on the large-diameter wheels, which were powered. Because of the unequal weight distribution, the small wheels had a tendency to derail at the slightest provoca- tion, thus making the maximum traction truck unsuited for high speeds. — *Collection of Howard E. Johnston.*

er changes were often sudden and temperatures were relatively mild throughout the year.

Another approach was the "convertible" car, which was little more than an open car equipped with removable side panels so that it could be changed into a closed car for winter operation. Orig- inally developed during the 1880's for a New York cable line, the convertible arrangement enjoyed only a modest success. Among its chief drawbacks were the nuisance of having to store the removable side panels during the summer season and the inability to quickly enclose the car in case of sudden weather changes. A few carbuilders attempted to overcome these deficiencies with convertible car designs in which both window sash and side panels slid into pockets in the roof of the car. These cars proved expensive to construct, however, and few were built.

By far the most popular variety of year-round car was the "semi-convertible" design. This represented a compromise between open and closed car arrange- ments. The semi-convertible was fitted with win- dow sash which disappeared into various types of wall or roof pockets, while the side panels below the windows remained fixed in place. The storage problem of removable sash was eliminated and the cars could be quickly enclosed in the event of a sud- den rain.

Except for the change to double-truck equipment

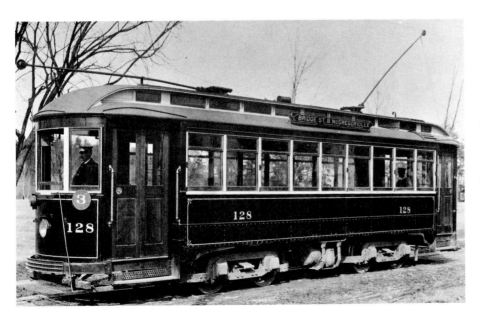

Plain lines and an impressive air of solidity characterized the trolley car of the pre- World War I era. This stur- dily constructed and commo- dious double-trucker of the Manchester (N. H.) Street Railway was delivered in 1913 by New Hampshire's Laconia Car Company. It seated 40 passengers and pro- vided standing room for 60 more. — *Collection of O. R. Cummings.*

A commonly required trolley car appurtenance of the earlier years of electric traction was some form of safety fender designed to scoop up wayward pedestrians. Above is the popular Eclipse Life Guard model applied to a car of San Francisco's Market Street Railway Company. The Duluth (Minn.) Street Railway car shown below was equipped with a much simpler model. — *Collection of Alfred E. Barker (above); Collection of Wayne C. Olsen (below).*

The interior arrangement of this roomy car turned out by J. G. Brill in 1911 for the People's Street Railway Company of Nanticoke & Newport (Pa.) was typical of much of the equipment of the period. Transverse "walkover" seats were upholstered in rattan. Hanging from the ceiling were the conductor's signal cord and fare register cords. — *Collection of Howard E. Johnston.*

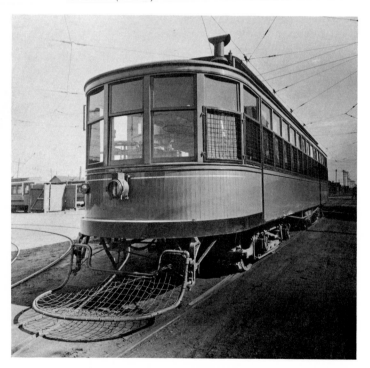

and the conversion to steel construction in place of wood, which began soon after the turn of the century, one of the most significant advances in streetcar design during the early 1900's was the development of greatly improved interior arrangements.

Until early in the century trolley cars were almost always double ended with a platform at either end. Passengers boarded and alighted from the rear platform and fares were collected by the conductor as he passed through the car. Not only were a good many fares missed by this haphazard system, but the conflict between boarding and alighting passengers often slowed operation. The problems of this arrangement became increasingly serious as the size of cars was enlarged, and street railway managers began to search for improved methods of fare collection and control of passenger flow.

The earliest solution was the "Pay-As-You-Enter" or "prepayment" car developed by the Montreal Street Railway Company in 1905. Passengers entered at the rear platform, paid their fare to the conductor before entering the body of the car, and left at a front entrance controlled by the motorman. In some P.A.Y.E. cars there was an exit at the rear platform also, with a rail arrangement to separate incoming from departing passengers. In order to furnish ample room for passengers waiting to pay their fares, an extra-large rear platform was provided. P.A.Y.E. cars were almost always arranged for single-end operation only, requiring the installation of a loop or wye to turn the cars at the end of the line.

The P.A.Y.E. design was an enormously popular

Perhaps the most ungainly electric cars of the entire traction era were the boxlike models turned out by the short-lived Barber Car Company of York, Pa. This double-truck Barber car, nicknamed "Black Charlie" by the line's employees, operated briefly on Pennsylvania's Sunbury & Susquehanna Railway around 1915. Inadequate springing in the massive trucks caused the car to bounce alarmingly, and derailments were frequent. — *Collection of Gene D. Gordon.*

one. Not only was fare collection improved and service speeded, but most traction companies found that better control of boarding and alighting greatly reduced the number of accidents. In Chicago, for example, a 54 per cent decrease in accidents was reported after the introduction of P.A.Y.E. cars. Kansas City reported a remarkable 67 per cent reduction in platform accidents.

Following the success of the P.A.Y.E. car a number of other configurations were advanced for controlling fare collection and passenger movement. The "Pay-Within" car, evolved by the Philadelphia Rapid Transit Company, was a variation of the P.A.Y.E. arrangement in which the conductor was located within the carbody facing the rear platform rather than on the platform itself. Another type of car developed in Philadelphia was the "Pay-As-You-Leave" car. Passengers entered at the front only and left the car at the rear only, paying their fares to the conductor as they departed from the car.

Still another design developed by the Philadelphia Rapid Transit Company and widely used there,

Perennial efforts were made to evolve a satisfactory self-contained electric car for service on lightly traveled street railway lines. One solution that finally met with some degree of success after years of experimentation was the battery-powered streetcar. Even though battery cars were notoriously docile in performance, a mild flurry of interest in them arose around 1910, after development of Thomas A. Edison's alkaline storage battery and improvements to the lead-acid type storage battery made them reasonably practical. This 24-seat Brill model was operated by the Concord Street Railway in North Carolina. — *Library of Congress.*

Transverse benches the full width of the open car gave it a tremendous carrying capacity. This was an early Baltimore (Md.) car. — *Collection of LeRoy O. King.*

The open car was popular for summer trolley riding. This nine-bench single-truck model carried Cincinnatians to Eden Park and the zoological gardens. The formidable fender was an unusual Cincinnati characteristic. — *Smithsonian Institution.*

as well as in Chicago, Buffalo, and Atlantic City, was the "Near-Side" car. Large double doors, one for loading and one for unloading, were provided at the front platform; and the conductor, who was located directly behind the motorman, collected fares from passengers as they boarded the car. A small rear door was used only for emergencies. By placing control of the doors with the motorman, the possibility of accidents owing to misunderstanding of signals from the conductor was eliminated, and the Near-Side cars enjoyed a particularly good safety record. Philadelphia alone bought 1500 of them.

The Peter Witt, or "Pay-As-You-Pass," car, which appeared about 1915, was another popular model. Named for the Cleveland (O.) street railway commissioner who developed the design, the Peter Witt car was arranged for front entrance and center exit. The conductor was located at the center of the car and passengers paid their fare either when leaving the car or before passing to the rear half. By devoting the entire front half of the car to space for unpaid passengers, the Peter Witt eliminated delays caused by passengers waiting to pay their fares as they boarded.

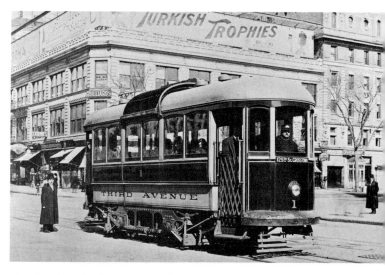

New York's Third Avenue Railway, which made extensive use of battery cars on its lightly traveled lines, also experimented briefly with this GE gas-electric streetcar around 1910. Power was obtained from a gasoline-engine-driven generator mounted on the car. Although the builder enjoyed success with its gas-electric cars for steam railroad and interurban railway service, the gas-electric streetcar failed to attract repeat orders. — *Collection of Frank E. Butts.*

Open trolleys were phenomenal crowd swallowers. A 14-bench car such as No. 96 of the Boston & Worcester Street Railway could seat 70 passengers with ease and carry scores more on the running boards. The Newburyport Car Manufacturing Company of Massachusetts built the big car in 1903. — *Collection of LeRoy O. King.*

This 12-bench double-truck open car built by J. G. Brill in 1906 for the Cape May, Delaware Bay & Sewell's Point Railroad in New Jersey was typical of larger open cars.

Gaily striped side curtains could be lowered for protection in the event of a sudden shower. — *Collection of Howard E. Johnston.*

Introduction of the tight hobble skirt early in the century made it all but impossible for fashionable ladies to board the standard single-step open car. Witness this lady's technique in boarding an open car. J. G. Brill saved the day with the patented two-step Narragansett open-car design. — *Culver Pictures, from the Library of Congress.*

Yet another car pattern that was widely used was the center-entrance-and-exit car. One of the chief advantages of this type of equipment was that it permitted a depressed floor opposite the center doors, enabling rapid loading and unloading and materially reducing boarding and alighting accidents. One car of this type, developed by the New York Railways Company in 1912, provided a floor level between the car trucks only 7 inches above the rails. Officially termed the "public welfare" or "stepless" car, the New York cars quickly became known as "hobble skirt" cars because of the manner in which they facilitated boarding of ladies attired in the then-popular tight skirts. Within a few years 176 of them had been built for New York alone, and similar cars were operated in other cities throughout the United States. Confusion between boarding and alighting passengers was a disadvantage of the center-entrance arrangement, although some designs attempted to obviate this by supplying separate doors for entrance and exit. Their chief handicap, however, became evident during the 1920's when street railway systems began to convert to one-man operation. Most lines found that end doors could not be installed without costly alterations and the stepless cars were quickly retired.

Throughout almost the entire history of electric traction there was a continuing search by street railway managers for equipment designs which would allow greater passenger-carrying capacity without a corresponding increase in labor costs, or "platform charges," as they were usually termed.

One of the most persistent, and consistently fruitless, efforts in this direction was the attempt to develop a suitable double-deck car. In spite of its widespread adoption in Great Britain, Europe, and

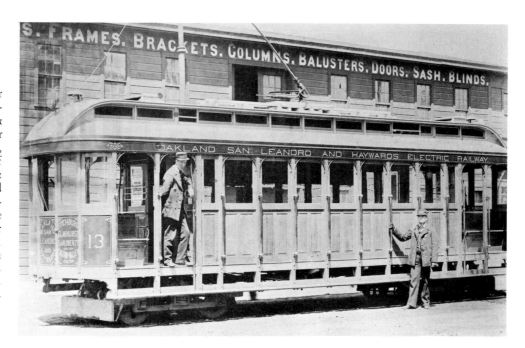

One of the earliest designs for a convertible car was produced by the Heacock & Lovejoy Convertible Car Company of Portland, Ore., in 1891. This was one of five cars using the Heacock & Lovejoy system constructed for the Oakland, San Leandro & Haywards Electric Railway in 1894 by Carter Brothers of Newark, Calif. Window sash and side panels raised into the roof in a manner similar to that of an overhead garage door. — *Collection of Erle C. Hanson.*

This single-truck car built by Jackson & Sharp for the Bergen County (N. J.) Traction Company around 1900 featured the short-lived convertible car system developed by the Duplex Car Company of New York. Sometimes known as a "barrel" car, the design employed curved window glass and side panels built like the roll top of a desk which slid into the roof on a curved track. — *Collection of Howard E. Johnston.*

The combination open and closed trolley which, presumably, provided accommodations to suit everyone, enjoyed considerable popularity on the West Coast. One of the most common types was the "California" car, which had a closed center section and was open at each end. It is represented here by Los Angeles Consolidated Electric Railway 103 about 1894. The car's configuration, locating the motorman between back-to-back longitudinal benches in the open section, was virtually identical to that of the cable cars of San Francisco's California Street Cable Railroad, which gave the car type its name. — *Historical Collections, Security First National Bank, Los Angeles.*

The repair shops of a major street railway company were the scene of a fascinating variety of work. These views depict a few of the operations in the Harvard shops of the Cleveland Electric Railway shortly after World War I. (Right) One end of a car is lifted by an overhead hoist to permit replacement of a truck. (Center) The carpenter shop was capable of repairing or replacing almost any wooden part of a streetcar. (Far right) This formidable piece of equipment was a huge jack used to straighten bent car frames. — *All photos, collection of Charles Goethe.*

A less common variety of combination open and closed car was this design built by St. Louis Car Company in 1912 for the San Diego Electric Railway. The car was divided between open and closed sections, one on either side of a center entrance. No. 125, first of more than 100 San Diego cars of this arrangement, is at the entrance to Mission Cliff Gardens. — *Historical Collection, Union Title Office, Title Insurance & Trust Co., San Diego.*

elsewhere, the double-decker never caught on in North America. The earliest known electric double-decker was the *Columbia*, turned out for Pittsburgh's Pleasant Valley line in 1890. *Columbia* seated second-story passengers on longitudinal benches on the open roof. Its carrying capacity must have pleased the management — on one occasion the car was reported to have transported 160 passengers — but evidently the car was less popular with the public, for the design was not repeated. A year later the Pullman Palace Car Company turned out several single-truck double-deckers for the Highland Park & Fruit Vale Railroad, an Oakland (Calif.) horsecar line. These were converted shortly afterward to electric operation and remained in service until about 1898. Passengers reached the open upper level by means of an ornate cast-iron spiral staircase. During the next few years the Pullman works turned out several large double-truck double-deckers, one of which ran for some time on the Jamestown (N. Y.) Street Railway. Minnesota's Twin City Rapid Transit Company converted three large suburban cars to double-deckers during 1904-1906 but removed the upper decks within a few years.

Similar experiments were tried on a number of street railways, but none was ever successful enough to warrant repetition. Apparently the traveling public balked at having to climb a flight of stairs to reach the upper level. Moreover, the streetcar lines

Ready for shipment, a batch of single-truck open cars was loaded aboard flat cars at American Car's St. Louis (Mo.) plant, one of the principal carbuilders. During the great years of electric traction, city car production sometimes exceeded 4000 annually. — *Collection of Stephen D. Maguire.*

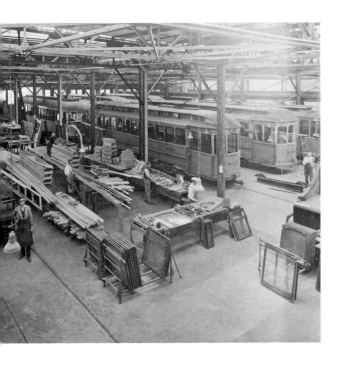 

found that the double-deckers were extremely slow to load and unload.

Despite its record of consistent failure, the double-decker idea was briefly revived shortly before World War I when development of "low floor" car designs suggested the possibility of double-deckers of greatly reduced over-all height. In 1913 the New York Railways produced a double-deck version of its low-floor stepless car that was promptly christened the "Broadway Battleship." Similar cars were built shortly afterward for the Columbus (O.) Railway, Power & Light Company and for Washington, D. C. None were particularly successful, and all were taken out of service after only a few years of operation.

About the same time, the Pittsburgh Railways experimented with a somewhat similar low-floor double-decker design that held over-all height to 14 feet

After its development at Montreal in 1905, the "Pay-As-You-Enter" (P.A.Y.E.) car was widely adopted by street railway systems. Passengers paid their fare as they entered at the rear, and left the car by either end. By eliminating confusion between boarding and alighting passengers, the arrangement speeded service and reduced platform accidents. No. 501 was the first of an order for 100 P.A.Y.E. cars delivered to The Milwaukee Electric Railway & Light Company in 1911 by the St. Louis Car Company. — *State Historical Society of Wisconsin.*

The entire front half of the Cleveland-originated Peter Witt car, represented here by Cleveland Electric Railway No. 33, served as an area for passengers who had not yet paid their fares. A conductor at the center collected fares as passengers passed him on the way to the exit doors or to seats at the rear. — *Both photos, Smithsonian Institution.*

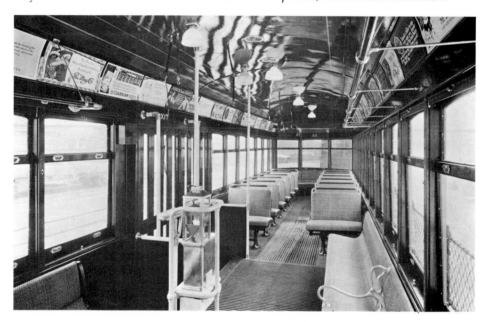

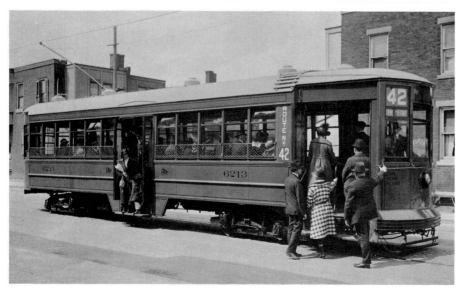

The "Near-Side" car, originated by the Philadelphia Rapid Transit Company in 1911, placed the conductor directly behind the motorman. Most Near-Side cars had both entrance and exit at the front, with a rear emergency exit. This model, photographed on Philadelphia's Route 42 about 1919, was provided with a center exit. — *Collection of Richard L. Allman.*

7½ inches. This trial was successful enough to encourage a repeat order for five double-deckers soon afterward, but the old problem of slow loading and unloading remained and the company finally took all six cars out of service in 1924.

The double-decker idea reappeared for the last time in the late 1920's when San Francisco's Market Street Railway produced a design for a car with a top deck that could be removed by a special lifting mechanism during periods of light traffic. Presumably the Market Street management took a look at the past history of double-deckers and promptly forgot the whole thing, for the unique removable-top double-decker never materialized.

Another recurrent approach to the desire for a high-capacity car that met with considerably greater success was the articulated car. Although several cars of this type were built during the early 1890's for Cleveland, the first important application of the idea was in a car constructed by the Boston Elevated Railway Company in 1912. This project took two old 20-foot single-truck cars, removed one platform from each, and suspended a center compartment between the two carbodies. Bostonians were soon calling the 62-foot 10-inch car "two rooms and a bath." Entrance was through the center compartment, which acted as a prepayment platform. The design not only provided a high-capacity unit operated by only a two-man crew and capable of negotiating Boston's sharp curves and narrow streets, but also permitted the company to recoup its considerable investment in a fleet of obsolescent but still serviceable single-truck cars.

So encouraging was Boston's experiment in articulation that during the next 3 years the company constructed 68 identical units from old single-truck cars, and between 1915 and 1919 built another 110 similar units from old double-truck cars. At least two other U. S. traction lines, the Portland (Ore.) Traction Company and the Virginia Railway & Power Company, built similar units; and the "two rooms and a bath" configuration also became popular in Europe, where its snakelike flexibility proved just the thing for narrow streets and sharp curves.

Several other large cities developed articulated equipment that employed two separate carbodies supported by a common truck at the center. Milwaukee and Baltimore rebuilt a number of old double-truck cars into units of this type. Milwaukee rebuilt its first car to this pattern in 1919 and had 33 of them on the streets by 1921. It found that the expense of the conversion was recovered in reduced labor costs in less than a year's time. During the late 1920's Milwaukee, Montreal, and Cleveland all ordered a number of three-truck articulated units seating a hundred or more passengers each. The record for the biggest streetcar of all, though, goes to an experimental four-truck, three-section articulated built for Detroit in 1924 by the Cincinnati Car Company. The 122-foot 8-inch monster seated 140 passengers and was run by a four-man crew.

A more common method of accommodating the crowds at rush hours or other peak periods was the operation of streetcar trains made up either of two or more motor cars operated in multiple unit or of a motor car and a trailer. Although train operation did not permit platform labor savings equal to those of articulated units, it avoided the costly investment represented by such specialized high-capacity equipment as the articulateds. Multiple-unit cars were

Brooklyn was among the many cities that employed the Peter Witt car design. Part of a 1930 order for the Brooklyn & Queens Transit Corp. is shown on the erecting floor of J.G. Brill's Philadelphia plant. — *Duke-Middleton Collection.*

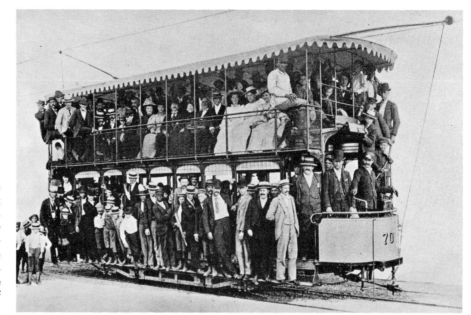

Double-decker No. 70 of the Terre Haute (Ind.) Street Railway boasted an almost incredible carrying capacity for a single-truck car. Shortly after the car was built in the late 1890's, however, the traction company removed the upper story. — *Collection of Howard E. Johnston.*

easily separated for individual service, and trailers were comparatively inexpensive units that could be stored during the off-peak periods.

Beginning with the general changeover to double-truck cars and the conversion to steel construction that started soon after the turn of the century, trolley cars had become increasingly large and heavy. Shortly after World War I, however, an entirely new type of car was developed which represented a complete reversal of the trend to larger and heavier

equipment. Beset by rising wage rates and other operating costs, and suffering from a small but growing competitive threat in the form of wildcat "jitney" buses and privately owned automobiles, the traction industry badly needed a car that could be more economically operated, particularly on lightly traveled routes.

The new streetcar was designed by Charles O. Birney, the engineer in charge of car design and construction for the Stone & Webster Corporation,

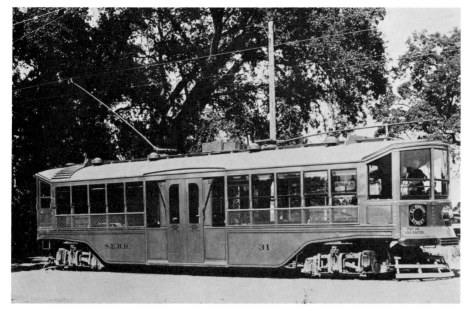

Devised by Frank Hedley and J. S. Doyle, general manager and superintendent of car equipment respectively for the New York Railways, the center-entrance "stepless" trolley had a floor only 7 inches above the rails. Aside from New York Railways itself, the largest user of the cars was the Southern Pacific Company, which purchased 36 of them from J. G. Brill in 1913 for service on several subsidiary electric lines in California. No. 31 was one of six stepless "dragons," as they were known in the West, operated by the Stockton Electric Railroad. — *Collection of William D. Middleton.*

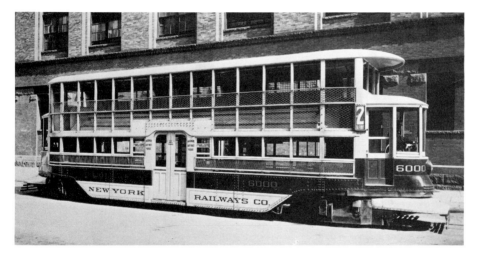

New York Railways' experimental "Broadway Battleship" double-decker of 1913 was developed from the company's stepless car design. The extremely low floor, together with a novel interior arrangement, held over-all height of the car to less than 13 feet — little more than that of a conventional single-level car. The car was not particularly successful, though, and the New York Railways never repeated the experiment. — *Library of Congress.*

operator of a number of street railway properties in Texas, Washington, and elsewhere in the United States. Birney's concept called for a small, extremely lightweight car that could be worked at low cost with a one-man crew. Because of the low operating cost, Birney argued, more frequent service could be given, with a resultant increase in traffic.

The "Safety Car," as it was called, was a single-truck car averaging about 28 feet in length and seating approximately 32 passengers. Although the first experimental model, constructed by the American Car Company in 1915, weighed only about 5 tons, the standard production models were somewhat heavier, weighing anywhere from 7 to 9 tons. Even

The roomy double-decker *Columbia* of the Jamestown (N. Y.) Street Railway is pictured at Celoron Park about 1893. The design, built by the Pullman Palace Car Company, represented the work of George M. Pullman and H. H. Sessions. The motorman's upper deck enclosure resembled a pilothouse. — *Collection of Charles Goethe.*

at that, Safety Cars weighed only about half as much per seat as most of the heavier equipment they replaced. One of the car's novel features was its "dead man control," which automatically brought the car to a halt if the operator released the controller or a special foot pedal without first setting the brakes.

The first Birney cars, as they became generally known, were placed in service in 1916, and by 1920 over 4000 of them had been built. Ultimately, more than 6000 were in service throughout the United States as well as in a number of foreign countries. Their initial success was almost phenomenal. Operating costs proved to be little more than half as much as for older, heavier cars. Running the new cars on a more frequent headway, most street railway companies realized substantial traffic increases. The experience of the Chicago North Shore & Milwaukee Railroad, which re-equipped its city services with Birney cars, was typical. After installing the cars on its local lines at Waukegan and North Chicago,

Boston's "two rooms and a bath" car, made up of two permanently coupled single-truck cars with a suspended intermediate section, was just the thing for snaking through narrow Hub City streets. The center section (above) acted as a pay-as-you-enter conductor's platform. — *Collection of LeRoy O. King (above); Collection of O. R. Cummings (below).*

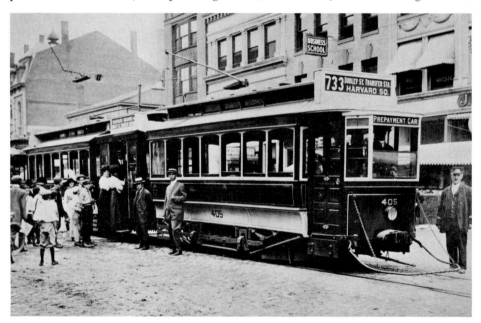

Ill., in 1919, the company was able to reduce headways from 15 minutes to 8 minutes. The improved service, together with reduced fares, brought a 39 per cent traffic increase in less than a year. The installation of Birneys on the North Shore's Milwaukee local line in 1923, along with a comparable increase in frequency of service, brought a traffic increase of 59 per cent and a revenue increase of 34 per cent in

only three months after the new cars entered service.

Even so, the standardized single-truck Birney proved to have its limitations. Because of the four-wheel design, the cars had poor riding qualities and were easily derailed. Propelled by only two 25 h.p. motors, the Birneys were notoriously underpowered. Several large cities that attempted to use Birneys on heavy traffic lines found the cars inadequate, and

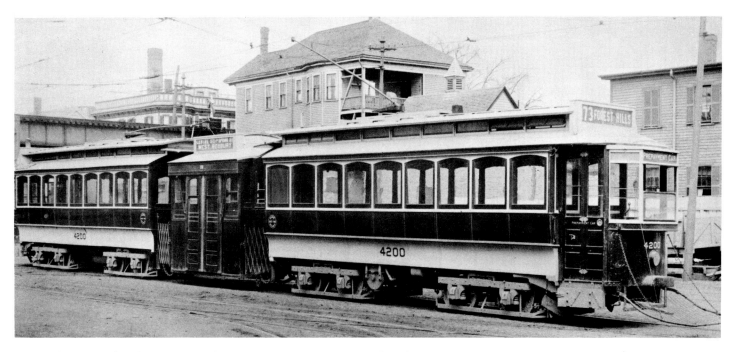

A later articulated car, Boston Elevated 4200, made use of obsolete double-truck cars. — *Collection of Allan H. Berner.*

most were soon relegated to unimportant lines or were sold to small city systems. Most important, the lightly traveled lines for which the Birneys were best adapted proved the most vulnerable to a growing trend to bus substitution that began during the 1920's. After reaching a peak of 1699 cars built during 1920, Birney production declined rapidly, and the last one was constructed in 1930.

Despite the somewhat limited success of the single-truck Birney, many of its features were widely applied to other equipment. A larger, double-truck version of the Birney developed during the 1920's proved quite popular, and was turned out in quantity for a number of systems. The "Safety Car" features of the Birney were applied to thousands of older cars to permit the economies of one-man equipment.

The years following World War I were troubled ones for the street railway industry. Costs continued to rise, private automobile ownership was growing rapidly, and the motorbus was beginning to pose a serious threat to the supremacy of the electric car. A recurrent theme in industrial history is that times of adversity often produce some of the greatest and most rapid advances in technology, and the traction industry's troubled times spurred a continuing development effort that was to result in unparalleled advances in the efficiency, performance, and comfort of the trolley car.

Increasing use was made of such materials as alloy steels and aluminum to produce extremely lightweight cars. The development of new motors and controls improved performance characteristics.

Several builders turned out new types of trucks which incorporated roller bearings, rubber cushioning, worm drive motors, and other features intended to improve riding qualities and reduce noise. Such passenger comforts as rubber-tiled floors and individual leather upholstered seats were introduced, and greater attention was given to the appearance of equipment.

Several carbuilders developed standardized car designs which were built, with variations, for street railway systems throughout the U. S. The Cincinnati Car Company's curved-side lightweight car, although it was developed primarily for interurban service, appeared on several street railway systems. The St. Louis Car Company produced a modern car called the "Rail Sedan" for several systems. Easily the most successful of these "standard" cars was J. G. Brill's "Master Unit," a lightweight car of advanced design and modern appearance constructed in quantity between the late 1920's and 1934.

A brief attempt was made to revive the four-wheel car during the late 1920's. One of the most interesting efforts in this direction was that of the Twin Coach Corporation, a leading motorbus manufacturer, which introduced an "automotive-type" streetcar in 1928. Built from the same jigs used for the company's bus production line, the Twin Coach trolley looked little different from the company's standard bus, and even employed identical automotive-type brakes and leaf springs. The most novel feature of the design was the use of wheels that turned independently on automotive-type steering knuckles, permitting a low floor and a considerably

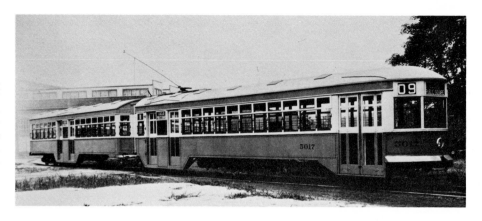

Cleveland's G. C. Kuhlman Car Company built 28 of these three-truck articulated cars for the Cleveland Railway in 1928. Each of the 101-foot, 40-ton monsters seated 100 passengers. Two conductors and a motorman operated each of the cars. — *Collection of Allan H. Berner.*

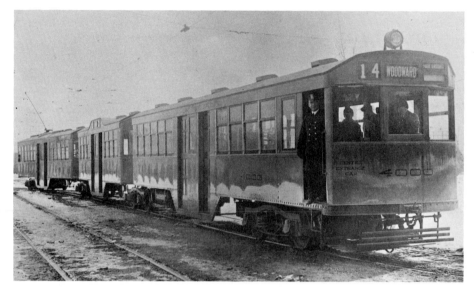

The biggest trolley of them all was this three-section articulated built for Detroit's Department of Street Railways in 1924. The 140-seat car was just right for auto plant rush-hour crowds but proved to be too large for off-peak services. — *Collection of Thomas J. Dworman.*

longer wheelbase for the car. This tended to eliminate the uncomfortable galloping motion that was characteristic of the usual four-wheel car. The company's promotional literature claimed that even though the bus-turned-trolley was hardly susceptible to flat tires, a wheel could be changed in a matter of minutes, just as on an automotive vehicle.

At about the same time, the St. Louis Car Company evolved a similar four-wheel "automotive-type" trolley, billed as the "New Birney," which carried the automotive treatment even to chromium-plated automobile bumpers. Neither the Twin Coach nor the St. Louis cars got beyond the demonstrator stage, however, and the four-wheel car idea was thereupon given up for good. The Twin Coach organization did make one further effort to invade the streetcar field the following year with a lightweight double-truck car of somewhat more conventional design. A single demonstrator operated for a few years in Brooklyn, but repeat orders never materialized and Twin Coach quietly retired from the streetcar business.

Throughout the 1920's the efforts to develop an improved streetcar were largely individual ones by equipment suppliers, carbuilders, or the traction companies themselves. But in 1929 an organization of street railway officials formed a new group — the Electric Railway Presidents' Conference Committee — to carry out an industrywide development program aimed at producing a new standardized streetcar design of radically improved appearance and performance. Headed by Dr. Thomas Conway Jr., one of the most noted executives in the traction industry, the Committee hired Prof. C. F. Hirshfeld, director of research for the Detroit Edison Company, as its chief engineer and authorized him to assemble a technical research staff and to proceed with development work.

Over a 5-year period more than a million dollars was spent on an exhaustive program of testing, research, and experimentation. A considerable amount of testing was carried out to develop the best possible lightweight body design. By experimentation the maximum acceptable rate of acceleration and other performance characteristics were determined, and such suppliers as General Electric and Westinghouse evolved the necessary motors and controls to meet the new specifications. Probably more at-

The single-truck "Safety Car" developed in 1915 by Charles O. Birney was a popular standardized streetcar. More than 6000 were built over a 15-year period. A 1920 modernization of The Milwaukee Electric Railway & Light Company's local lines at Racine, Wis., included 25 of them. — *State Historical Society of Wisconsin.*

tention was given to development of an improved truck design than any other feature of the new car.

The Committee's first car to take the rails, the Model "A" PCC (Presidents' Conference Committee) car, was a modern carbody borrowed from the Brooklyn & Queens Transit Corporation for the purpose of testing a new truck design and other electrical equipment. In 1934 an entirely new experimental car, the Model "B" PCC car, was ordered from Pullman-Standard. It incorporated an extremely lightweight streamlined carbody, spring suspended motors, eddy-current brakes, magnetic track brakes, "floating" type control, and improved heating, lighting, and ventilating systems. Employing newly developed high-tensile steel for carbody construction, the experimental car weighed only 31,000 pounds.

By the following year the Committee's work had advanced to the point where a specification for a production-model car could be presented to the carbuilders. The St. Louis Car Company was finally persuaded to undertake some of the remaining de-velopment work and to manufacture the car. The resulting production-model PCC bore little resemblance to any previous streetcar. Utilizing a stream-lined carbody of welded high-tensile steel, the standard PCC weighed about 33,000 pounds — far less than any previous car of comparable capacity and performance. Provided with comfortably cushioned seating and improved heating, lighting, and ventilating systems, and possessed of unparalleled riding qualities, the PCC represented an entirely new level of passenger comfort. The new trucks, featuring rubber-cushioned wheels and extensive use of rubber insulation, were remarkably quiet in operation. Four 55 h.p. motors provided the PCC car with the highest power-to-weight ratio in street railway history plus exceptional speed and acceleration characteristics. A dynamic braking system, which used the motors for braking action, supplemented by magnetic track brakes and air brakes, provided a comparable improvement in braking performance.

The PCC car won an immediate triumph with

Fresh from the paint shop, seven brand-new Birneys were lined up on a string of flat cars awaiting shipment to Brooklyn, N. Y., from the Philadelphia plant of carbuilder J. G. Brill. — *Duke-Middleton Collection.*

both car riders and the street railway companies. Great throngs inspected the new cars when they were placed on display, and soon after their introduction the traction companies were reporting traffic increases of as much as 33 per cent. Schedule speeds on PCC-equipped lines were increased by as much as 15 per cent, and most lines reported reduced accident rates, power consumption, and labor and maintenance costs.

The Brooklyn & Queens Transit Corporation, which had participated in much of the development work for the PCC, was the first system to purchase the new car, with an order for 100 placed in 1935. Major systems throughout the U. S. and Canada

soon followed suit, and by 1940 some 1400 PCC cars were in service. Continuing improvements, most notably a change to all-electric operation, were made to the basic design throughout the more than 15 years that PCC cars were being turned out. The peak year for PCC orders was reached in 1946, when some 800 cars were constructed; and by 1951, when PCC car production ended in North America, nearly 5000 of them had been built. Toronto, the largest operator of PCC's, had 745, over half of which are still in service. Chicago and Pittsburgh each had nearly 700 PCC cars, Philadelphia had 559, and Washington had nearly 500. A few PCC's were built in the U. S. for overseas systems, and hundreds

Typical of the improved car designs of the 1920's was this lightweight suburban car for Wheeling, W. Va. — one of 15 delivered in 1927 by the Kuhlman works at Cleveland, O. Interior appointments included rubber-tile floors, seats upholstered in Spanish grain leather, and a Philippine mahogany finish. — *Collection of William D. Middleton.*

Following a disastrous car-barn fire in 1924, the Grand Rapids (Mich.) Railway sponsored a competitive trial of several new streetcar designs before ordering a new fleet of cars. The experimental car *Minnesota* was delivered by the short-lived Light Weight Noiseless Electric Street Car Company, which produced several orders during the mid-1920's in the Snelling Shops of the Twin City Rapid Transit Company at St. Paul, Minn. The car weighed 12 tons, and its truck design featured inboard roller bearings. — *State Historical Society of Wisconsin.*

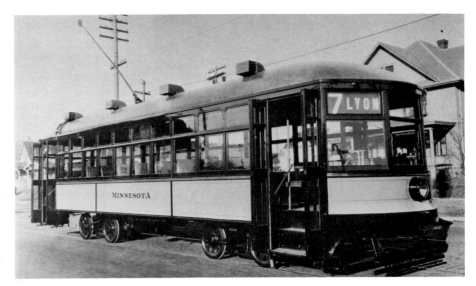

more were built abroad utilizing various PCC car patents. Trucks and other components originally evolved for the PCC car were also used on a number of rapid transit cars.

Coincident with development of the PCC, several independent efforts were made to create a modern streamlined car. In 1934 J. G. Brill and Pullman-Standard each delivered an experimental streamliner to the Chicago Surface Lines. Both cars incorporated a number of innovations that were shortly to become standard on the production-model PCC, and the Pullman-Standard car was notable for the use of all-aluminum carbody construction. Neither car was sufficiently successful to warrant repetition,

however, and when Chicago Surface Lines commenced a large-scale equipment modernization program 2 years later, it was with PCC cars. Also in 1934, Detroit's Department of Street Railways constructed an extremely lightweight experimental streamliner in its own shops. The car was considered quite a success, but its technical features were nowhere near as advanced as those then under development for the PCC and the experiment was not repeated.

Impatient to begin an equipment modernization program, Capital Transit Company of Washington, D. C., divided an order for 20 streamlined cars between J. G. Brill and St. Louis Car Company in

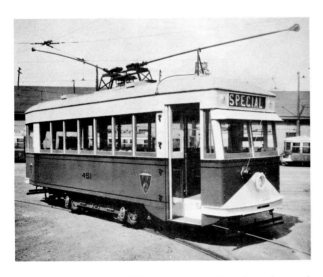

An experimental rebuilding job by the Haselton shops of the Mahoning & Shenango Railway & Light Company at Youngstown, O., produced this ultramodern Birney car in 1928. Although the effort was not repeated, the exterior styling and such interior features as individual leather upholstered seating were applied to an order of "Master Unit" cars delivered a short time later by the G. C. Kuhlman Car Company. — *Collection of O. F. Lee.*

Another entry in the Grand Rapids design competition was this "Electric Coach" built by the G. C. Kuhlman Car Company at Cleveland. An exceptionally lightweight design, the car weighed less than 13 tons. The advanced truck design featured inside roller bearing journals, clasp band brakes, and rubber-cushioned wheels. The car was painted in Ohio State University's scarlet and gray colors. — *Collection of Charles Goethe.*

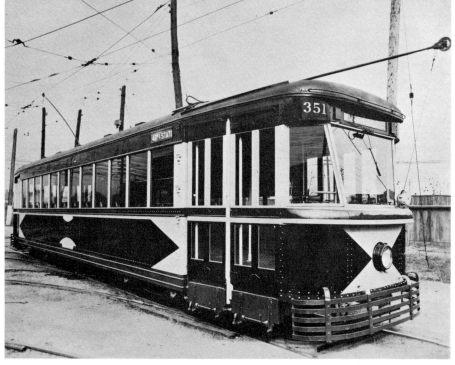

St. Louis Car Company's "Rail Sedan" was one of several standardized lightweight designs produced by car-builders during the late 1920's. No. 351 was one of five built in 1927 for the East St. Louis & Suburban Railway. Its advanced features included cushioned wheels and a load equalized braking system. In keeping with an emphasis on passenger comfort and appearance, the car was equipped with leather upholstered seats and finished in a snappy orange, cream, and red color scheme. The head-on pose with a Dodge sedan (above) was intended to show the utility of the Rail Sedan's automotive-type spring bumpers. — *Both photos, collection of William J. Clouser.*

1935. Although the cars were entirely satisfactory, and remained in service for more than 20 years, the PCC car marked such a radical advance that Capital Transit turned to the standard production-model PCC for subsequent orders.

When the PCC car went into quantity production in 1936, two builders — St. Louis Car Company and Pullman-Standard — were licensed to build it. Instead of taking up PCC car production, J. G. Brill of Philadelphia, which had been the leading street

New WEIGHT REDUCTION
An Epoch In Design

Automotive Practice
Arrives for Street Cars

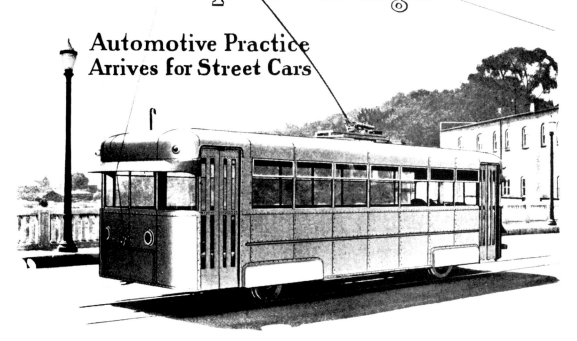

Buslike styling of the experimental four-wheel "automotive-type" streetcar of 1928 was not coincidental. The builder, bus manufacturer Twin Coach, employed the same jigs used for bus production to assemble the car. A second Twin Coach experimental car built in 1929 (below) was a more conventionally arranged double-truck car but retained bus styling. Although neither experimental brought production orders, many features of the cars appeared in the PCC streamliner of the mid-1930's. — *Collection of Wayne C. Olsen (above); Collection of Stephen D. Maguire (below).*

Pittsburgh Railways experimental car No. 6002, built by the Osgood Bradley Car Company in 1929, represented one of the most advanced designs of the 1920's. Constructed largely of aluminum, the car weighed only 13½ tons. Timken-Detroit Axle Company trucks featured four 50 h.p. longitudinally mounted motors. Pedal-operated controls included dynamic braking. — *Collection of LeRoy O. King.*

railway carbuilder ever since the advent of electric traction, elected to go its own way with an independent modern car design. Convinced it could turn out a car superior even to the PCC, Brill produced the first model of a streamlined car called the "Brilliner" in 1938 for the Atlantic City & Shore Railroad, which a short time later increased its Brilliner fleet to a total of 25 cars. The Brill streamliner looked little different from the PCC car, but its performance was something else again. Aside from

Produced in quantity for systems throughout the United States, J. G. Brill Company's Master Unit car was the most popular of the standardized modern car designs that preceded the PCC streamliner of the 1930's. This double-end Master Unit was built for the Portland (Ore.) Traction Company. — *Duke-Middleton Collection.*

the Atlantic City orders, only five other Brilliners were ever built; and while St. Louis and Pullman busied themselves with record orders, Brill vanished from the carbuilding scene after filling an order for 10 suburban cars for a Philadelphia line in 1941.

Pullman-Standard built this Model "B" streamliner in 1934 as a test vehicle for the Presidents' Conference Committee. Most of its features, including welded high-tensile steel body construction, "floating" control, and magnetic track brakes, were later incorporated into the production-model PCC. The car's eddy-current braking system proved disappointing, however, and after brief periods of experimental operation in Chicago and Brooklyn the car was scrapped. — *Chicago Architectural Photographing Company, from Stephen D. Maguire (above); Courtesy Railroad Magazine (below).*

In 1935 the Brooklyn & Queens Transit Corporation was the first system to sign up for the new PCC streamliner with a 100-car order. No. 1001, the first production-model PCC, was delivered by St. Louis Car Company in 1936. After 20 years of service, the pioneer streamliner was retired to the Branford Trolley Museum at Short Beach, Conn., following abandonment of street railway service in Brooklyn. — *General Electric Company.*

PCC car production reached a peak in the years just after World War II. These standee-window, all-electric models were part of an order for 100 Philadelphia cars under construction at St. Louis Car Company in 1947. — *St. Louis Car Division of General Steel Industries.*

Chicago Surface Lines, which bought 683 PCC cars between 1936 and 1948, was one of the largest operators of the streamlined trolleys. No. 4063 was built by Pullman-Standard in 1947. Larger than standard PCC's, Chicago's cars were arranged for two-man operation. — *Collection of William D. Middleton.*

Blue-and-silver "Blue Goose" streamliner No. 4001 was built for Chicago Surface Lines by Pullman-Standard in 1934. The aluminum-bodied experimental had cushioned wheels, magnetic track brakes, and PCC-type control. The Blue Goose had a tendency to break down frequently, tying up the streets, and was removed from service in 1941 after only 7 years of operation.—*Ed Frank, from Robert W. Gibson.*

Detroit's homemade light-weight streamliner of 1934 incorporated such features as welded steel construction, foot-valve-operated air brakes, and indirect lighting. The 39-seat car weighed only 12 tons.—*Collection of Thomas J. Dworman.*

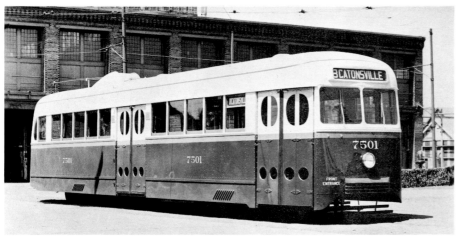

J. G. Brill's "Brilliner" stream-lined car was an unsuccessful rival of the PCC car. Baltimore Transit Company, already the owner of a good-sized PCC fleet, took delivery of sample Brilliner No. 7501 in 1939. Performance failed to match that of the PCC's, however, and subsequent orders went to Pullman-Standard for PCC's. — *Collection of LeRoy O. King.*

Recoiling in mock fright, these Brooklynites look aghast at the trolley window that has just been shattered by a rock thrown by a boy. The windows of passing transit vehicles have historically proven irresistible to a boy with a rock or snowball. This scene was posed for a safety campaign of the Brooklyn Rapid Transit Company. — *Library of Congress.*

Life on the Cars

TO a casual observer in the trolley's declining years, when streetcars were generally aged, docile vehicles operated by employees who themselves more often than not were getting on in years, employment on the cars must have seemed a tranquil occupation indeed. That this is far from the case is amply documented by the historical record.

In the early years, when traction was a vigorous, growing industry, the job of running the cars was a much more demanding one than it was to become later. It was a job for a young man with a sturdy constitution. Until enclosed vestibules came into common use after the turn of the century, conductors and motormen alike were exposed to the rigors of the weather in all seasons, frequently for the length of a workday that lasted 12 hours or more. As long as the open cars remained in service, conscientious fare collection required of conductors the utmost agility in order to negotiate the exposed running boards. Before air brakes came into general use a sturdy physique was essential to a motorman, who was expected to bring a heavy car to a halt with only hand brakes at his disposal. In a time when public behavior tended to be more boisterous than it is today, facility with a controller handle or a switch iron was a prerequisite if a trolley crew

Employment on the street railway was a highly respected occupation in the early years of electric traction. This young Duluth (Minn.) trolley man was fairly bursting with pride in his brass-buttoned uniform when he posed for a studio photographer in 1910. — *Collection of Wayne C. Olsen.*

hoped to maintain order in a car loaded with Saturday night revelers.

A job in the street railway service was a highly prized one. A handsome blue uniform with brass buttons gave a man an air of authority, and the work was considered vastly superior to occupations that required manual labor. Understandably, the trolley companies demanded the highest standards of appearance and deportment from their operating employees. A typical early rulebook prohibited any kind of profane or vulgar language, smoking, gambling, or reading of newspapers and magazines while on duty or on company premises. Rules regarding drinking were especially severe. Drinking to excess at any time, constant frequenting of drinking places, and even appearing in a saloon while in uniform were considered grounds for dismissal.

The employment of women as conductors or motormen was not infrequent, particularly in periods of wartime manpower shortages. One of the earliest reported uses of women in street railway service was in Chile in the early 1880's, when young women were employed as horsecar conductors to replace men drafted into the army during the war with Bolivia and Peru. The lady conductors wore an outfit consisting of a Panama hat, a blue flannel uniform, and a many-pocketed white pinafore reaching from breast to ankles and trimmed in dainty frills.

In the United States, women were widely employed in streetcar operation during both World Wars, and in some cases continued to work as conductors and motormen long after the war was over. There was at least one instance of a husband and wife trolley crew. During World War II, Reuben Lindquist, a Twin City Rapid Transit motorman,

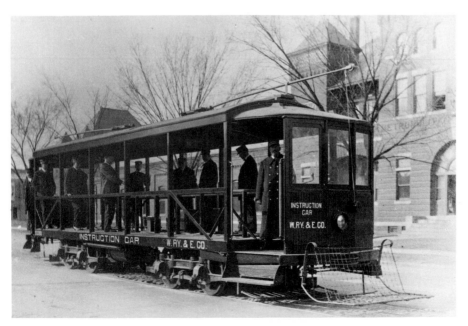

Early motorists were wary of the Washington Railway & Electric Company's special instruction car, which rolled through the streets of the national capital training prospective motormen in the intricacies of streetcar operation. Most larger street railway systems had some such instruction car. — *Collection of LeRoy O. King.*

These three veteran female trolley motormen, originally hired during the manpower shortage of World War I, were still running Baltimore trolleys when the first PCC cars came along in the late 1930's. — *Courtesy of Railroad Magazine.*

In the earlier years, company-sponsored recreational activities were common. This was the Duluth Street Railway band of the 1920's. — *Collection of Wayne C. Olsen.*

persuaded his wife to apply for a position when the company began hiring women. After landing a job as a conductor, Mrs. Lindquist managed to get assigned to her husband's car.

On one occasion women were employed as trolley car hostesses in the manner popularized by airlines and the new steam railroad streamliners during the 1930's. In 1941 the Birmingham Electric Company hired several girls to ride the company's trolleys wearing band uniforms and caps and "hostess" armbands. Startled streetcar riders were offered hot coffee and magazines. The device was only a publicity stunt intended to promote trolley riding, and the girls soon vanished from the cars.

The rise of the street railway more or less coincided with the growth of organized labor, and street railway systems were involved in some of the bitter strikes that characterized the union drive for recognition and strength. Strikebreaking was a recognized tactic on the part of street railway companies. A regular advertiser in the pages of *Street Railway Journal* early in the century was the detective and strikebreaking firm of Waddell & Mahon that proudly claimed "we have never lost a strike," and "call on us if you anticipate a labor disagreement." The Waddell & Mahon operatives were especially proud of their handling of a 1907 Birmingham strike, modestly pointing out in their advertising copy the noteworthy "efficiency and dispatch with which this strike was handled and broken up."

An example of a particularly violent strike is that which occurred on the Denver Tramways in 1920. After granting the newly organized platform men a 10-cent raise, the company found that it was suffering heavy losses and proceeded to cut wages back to their original level. The union men promptly began a bloody strike. On the first day, strikers killed two men and wrecked five cars in citywide fighting. Five days later union mobs stopped 12 cars, beat their crews, and demolished the cars, after which they wrecked one of the city's newspaper offices. Federal troops were finally called out after strikers stormed the carbarns with bricks and guns, and bombed cars stored in the yards. Thereafter two armed soldiers rode each of the company's cars until a sufficient number of old employees returned to work or until strikebreakers were hired to restore service to a normal level and the strike was broken.

A more recent labor dispute in New Delhi, India, was handled in a much more peaceable, though whimsical manner. On the appointed day over a thousand of the city's trolley motormen and conductors showed up for work dressed only in their underwear. Attached to each man's shorts was a notice informing the public that he wanted more pay and a free uniform from the company. The temperature was 110 degrees, so there was little risk to health

owing to exposure. Reportedly, the company's women conductors did not participate.

Although the era of the train robber had long since ended, a surprising number of instances were recorded of attempts to hold up the electric cars in imitation of the Jesse James style. Needless to say, such attempts usually took place on a stretch of deserted suburban track rather than in crowded downtown districts. At Richmond in 1900, for instance, holdup men blocked a suburban line with a pile of stones in order to stop a trolley at a deserted spot. The motorman and conductor were quickly taken by surprise when they left the car to remove the obstruction. Another method employed to halt a car was for one or more of the holdup men to ride the car and simply pull down the trolley pole at the desired location. One attempt of this kind at Lima, O., in 1900 was thwarted by an intrepid motorman who providently had a revolver in his possession. When two holdup men halted the car at a deserted location, the motorman drew his revolver and sent the bandits scrambling for a nearby wood pursued by a hail of lead.

In still another holdup attempt, on New Jersey's Bridgeton & Millville Traction Company, four bandits were set upon by passengers and thrown from the car, which continued on its way in a shower of stones hurled by the chagrined thugs.

At Seattle in 1910 a trolley was successfully held up in the heart of town. Four young men stopped a Seattle Electric Company car at First Avenue South and Spokane Avenue at 1 a.m. and relieved the passengers of $1500 in money and jewels. All four were later apprehended and sentenced to the state penitentiary.

A Cleveland Electric Railway conductor was separated from his cash in more subtle fashion in 1900. On two consecutive mornings the conductor was confronted by a passenger who boarded at the same spot and tendered a $20 bill in payment of his fare. Unable to change the bill, the conductor allowed the man to ride free. Anticipating a repetition on the third morning, the conductor secured $20 in nickels and gleefully waited for his man. The passenger boarded at his usual corner and again proffered the $20 bill. This time the conductor promptly accepted it and presented $19.95 change in nickels to the amusement of passengers on the car who thought it a first-rate joke. The conductor's enjoyment quickly vanished when he turned in the bill at the office and was told it was counterfeit.

Operating as it did almost entirely in public streets, the trolley was particularly vulnerable to traffic mishaps. Although the streetcar's inability to deviate from its fixed path and its relatively sluggish braking action often made avoiding accidents difficult for trolley men, the electric car's greater

A dramatic rescue by an alert policeman saved a boy from the consequences of careless playing in the street.

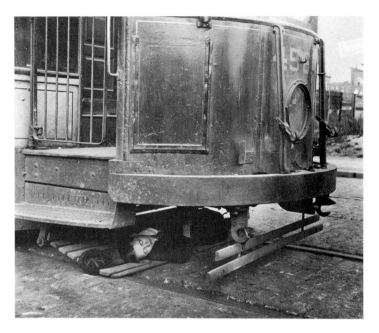

A narrow squeak for another negligent youngster, who has been scooped up in this trolley's "life guard" fender. The life guard, normally carried in a raised position, was dropped to rail level by a mechanical linkage whenever the guard at the front struck an obstruction.

Although the trolley car's superior size and weight normally provided ample protection for its passengers in the event of street accidents, such mishaps were still the source of numerous and costly claims and no little amount of bad publicity. This set of photographs, posed on the Brooklyn Rapid Transit Company as part of a safety campaign around 1915, depicts some of the street accident hazards faced by trolley men.

This scene illustrated the tragic result of carelessly riding a scooter in a busy street.

Hitching rides on the back end of trolleys, a favorite pastime for boys everywhere, was something to be discouraged. As we are shown so graphically here, the practice could have unfortunate consequences. — *All photos, Library of Congress.*

Crossing collisions with steam railroad trains represented some of the most serious accidents in street railway history. In this early New Jersey scene, a Public Service Railway work car has arrived to help pick up what little remains of Raritan Line trolley No. 524 after the car unsuccessfully contested the Chimney Rock spur crossing with a Central Railroad of New Jersey locomotive. — *Collection of Howard E. Johnston.*

"Accidents That Happen Daily" was the title of this lurid drawing from a National Railroad Trolley Guard Company advertisement in a 1911 issue of *Electric Railway Journal*. The firm specialized in the manufacture of a "trolley guard" designed to prevent dewirements at hazardous points. — *Collection of William D. Middleton.*

Left unattended while its crew enjoyed a smoke at the end of the line, Manchester (N. H.) Street Railway trolley No. 82 rolled off down Derryfield Hill, narrowly missed another trolley, and finally crashed into the front of a furniture store after failing to negotiate the curve at Bridge and Elm streets. Here the battered trolley is extricated from the wreckage of the 1912 mishap. — *Collection of O. R. Cummings.*

Thirteen died and a score were injured in this smashup at the end of a wild runaway on the Mountain Lake Electric Railroad at Gloversville, N. Y., in 1902. Running at an excessive rate of speed with a load of Fourth of July excursionists, closed car No. 5 (right) overtook and collided with open car No. 1. Both cars then ran out of control at an estimated speed of 60 mph on the 11.5 per cent grade between the Mountain Lake resort and Gloversville before derailing on a curve at the bottom. Damage claims bankrupted the line. — *Collection of William D. Middleton.*

A runaway trolley of the Carbon Transit Company almost made it into the lobby of a Lehighton (Pa.) hotel. This kind of mishap was a constant and dangerous threat in the anthracite country of eastern Pennsylvania. The hilly terrain was a frequent cause of many such accidents. — *Collection of Howard E. Johnston.*

Excitement ran high in Superior, Wis., in 1914 when the Billings Park trolley derailed on the Great Northern viaduct, crashed through the guard rail, and dropped to the ground. — *Collection of Wayne C. Olsen.*

This Duluth Street Railway trolley tied up Duluth-Superior traffic after a 1913 derailment on the approaches to the Interstate Bridge.—*Collection of Wayne C. Olsen.*

size and weight in comparison with almost anything else on the street at least minimized the chances of injury to its passengers. Even in the most violent collisions with other vehicular traffic, the trolley usually came away with little more than some scratched paint and a damaged fender.

In the earlier years of electric traction, of course, horse-drawn vehicles were the principal hazard. Until the horses became accustomed to the electric cars, the animals tended to be skittish, and often a startled horse would overturn his carriage or wagon without ever being touched by the offending car.

In one early accident recorded at Minneapolis in 1893, a trolley en route downtown from Fort Snelling was charged by a runaway team of horses. One of the horses plunged over the front dash of the car, through the door, and fell dead on the floor, evidently of fright. The startled motorman narrowly escaped instant death by jumping out of the path of the crazed beast. "It was one of the liveliest and most unusual accidents on record," concluded a news account.

Although the electric cars customarily came out best in street collisions, in a few instances the trolley was at a decided disadvantage. A relatively recent accident of this kind, and one of the most tragic, occurred in Chicago in 1950. A PCC streamliner packed with rush-hour passengers split a switch and collided with a gasoline truck near 63rd and State streets. In the ensuing explosion and conflagration the trolley was destroyed, nearby residences were set afire, and 33 passengers lost their lives.

One type of collision to which the trolley cars seemed particularly prone was the grade-crossing crash with steam railroad trains. These often resulted from the inadequacy of warning signals; another frequent cause was an untimely dewirement of the trolley pole, which left a car stranded without power in the path of an approaching train. So serious was this latter hazard regarded by street rail-

Nothing tied up rush-hour traffic quite like a strategically located derailment. Seven trolleys waited while emergency crews rerailed this Albany (N. Y.) car on North Pearl Street in 1944. — *Collection of Jim Shaughnessy.*

145

Passengers on this Rhode Island Company trolley had a narrow escape in 1921 when the Providence-Attleboro car derailed and plunged off Lebanon Bridge into Ten Mile River. Underbody equipment caught on the bridge structure and kept the car from going all the way into the river. Motorman Percy Titus escaped through a broken window, waded ashore, and joined the conductor in aiding passengers. — *Collection of Richard L. Wonson.*

One of the worst accidents in New England traction history was this 1903 head-on collision not far from Pelham Center, N. H., between two open cars of the Hudson, Pelham & Salem Electric Railway. The two cars, traveling between Nashua and Canobie Lake Park, met on a blind curve with lethal effect. The cars collided with such force that both roofs collapsed onto the terrified passengers, adding materially to the casualty toll and greatly hampering rescue efforts. Six persons were killed and 72 injured. — *Collection of O. R. Cummings.*

This New York Railways trolley landed with a devastating jolt in 1915 when the temporary shoring and planking supporting the street gave way during construction of the Broadway subway. — *Collection of Jeffrey Winslow.*

waymen that a special protective mesh, mounted above the trolley wire to keep the pole in contact in case of dewirement, was frequently installed at steam-railroad crossings.

Typical of grade-crossing accidents was a 1927 collision at Superior, Wis., between a Billings Park streetcar and the Great Northern Railway's crack *Gopher*. Accounts differed concerning the cause of the accident, the most likely being that the crossing watchman lowered the gates after the streetcar was on the crossing, knocking the trolley pole from the wire and stalling the car in the path of the train. The passenger train, traveling at a speed of over 25 mph, demolished the wooden streetcar. Seven persons were killed and another 16 seriously injured. Among the dead was the locomotive fireman, who was fatally injured when he jumped from his locomotive in an effort to escape the collision. The crossing watchman narrowly escaped death when his watchtower was toppled by flying wreckage and burst into flames, ignited by coals from a heating stove.

Perhaps the most common cause of serious street railway accidents was the runaway car, and traction history is filled with harrowing tales of cars hurtling downhill out of control after brake failure or some similar mishap, almost invariably derailing and wreaking havoc before finally coming to rest. One of the most serious accidents in the early years of electric traction occurred at Tacoma, Wash., in 1900 when a crowded car inbound from South Tacoma and Spanaway Lake with a Fourth of July crowd lost its brakes on the Delin Street hill. After derailing at a sharp curve at the bottom of the grade, the trolley hurtled into space over a deep gully and landed on its roof after a fall of 75 feet. The heavy car trucks and motors crashed through the floor of the car, crushing many of the occupants. Forty-one passengers lost their lives, and more than 50 were injured.

A runaway trolley on Cleveland's Scranton Road line in 1916 set in motion a chain of mishaps. After derailing on a sharp curve at the foot of a long, steep grade, the runaway car crashed into the end posts of a 105-foot iron truss bridge, causing its collapse onto the tracks of the Baltimore & Ohio Railroad 23 feet below. A second trolley entered the span just as it failed and, together with the wreckage of the bridge, crashed onto the steam railroad tracks. Miraculously, only two persons lost their lives.

The worst accident in street railway history took place at Mexico City in 1953 as the result of a runaway on a single-track suburban line. After failing

147

Because of the difficulty in reaching a trouble scene with rail work equipment, most street railways preferred off-rail emergency equipment. (Above) This horse-drawn tower wagon of the San Diego Electric Railway was all set to gallop off to the scene of trouble. (Right) A truck-mounted model was used by the Toronto Transportation Commission in 1931. — *Collection of Frederick W. Reif, from Eric Sanders (above); Toronto Transit Commission (right).*

to wait for an outbound car in the siding at the top of a steep grade, an inbound car lost its air brakes and plunged head-on into the approaching car with brutal force. Both cars left the rails and rolled down a mountainside. Of some 200 passengers aboard the two cars, 66 were killed and close to 100 received serious injury.

One spectacular runaway that ended without serious property damage or any casualties was an incident described as "the great tram chase," which took place at Southampton, England, in 1942. A 15-year-old boy managed to set in motion two trolley cars left unattended in a storage track. Observing the two cars rolling downhill on The Avenue, a truck driver named Jesse Clark gave chase with his 5-ton lorry loaded with 6 tons of sand. By the time Clark caught up to the runaways they were traveling at better than 40 mph. Blowing his horn and frantically waving oncoming traffic out of the way, the truck driver finally managed to pass the speeding cars, pulled in front of them, allowed the leading car to overtake him, and then carefully braked all three vehicles to a halt. A bit of scraped paintwork was the only mark Clark's lorry had to show as a result of the spectacular chase and rescue.

Several street railway lines with particularly perilous grades equipped their cars with such devices as dynamic braking or magnetic track brakes to supplement ordinary braking equipment. Another safe-

ty measure was the installation of periodic derails that could be released only if a car was moving at a safe speed. The Lake Burien line of the Seattle Municipal Railway had a particularly dangerous 4.5 per cent grade with a sharp curve at the bottom, so the railway installed a safety siding which had a 15 per cent reverse grade to stop runaway cars. Shortly after installation of the safety siding, a descending car ran out of control; it reached an estimated speed of 60 mph before being diverted into the siding and safely brought to a halt. The motorman and eight passengers, who crouched on the floor during the wild ride, escaped injury. Only the conductor, who lost his nerve and jumped, was hurt.

A scattering of miscellaneous causes account for several of the more serious accidents recorded in street railway history. Second only to the Mexico City disaster of 1953 among North American street railway wrecks was an 1896 crash at Victoria, B. C. An overloaded iron bridge collapsed under the weight of a heavily loaded trolley carrying part of the crowd en route to a Queen's birthday celebration. The car plunged 75 feet to the bottom of a gorge, killing 54 of the 80 passengers aboard.

What was probably the worst trolley disaster in the United States took place in 1916, when the motorman of a heavily loaded Boston car failed to stop at the gate guarding the open Summer Street draw-

The carbarn fire was a distressingly frequent occurrence in street railway history. This was the wreckage of a 1923 blaze that destroyed the Columbia Street carhouse of the Chicago, South Bend & Northern Indiana Railway at South Bend with a loss of eight cars. Full service was restored three days later with nine cars hastily purchased from Cleveland. Only 4 years earlier the same carbarn had burned down with similar results. On that occasion replacement cars were bought from Akron. — *Van-Zillmer Collection.*

A Cleveland flood during the 1950's stranded this two-car Shaker Heights Rapid Transit train. City firemen in a boat rescued the helpless passengers and crew. — *Cleveland Plain Dealer, from Railroad Magazine.*

Virtually hidden in a cloud of snow, a rotary sweeper of the Regina (Sask.) Municipal Railway cleared a car line of a light snowfall in 1947. — *Collection of Allan H. Berner.*

The Berkshire (Mass.) Street Railway had to call out its snowplow to clear the line between Glendale and Housatonic after the Housatonic River overflowed and left the railway track covered with ice. — *Collection of Howard E. Johnston.*

The severe winter of 1919-1920 proved too much for Massachusetts' financially shaky Blue Hill Street Railway. Matters came to a head during the severe blizzard of February 5, 1920. As crews struggled to rescue snowbound trolleys, the powerhouse coal supply ran out and the trolley wire went dead. This car and a snowplow were stuck fast in drifts on Ponkapoag Hill for more than a month. The railway never resumed operation. — *Collection of Carl L. Smith.*

A little Taunton snowplow of the Georgetown, Rowley & Ipswich Street Railway led two single-truck trolleys through deep drifts near Byfield, Mass., as the crew looked on. — *Collection of LeRoy O. King.*

bridge. The car crashed through the gate and toppled into the Fort Point Channel, turning end over end before coming to rest in 30 feet of water. Forty-five passengers were drowned.

What must be regarded as one of the most unusual accidents in trolley history occurred at Brooklyn in 1900. As a result of heavy rains, settlement took place in some new earth fill under a double-track car line, lowering the inner rail of each track by several inches. Two cars traveling in opposite directions leaned inward simultaneously as they met on the uneven track. The corner of the roof of one car caught under the roof of the other and ripped out every roof support on one side before the cars could be stopped. Terrified passengers crawled under their seats for safety as the car roof crashed down on them. Somehow, all aboard the car escaped injury.

In addition to experiencing the perils of accidents, the street railways were exposed to the year-round hazards of fire, flood, and storm. Fire in particular posed a continuing threat to the traction companies. On those lines which employed some type of coal-burning heaters on their cars, fire aboard the cars was a frequent occurrence. The folklore of the street railway is filled with accounts, some of them more than likely true, in which a cool-headed trolley crew ran their blazing car to the nearest firehouse, where the flames were extinguished by quick-acting firemen. Far more serious in its consequences was the carbarn fire, which appears as a recurring theme in street railway history. According to the *National Fire Prevention Quarterly*, there were 240 serious fires at North American street railway carbarns or workshops between 1897 and 1940.

The classic carbarn fire was a nighttime happening, breaking out perhaps as the result of a discarded cigarette or an electrical fault. The cars themselves were a highly combustible mixture of wood, grease, paint, and varnish, and the carbarn structures were often no better. Even if the fire was promptly discovered, damage to the trolley wire or power failure frequently made it impossible to run the cars out in time. With this eventuality in mind, a Massachusetts trolley company, the Athol & Orange Street Railway, when reconstructing its carhouse in 1896 placed the storage tracks on a slope from rear to front in order that cars could be run out without power in the event of fire.

Typical of the consequences of a major carhouse fire was the experience of the Georgetown, Rowley & Ipswich Street Railway of Massachusetts in 1901. On the night of February 20 fire broke out in a car stored in the company's Byfield carbarn and swiftly

Snow removal in the wake of a severe blizzard required a major effort on the part of the street railway companies. From 75 to 100 of these horse-drawn snow removal boxes were in operation at Ottawa, Canada, after each snowstorm. A V-bottom and hinged sides facilitated unloading at the snow dumps, which were conveniently located close to trolley lines. Teamsters who provided the service were paid in the form of a disk for each load. These were later exchanged for cash at the company's general office. — *Ottawa Transportation Commission.*

After experiencing increasing difficulty in hiring sufficient horse teams for snow removal, the Ottawa Electric Railway bought a fleet of Model T Ford trucks, equipped with oversize boxes, which bore the brunt of snow removal requirements for some 25 years after their purchase in 1918. — *Ottawa Transportation Commission.*

spread to the other cars stored in the building, as well as the building itself. By dawn only three walls of the carbarn remained standing, and 16 trolleys and three snowplows had been reduced to smoldering embers and twisted metal. So quickly had the flames spread that workmen had been able to push only a single car to safety, and even that was badly scorched. Until new cars could be purchased the company was able to maintain service only by means of equipment borrowed from two neighboring street railway companies. In the declining years of electric traction such a disastrous event was sufficient to bring a permanent end to streetcar operation on more than one hard-pressed system.

Weather conditions frequently raised havoc with street railway operations. Wind and thunder storms often damaged the overhead trolley wire, and sometimes tracks were inundated by floods. Probably no weather condition gave more trouble — at least in northern locations — than snow. Most street railway companies took seriously their obligation to provide dependable public transportation, and maintained fleets of snowplows, sweepers, scrapers, and other snow-fighting equipment which was hurled against the elements in an effort to keep the car lines open.

Usually the battle against a blizzard began with the dispatching of extra cars to run up and down the tracks just to keep them open. Track men were sent out to keep switches clear. As the snow became heavier, the big rattan-broomed rotary sweepers went into action, followed by snowplows if the going got really rough. In the aftermath of exception-

ally heavy snowfalls the trolley companies had to organize a massive snow removal effort to remove drifts and the windrows thrown up by the plows in streets on which the cars ran. Even when the trolley lines were successful in keeping their tracks open, maintaining satisfactory service was sometimes difficult during and after a heavy snow. Often the car tracks represented the only cleared path in principal thoroughfares, and the trolleys were forced to contest their right of way with all manner of street traffic.

During the late 1920's the Duluth (Minn.) Street Railway, which contended with extremely severe winter weather conditions, designed and built an unusual piece of equipment for removing the heavy accumulations of ice and snow that built up in the company's tracks during the long Minnesota winter. Nicknamed *Goliath* by company employees, Duluth's ice-breaker was a heavy four-wheel vehicle that could be pushed or pulled through the streets by another piece of equipment. A large cast-iron roller, 2 feet in diameter and weighing 6 tons, was suspended between the unit's axles. Mounted on the roller were diagonal cutters, similar to the cleats mounted on the wheels of an old-fashioned steam tractor; these helped to break up troublesome accumulations of ice. *Goliath* was reported to be extremely noisy, and residents complained that windows rattled and the ground shook as it passed through the streets.

Life on the cars, it would seem, provided plenty of excitement.

One of the greatest snowfalls in Seattle history paralyzed street traffic throughout the city in January 1916. A line of Seattle, Renton & Southern trolleys was stalled in deep snow on Fourth Avenue. — *Collection of Robert S. Wilson.*

153

A parade of battered old trolleys, handsomely decorated in flags and bunting, marked the end of 57 years of streetcar service at Knoxville, Tenn., in 1947. — *Collection of Allan H. Berner.*

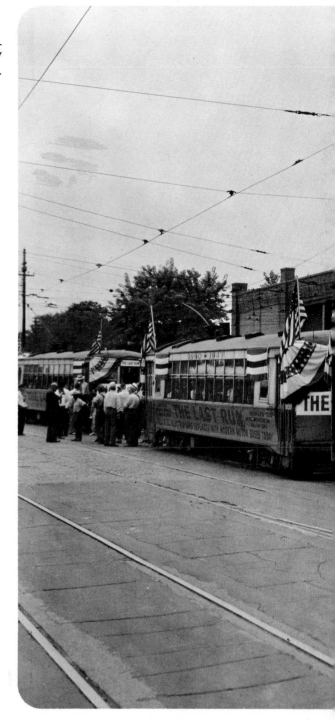

The Trolley Vanishes

DIRECTLY, at least, the trolley car was usually displaced by the motorbus, or on occasion that hybrid vehicle, the trolley bus. In a larger sense, however, the trolley was a victim of the automobile. As America made a swift transition from a mass-transportation- to a private-transportation-oriented way of life in the years after World War I, the street railway became increasingly superfluous. As a growing number of families took to the streets in their own automobiles, the demand became less and less for the kind of high-capacity mass transportation the streetcar provided, and the operating companies quickly learned that the newly developed motorbus provided a more economical way of transporting whatever traffic remained.

Made mobile by their automobiles, Americans no longer were tied to a trolley line; and the new suburbia, almost totally dependent upon private transportation, began to spring up in the outer reaches of the American city. Even if the street railways had been financially able to build new extensions — which they weren't — they would have found it impossible to economically serve the scattered population char-

acteristic of the new automobile-oriented suburbs.

The potential competitive threat of the automobile was being weighed and considered as early as the turn of the century. Said a 1900 Louisville *Courier-Journal* editorial of the vehicle: ". . . It has never been put to practical use, though it has become to some extent a fashionable fad. How large a use can be made of it for carrying passengers and freight cannot be foretold with certainty, but it is reason-

ably sure it can never compete with streetcars."

During the same year, the *Street Railway Journal*, taking note of a new automobile stage line that was providing a regularly scheduled service at Cleveland, commented, "It is not thought, however, that automobiles can ever practically compete with electric cars in Cleveland."

For well over another decade the automobile remained little more than a curiosity or, upon occa-

sion, a traffic nuisance. Street railway traffic continued to grow at an encouraging rate, and the only cause for alarm among the trolley men was an unhealthy upward trend in operating costs.

Oddly enough, an economic depression shortly before World War I brought the first real competition from the automobile. Beginning in Los Angeles about mid-1914, unemployed motorists began to solicit passengers along streetcar routes for a five-

Downtown Peoria was nearly deserted on an October evening in 1946 as an Illinois Power Company Birney waited for a traffic light at Adams and Main streets on a trip over the Knoxville route. It was the last night of trolley operation in Peoria. — *Paul Stringham.*

Except for the electric car itself, no other development in street railway history met with public enthusiasm comparable to that afforded the PCC cars. A crowd jammed downtown St. Louis streets in 1940 for the debut of 50 new PCC's. — *Collection of William J. Clouser.*

cent fare. The "jitney" craze, as it was called, spread rapidly. By the end of the year nearly 800 jitneys were operating in Los Angeles alone, and at the height of the fad in 1915 an estimated 6000 to 10,000 jitneys were running in U. S. cities.

For a time the jitneys posed a serious threat to the earnings of street railway systems. Operating only when and where there was traffic, the jitney drivers made no effort to provide the scheduled, all-day service that was required of the traction companies, but simply skimmed off the "cream" of the peak-hour traffic. The experience of the Los Angeles Railway was typical of that of the harder hit large city systems. By the end of 1914 LARy was losing an estimated $600 a day in revenues to the jitneys, and the company was forced to cancel an ambitious car rebuilding program and lay off a hundred men in its shops. During 1915 jitney losses totaled an estimated half million dollars. The company halted all track extensions and canceled its new carbuilding program.

The trolley companies fought back against the jitneys as best they could. The Richmond (Va.) street railway company put on its own jitney fleet in an effort to drive the private owners off the streets. The public seemed to resent this strategem; and the trolley company's "one-eyed jitneys," as the distinctive single-headlight Briscoe automobiles used were called, never proved popular. The San Diego Electric Railway simply suspended service on several routes hard hit by jitney competition. The Eastern Massachusetts Street Railway, announcing "war to the finish" against unregulated jitney competition, threatened to discontinue service in cities where jitneys were allowed to "run wild." The most frequent anti-jitney tactic, however, was simply a vigorous campaign carried on by the streetcar companies

World War II brought unaccustomed activity to U. S. trolley systems. Los Angeles Railway's South Park shops were the scene of intense activity in 1942 as cars were readied for wartime service.—*Collection of Donald Duke.*

for some licensing and regulation for the jitneys.

After 1915 the craze began to subside. Finding that jitney driving was not a very profitable occupation, many of the drivers dropped out, although for a time it seemed there was always a new one ready

Trolleys got their first real automotive competition in the jitney craze around World War I. Two open cars and an early jitney roll through an intersection in Washington, D.C. — *Collection of LeRoy O. King.*

to go into business when another quit. Improving business conditions helped too, as many drivers went back to more remunerative jobs. Most important, more and more regulatory bodies began to see the wisdom of the trolley companies' argument that permitting unregulated competition to weaken a city's mass-transportation system was not in the long-term public good. As soon as the jitneys were required to obtain licenses, post bonds, and maintain some degree of regular service, most of them vanished from the streets. Before the end of 1916 the situation was

encouraging enough for street railway executive Dr. Thomas Conway Jr. to remark that "the plague has run its course." By 1921 only an estimated 2000 to 3000 jitneys remained in operation in the United States.

In a few areas, though, the jitneys hung on tenaciously. As late as 1925 private jitney buses still accounted for fully 25 per cent of the mass transport traffic at Norfolk, Va., before they were finally driven out of business. In Honolulu, jitney competition did not succumb to regulatory control until 1940,

In its declining years, trolley No. 3 of Mount Mansfield Electric Railway reposed forlornly in a ramshackle carbarn at Stowe, Vt. The line's cars made their final runs through the Green Mountain countryside in 1932. — *Collection of Howard E. Johnston.*

A cheery sight on a wintry day was Elmira (N. Y.) Birney No. 117 as the little trolley bravely fought her way through a January 1939 blizzard. Abandonment of the system was barely two months away. — *Collection of Allan H. Berner.*

Southbound to Drake, a Pittsburgh Railways interurban PCC car raced along under the thunderhead of an approaching storm in 1959. Trolleys remained the principal mode of Pittsburgh public transportation into the 1960's, but declined rapidly after the new Port Authority of Allegheny County took over in 1964. By early 1967 only 58 track-miles and little more than 100 active cars remained. — *F. W. Schneider III.*

less than a year before the trolleys themselves vanished from the streets.

On a few occasions jitney service was used as a weapon against the street railway companies during strikes. In a 1916 strike at Wilkes-Barre, Pa., striking trolley men organized both a streetcar boycott and a competing jitney service. When the Denver Tramways attempted to maintain service with nonstrikers and strikebreakers during a bitter 1920 strike, the union retaliated with a free jitney service operated by automobile-owning strikers. After Portsmouth (Va.) trolley men organized a jitney service during a 1922 strike, they found the business so profitable that they kept right on operating it even after the strike was settled. Eventually the trolley company was forced to close three lines.

Even though the jitneys had no lasting effect on the traction companies, the World War I period found the industry facing grave problems. Although street railway mileage and passenger traffic were still growing, profits had begun to drop. Often extensions of service into new territory at the same

Two old trolleys of the Northern Indiana Railway met on the Notre Dame line at South Bend in the summer of 1940. Streetcar operation in the Indiana city ended shortly afterward. — *Van-Zillmer Collection.*

uniform fare contributed to the decline in net earnings. Most street railways were confronted with an increasingly heavy tax burden. Labor and material costs were rising rapidly; during the World War I period they almost doubled. To make matters worse, many companies were obliged by their franchises to operate at a fixed five-cent fare that had been in effect for many years, and regulatory bodies showed little inclination to change it. There was a growing number of street railway receiverships, and the situation became so serious that President Wilson appointed a Federal Electric Railway Commission to investigate conditions in the industry. In due time the commission reported that the industry was indeed in serious financial difficulty, and submitted a number of recommendations that helped somewhat, at least where they were heeded.

Meanwhile, there were some other encouraging developments in the industry's search for ways to get

costs in line. The Birney Safety Car, developed in 1915, was a huge success at cutting costs and increasing earnings on lightly traveled lines. Even more important, the thousands of Birney cars demonstrated that one-man operation was entirely practical. Soon street railways were ordering large numbers of new cars or rebuilding older equipment for one-man operation.

Throughout the 1920's unaccustomed activity on the part of both the carbuilders and the larger street railways was directed toward the development of improved equipment. More interest than ever before was shown in providing greater passenger comfort, imaginative new color schemes were applied to equipment, and merchandising and traffic promotion assumed new importance. The Electric Railway Presidents' Conference Committee, organized in 1929, put 5 years and a million dollars into a research effort aimed at development of a radically new trol-

Although its regular services had long since been operated exclusively with PCC cars, Washington (D. C.) Transit Company retained a few older cars for occasions such as this 1957 outing of the Washington Electric Railway Historical Society. All trolley operation in the nation's capital ended early in 1962. — *John J. Bowman Jr.*

Iowa's last trolley line was a suburban route operated between Waterloo and Cedar Falls by the Waterloo, Cedar Falls & Northern Railroad. During its last decade of operation the line was served by three former Knoxville (Tenn.) lightweights built in 1930 by Perley A. Thomas. One is shown near Cedar Falls in the spring of 1954. — *William D. Middleton.*

Refurbished in its original colors, San Francisco Municipal Railway's first trolley reappeared in 1962 to celebrate the city-owned system's 50th anniversary. By this time regular service was being provided with a fleet of 105 postwar PCC streamliners. — *James C. Wren.*

ley car. From this emerged the technical triumph of the PCC car, which was produced by the thousands over a period of 15 years.

Even as the trolley was enjoying its years of greatest triumph, its eventual successor, the motorbus, was already making a name for itself. The first big success for the bus was on New York's Fifth Avenue, where in 1908 a fleet of French-built double-deckers was installed in place of the Avenue's old horse-drawn omnibuses. Trolley cars had never been permitted on the exclusive thoroughfare.

The jitney craze led to the development of better-designed buses, and by the early 1920's a few street railway companies had timidly tried out the bus for service on lightly traveled outlying lines. As late as 1922 only some 370 buses were being operated by street railway companies. But in 1924 alone streetcar companies bought 1200 new buses and tripled their annual bus mileage. Another 1800 were bought in 1925, and annual bus traffic was doubled over that of the preceding year. Bus transportation was solidly on the path to success. By 1932 some 15,000 buses were in service, transporting more than a billion passengers annually. Only 5 years later the number had almost doubled, and annual bus traffic was running

A Dallas trolley rattled across the Tenth Street bridge on the last day of operation on the Trinity Heights route in August 1949. Streetcar operation continued elsewhere in Dallas for 10 more years. — *George A. Roush.*

By 1967 the sole surviving American example of conventional streetcar operation was the St. Charles line of the New Orleans Public Service Company. Trolley No. 948, a two-man standard car built by Perley A. Thomas in 1924, rolls past Tulane University and an elaborate fountain in Audubon Park. — *F. W. Schneider III.*

163

Operating a fleet of 165 narrow-gauge streamliners, Los Angeles was among the major users of PCC's until all trolley operation ended in 1963. This PCC lineup waited for "P" line service in 1951. — *Donald Sims.*

Threatening the supremacy of the streetcar as well as the motorbus was the hybrid vehicle known as the "trolley bus" or the "trackless trolley," whose proponents argued that it combined the best features of both. These early trackless trolleys, introduced on Staten Island in the 1920's, resembled diminutive streetcars mounted on rubber tires. — *Library of Congress.*

Aged trolleys rumbled through downtown streets on Denver's last day of streetcar operation on July 1, 1950. — *Courtesy of Electric Railroaders' Association.*

A decorous ceremony at the Vassar College terminal of Poughkeepsie's Main Street line in 1935 marked the last run of the Poughkeepsie & Wappingers Falls Railway Company. — *Collection of Allan H. Berner.*

Their long years of service over, Los Angeles trolleys were stacked three deep in a Terminal Island junkyard in 1960 awaiting conversion to scrap metal. — *Gary G. Allen.*

A usual part of the scrapping process for old trolleys was burning to remove unwanted materials. After the remains cooled, the junkman carried away the usable scrap metal that was left. These surplus Third Avenue Railway cars were put to the torch at the company's Garden Avenue yard in 1940. — *Jeffrey Winslow.*

With their trolley poles reaching vainly upward, a group of Lehigh Valley Transit streetcars were consumed by roaring flames at a Bethlehem Steel Company scrapyard in 1953. — *Collection of Allan H. Berner.*

In a bucolic Connecticut setting far removed from its original urban environment, ex-Montreal Tramways car No. 2001 traveled out to Short Beach in Sunday afternoon excursion service on the Branford Electric Railway in the fall of 1970. — *William D. Middleton.*

well in excess of 3 billion passengers a year. The rise of the motorbus seemed relentless.

The reasons for the success of the bus were many. Its operating costs were low, and no costly maintenance of track and overhead systems was required. The ability of the bus to swoop into the curb to pick up passengers was a safety asset, and its independence of fixed routings was regarded by many as a decided advantage over the trolley car. In an automobile age the lumbering trolley car seemed very much out of date, and motorists everywhere complained about rough trolley tracks and the hindrance to free traffic flow represented by safety islands for car riders.

By the early 1930's the trolley car had for the most part vanished from the smaller American cities, and even in the larger cities the bus was playing an increasingly important role on lightly traveled routes.

A major victory for the bus came in 1933 when San Antonio, Tex., with a population of over 200,000, became America's first large all-bus city.

The trolley car's greatest advantage was on routes of heaviest traffic, and it was here that it survived longest. The roomy cars were capable of packing in passenger loads far exceeding anything with which a motorbus could cope, and the high fixed costs of maintaining track and overhead were spread over a greater number of passengers. Indeed, many proponents of the "balanced" transit system maintained that each type of vehicle had its own area of best application and that the trolley car remained superior to all others for heavily traveled routes. The thousands of PCC cars placed in service beginning in 1936 were largely applied to this kind of service, and on many big city systems the trolley car seemed to have retained a permanent place.

In a dramatic example of after-dark photography, three retired New England trolleys met on the Connecticut Electric Railway's operating museum trackage in the Connecticut woods at Warehouse Point. — *Jim Shaughnessy.*

World War II halted for a few years the decline of the street railway, and elderly trolley cars of every description that had somehow escaped earlier scrapping were pressed into service to accommodate a tremendous wartime traffic. Once the war was over, however, traction's decline resumed. Despite record PCC car production in the years immediately after the war, the number of active cars and total track-miles were rapidly reduced. By 1951, when domestic streetcar production ended with a 25-car PCC order for San Francisco, it had become evident that the street railway, in its customary form at least, was on the way to extinction in North America.

Despite the superior qualities of the PCC car, the remaining street railway operations were becoming increasingly uneconomical. Even though the American urban population was growing at a rapid rate, the volume of public transportation traffic continued to decline, and fewer and fewer lines enjoyed sufficient patronage to warrant streetcar operation.

The cost of new trolleys was substantially higher than that for mass-produced motorbuses, and many cities found that growing traffic congestion made it almost impossible for the more expensive PCC cars to realize their superior earning potential. Chicago was a notable example. By 1953, when the newest of its 683 PCC cars was barely 5 years old, the Chicago Transit Authority came to the conclusion that traffic congestion had so hampered its surface lines that continued trolley operation was hopelessly uneconomical. During the next 5 years some 570 of CTA's newest PCC's were sold to the St. Louis Car Company for scrapping and reincarnation as PCC-type rapid-transit cars, and all Chicago trolley operation was ended by the summer of 1958.

By the early 1950's trolleys were even disappear-

Ready for a weekend excursion over the Connecticut Electric Railway near Warehouse Point, Conn., former Connecticut Company 15-bench open car No. 840 loads at the museum's terminal in September 1970. The car was built by J.M. Jones' Sons of West Troy, N.Y., in 1905. —*William D. Middleton.*

The oldest and largest operating trolley museum is that of the Seashore Electric Railway at Kennebunkport, Me. Former Philadelphia Rapid Transit No. 6618 rattled over the museum's rural main line on a spring afternoon in 1971. Built by J.G. Brill in 1911, the car was one of the popular "Near-Side" type developed by the Philadelphia company. — *William D. Middleton.*

ing from many of the major cities that had adopted the PCC car in large numbers. San Diego, one of the earliest cities to acquire PCC's, ended streetcar operation in 1949. Cincinnati gave up trolleys in 1951, and Birmingham and Cleveland followed a year later. Notwithstanding the purchase of a large fleet of postwar PCC's, Minneapolis and St. Paul trolleys were gone by 1954. The Detroit, Brooklyn, and Vancouver systems folded up in 1956. Kansas City cars made their last runs in 1957, and 2 years later the Dallas system was also gone.

By mid-1967 trolleys remained in only a handful of North American cities. Large fleets of PCC cars continued to operate in Toronto, Boston, Philadelphia, Pittsburgh, and San Francisco. At Newark and Cleveland, PCC cars provided service on lines of semi-rapid-transit character. In New Orleans, standard two-man cars continued to operate over a single route that afforded the only surviving Amer-

ican example of conventional trolley operation. At El Paso an aging fleet of PCC cars still rattled across the Mexican border to Ciudad Juarez in an international operation with a tenuous future, and in Mexico itself the cars still ran only at Mexico City, Tampico, and Veracruz.

The departure of the streetcar from the streets of the American city almost invariably was an occasion for some form of municipal celebration and often a good deal of public nostalgia. On a few occasions the departure of the trolleys was made the excuse for uninhibited hooliganism by local riffraff. The most notable example was the "last run" celebration on the Norfolk (Va.) system of the Virginia Transit Company in July 1948.

The company's last regular run left downtown Norfolk for Ocean View at 12:40 a.m. on July 11 crowded with drunks attracted to the affair. Soon after the trip got under way the celebrants ripped down the advertising placards in the car, and then proceeded to wrench down the standee straps. Next someone pulled out the rear roller sign and began tearing it to pieces. Then a seat handle was used to smash out the car's rear window, and soon afterward the car's seats were torn loose one by one and hurled through broken windows. The car limped into Ocean View at 1:30 a.m. with every light broken, including its headlight, and with but a single window unsmashed. By the time police arrived in response to a riot call, all but two of the hoodlums had escaped into the darkness. An hour later a second trolley arrived to tow the battered "last car" back to the carbarn.

There were several occasions, too, when the trolleys faded from the scene in the midst of acrimonious conflict between the streetcar company and local authorities. One early case in 1920 involved the Eighth Street local line operated at Goshen, Ind., by the Northern Indiana Railway. The line was a consistent money loser, but the city council regularly refused the company permission to abandon it. Finally, after learning that the local judge would be out of town for a weekend and things would be pretty quiet in Goshen, the company decided to act. A crew of men hastily brought in on Friday evening worked through the night and into the next day tearing up the rails and pulling down the overhead. By the time local authorities realized what was happening and halted the work, the destruction was a *fait accompli* and the line never resumed operation.

A somewhat different incident occurred at Council Bluffs, Ia., in 1948. After the Omaha & Council Bluffs Street Railway had rejected a proffered new franchise, the city awarded one to a new bus company instead. Protected by a court injunction, the streetcar company continued to operate its cars on the interstate line to Omaha in competition with the new bus service. Just to be on the safe side, the trolley company ran its own bus service as well, giving Omaha-Council Bluffs travelers a surfeit of service while the dispute lasted. When the injunction protecting the trolley operation ended at noon on September 25, Council Bluffs police forced the cars into the barn one by one; and on this note the trolley era ended in Council Bluffs.

In a majority of cases, however, the trolley car made its departure in a suitably dignified manner. Frequently a Sunday rotogravure spread, depicting transportation progress from horsecar to bus, would appear to underscore the occasion with appropriate nostalgia. The last days of operation were usually marked by a noticeable increase in riding as sentimental old-timers journeyed for the last time, or parents hurried to give their children their first and only trolley ride. Typically, the last cars were decorously draped in bunting or black hangings, although occasionally there were lapses in taste in the form of lugubrious faces or similar decorations painted on the cars. Quite often the old cars were paraded, generally followed by a string of the shiny new buses that were taking over. In more recent years, as trolley enthusiasts multiplied, at least one chartered car was usually on hand to transport the faithful over the system for the last time; and on the occasion of any major abandonment, a good deal of more or less good-natured jockeying took place among rival fan groups for the privilege of operating the very last car.

An unusual variation in the customary "last day" celebration marked the end of trolley operation at Atlantic City, N. J., on December 28, 1955. The trolley company decided to contribute the entire day's revenues to the Atlantic City hospital, which stationed its most attractive nurses aboard the cars to hand out suitable "last day" certificates to every rider.

The decline of trolley operation in North America was characterized by a growth of organized interest in the preservation of the history of the street railway era. Three national railway enthusiast organizations formed during the 1930's devoted their activities to electric railways, and dozens of local organizations occupied themselves with similar interests. The pursuits of the traction enthusiasts included the operation of excursions over remaining electric railway properties, the compilation of exhaustively detailed historical publications, and the collection of maps, timetables, and other traction memorabilia.

The ultimate achievement of the fans was the preservation of the trolley car itself. The first group formed for this purpose was the Seashore Electric Railway, organized at Kennebunkport, Me., in 1939. By 1967 more than 40 similar organizations had been established in the U. S. and Canada — almost all of them volunteer in character — which had preserved over 400 items of electric railway equipment of every description. A dozen or more of the museum groups were operating traction equipment over their own trackage or were at the point of doing so. Indeed, by the beginning of 1967 there were as many operating trolley museums as there were surviving trolley systems in North America.

Return of the Trolley

Inbound to Public Square in January 1986, Breda articulated light rail vehicle No. 828 accelerated away from the East 116th Street station on the Greater Cleveland Regional Transit Authority's rebuilt Shaker Heights light rail system. — *William D. Middleton.*

Packed with Shaker Heights commuters, a Van Aken
Express burst forth from the subterranean depths of
Cleveland Union Terminal in 1954. Ex-Twin Cities PCC
No. 68 led the four-car train. — *Herbert H. Harwood, Jr.*

Nearing the end of the long ten-mile climb out of Cleveland
Union Terminal to Shaker Heights, Pullman-built PCC car
No. 81 approached the East 116th Street station in 1955 on
a run to Green Road. Cleveland's St. Luke's Hospital is in
the background. — *Herbert H. Harwood, Jr.*

EVEN as the trolley car in its traditional form was rapidly vanishing from the streets of the American city, the urban electric railway was beginning a modest resurgence. The trend toward urbanization of America, which had continued without pause ever since the formation of the republic, had, if anything, accelerated in modern times. The need for urban transportation was a constantly growing one, then, and if the traditional trolley car had become unable to satisfy it, the motor bus and the private automobile were not doing much better at the job.

Despite almost universal automobile ownership and a massive urban highway program in the years after World War II, the millenium never arrived. No matter how vast the expenditure for highways and parking facilities, only rarely were America's urban centers able to do much more than stave off total traffic strangulation. Disenchanted with the notion that the expressway provided the total answer to the urban transportation requirement, America's cities began showing renewed interest in electric traction.

One form in which the trolley had successfully survived in a few cities was in what was sometimes called the "limited tramline" concept, a form of trolley operation that represented a compromise between the extremes of conventional streetcar operation in public thoroughfares and a full-fledged rapid transit system. Limited tramline, or what is now generally known as "light rail," typically operates in some form of private right-of-way, reserved median, or even subway to avoid the constraints of competing vehicular traffic. Grade crossings are typically provided instead of costly grade separations. Stations are usually more widely spaced than those in ordinary streetcar service. Light rail rolling stock generally operates at higher speeds and offers a greater carrying capacity than most trolley equipment, and is commonly equipped for multiple-unit operation in trains.

What is perhaps the best early North American example of the limited tramline or light rail concept is a remarkable electric railway completed at Cleveland in 1920. Conceived by Cleveland's renowned real estate and railroad tycoons, the brothers Oris P. and Mantis J. Van Sweringen, the Cleveland Interurban Railroad, later the Shaker Heights Rapid Transit, was constructed to provide rapid transportation between downtown Cleveland and the exlusive new residential community the Van Sweringens were promoting at suburban Shaker Heights. The inner portion of the 15-mile line, which terminated at the expansive Cleveland Union Terminal, was constructed to high standards characteristic of a heavy-duty rapid transit system, while two outer branches of the system were laid in the broad center medians of Shaker and Van Aken boulevards, much like conventional trolley trackage in a similar circumstance.

Boston's MTA extended its Green Line light rail system to Riverside over a former Boston & Albany branch in 1959. On the line's July 4th opening day, picture window PCC No. 3820 raced past the Newton Reservoir outbound to Riverside. — *F.W. Schneider, III.*

Boston MTA PCC No. 3292, outbound to Riverside, met inbound PCC No. 3318 at Newton Highlands station soon after the line's 1959 opening. The station, at the left, was one of two retained from the line's B&A commuter railroad days. — *F.W. Schneider, III.*

Pittsburgh Railways interurban PCC's met at Cremona siding, south of Drake on the Washington interurban line, in the summer of 1952. A year later the line was cut back to a long suburban route terminating at Drake, which still operates as part of Pittsburgh's modernized light rail system. — *Duke-Middleton Collection.*

En route to downtown Pittsburgh from Castle Shannon and Library on Pittsburgh's South Hills private right-of-way, PCC No. 1715 had just crossed the Warrington Avenue bridge south of South Hills Junction in 1957. — *C.L. Siebert, Jr.*

Initially, a fleet of leased Cleveland Railway trolleys, equipped for multiple-unit operation, was used on the line. These were replaced after World War II with multiple-unit PCC cars.

Indeed, in nearly every North American city in which the trolley car continued to operate into the 1960's, the cars had survived largely as a result of operating conditions which provided, at least in part, the freedom from general street traffic contemplated in the limited tramline concept.

At Boston, the Massachusetts Bay Transportation Authority's "Green Line" network of PCC-equipped trolley lines in the southwest area of the city operated largely in private right-of-way to reach downtown Boston via the Tremont Street subway. Similarly, PCC cars of the principal surviving lines at Philadelphia reached City Hall from West Philadelphia through a long trolley subway.

Boston was Pullman's largest PCC streetcar customer, buying 320 units from 1941 to 1951. MBTA No. 3264 was photographed on the Arborway Line while taking on passengers at the Peter Bent Brigham Hospital stop in 1982. — *F.W. Schneider, III.*

San Francisco's Municipal Railway continued to operate PCC cars well into the 1980's. No. 1031, part of the last U.S. PCC car order in 1952, ran outbound on the J Line in Mission Dolores Park in October 1981. — *William D. Middleton.*

In Pittsburgh, almost all of the city's surviving car lines operated to the city's South Hills suburbs through the long Mt. Washington trolley tunnel and beyond the tunnel on private right-of-way. San Francisco's remaining trolley lines benefitted similarly from long tunnels and extensive private right-of-way which permitted a standard of service that could not be approached by motor buses. Several of Mexico City's remaining PCC-equipped lines had extensive sections of reserved center median. Even at New Orleans, where trolleys of 1920's vintage continued to operate, the remaining car line operated principally in a reserved median.

Only Toronto, which retained the largest trolley system in North America, continued to operate a large PCC car fleet on a conventional system with track located largely in paved streets.

By the beginning of the 1970's, there was increasingly serious interest in light rail as an alternative to either motor transit or costly heavy rapid transit systems.

This new interest manifested itself first in projects to rebuild, modernize, and sometimes extend, the aging trolley systems that had survived in more than a half dozen North American cities. During the 1970's and into the 1980's track, power supply systems, signalling, stations, and structures were extensively rebuilt to standards equal to, or approaching, those of the new light rail technology on the trolley systems at Boston, Newark, and Philadelphia.

Mexico City's Servicio de Transportes Electricos del D.F. rebuilt a number of its fleet of secondhand PCC's during the 1970's. Rebuilt No. 2216, a former Detroit PCC, waited at STE's Xochimilco terminal in 1976. — *William D. Middleton.*

America's last surviving conventional trolley line rolls on at New Orleans. No. 933, a 1923 Perley A. Thomas product, made a passenger stop at Lowerline Street, inbound to Canal Street on the tree-lined median of St. Charles Avenue in January 1987. — *William D. Middleton.*

177

Regional Transit Autthority No. 962, a 1924 Perley A.
Thomas product, made a passenger stop at St. Charles
Avenue opposite Lafayette Square in 1987. The car was
outbound from Canal Street. — *William D. Middleton.*

Dating back to the electrification of the St. Charles Line in
1893, the Carrollton car barn remains a still serviceable,
enduring artifact from the opening years of the electric street
railway era. Inside the barn and shops, streetcar maintenance
is carried on with tools and methods little changed in more
than a half century. (RIGHT) Two venerable Thomas cars
laid over at the outer terminal of the St. Charles Line at South
Carrollton and South Clairborne avenues in January 1987. —
Both William D. Middleton.

178

Two of the Crescent City's durable Perley A. Thomas cars passed in the night on the Canal Street median in 1959. The Canal Line was abandoned five years later, leaving the St. Charles Line as the last survivor of a once-great New Orleans streetcar empire. — *F.W. Schneider, III.*

A Streetcar Named New Orleans

St. Charles Line car No. 962 turned from the St. Charles Avenue median to round Lee Circle on its way downtown to Canal Street on a January morning in 1987. — *William D. Middleton.*

Inbound from the Taraval Line, San Francisco PCC No. 1146 emerged from the Twin Peaks Tunnel in 1969 to begin the long run down Market Street to the East Bay Terminal. This portal at Castro Street has since vanished with the linking of the Twin Peaks Tunnel to the new Muni Metro subway under Market Street. — *Harre Demoro.*

At San Francisco the Municipal Railway gained the advantage of a long Market Street trolley subway, built as part of the regional Bay Area Rapid Transit project, replacing surface trackage for the entry of its five light rail routes into downtown San Francisco. At Pittsburgh, a new downtown subway and complete reconstruction of major portions of the city's old South Hills trolley lines was giving the city the equivalent of an almost entirely new light rail system. At Cleveland, the Greater Cleveland Regional Transit Authority completed an all-but-complete rebuilding of the Shaker Heights light rail lines to modern light rail standards during the early 1980's. By the mid-1980's, a major rebuilding of Mexico City's remaining trolley lines to modern light rail standards had begun.

As the rebuilding of these older systems neared completion in the mid-1980's, many were beginning to make plans for new light rail lines. Boston's MBTA had two new routes for its Green Line light rail system under study. At Pittsburgh, a proposed Spine Line Corridor project would extend light rail service north and east from the city's new downtown light rail subway. San Francisco's Municipal Railway had long-range plans for extensions from its Muni Metro light rail system. Mexico City's plans for a rebuilt light rail system included two new rail lines. And Toronto was ready to begin work in 1987 on a new Harbourfront light rail line.

A new downtown subway opened in 1985 helped Pittsburgh's Port Authority Transit convert its surviving South Hills trolley lines into a modern light rail system. PCC No. 1754 handled morning rush hour passengers at the Steel Plaza station in January 1986. — *William D. Middleton.*

A portion of Pittsburgh's new downtown subway plan included a ramp which carried the trolley line from the east portal of the Mount Washington trolley tunnel to the Panhandle Bridge approach. This new route bypassed the old Smithfield Bridge crossing of the Monongahela River into downtown Pittsburgh. — *F.W. Schneider, III.*

North America's remaining trolley lines had been well served by the extraordianry PCC car, but as the PCC survivors approached ages of 30 and 40 years their replacement became an increasingly urgent requirement. The first attempt at a new generation of light rail vehicle was the U.S. Standard Light Rail Vehicle (SLRV), a high capacity, high performance articulated design developed by the Urban Mass Transit Administration. Unfortunately, this idea for a new standard vehicle to replace the PCC never worked out. San Francisco and Boston joined forces in 1973 with an order for 275 of the new SLRV's that went to Philadelphia aerospace manufacturer Boeing Vertol. Part of the Boston order eventually went to San Francisco after Massachusetts Bay Transportation Authority (MBTA), dissatisfied with performance of the cars, cancelled the final part of its order. No one else ever ordered the standard light rail vehicle, although more recently MBTA has ordered 100 similar cars of a much-improved design from Japan's Kinki Sharyo for 1986-87 delivery.

A fleet of 275 U.S. Standard Light Rail Vehicles was being assembled at Boeing Vertol's Philadelphia plant in 1975. Boston's MBTA was scheduled to get 175 of the SLRV's, while the remainder of the order was for the San Francisco Municipal Railway. — *F.W. Schneider, III.*

Resplendent in bright red and orange colors, SLRV's for San Francisco's new Muni Metro light rail system took shape at Boeing Vertol's Philadelphia plant in 1975. San Francisco later augmented its 100-car SLRV fleet with 30 cars from a cancelled portion of the Boston order. — *F.W. Schneider, III.*

San Francisco

San Francisco Municipal Railway Boeing Vertol light rail vehicle No. 1220 was photographed on a 1978 test run at the Muni Metro's Embarcadero subway terminal. Regular operation of the subway was still two years away. — *Harre W. Demoro.*

Two of Muni's Boeing Vertol light rail vehicles pass one another during test runs of the new cars, near St. Francis Circle (near the portal of Twin Peaks Tunnel). Finally on February 18, 1980, with no ceremony or fanfare, the SLRV's began to use the new Muni Metro subway. — *Harre W. Demoro.*

The Twin Peaks tunnel was linked with downtown San Francisco by a new Market Street subway to convert the Municipal Railway's surviving trolley lines to the modern Muni Metro light rail system. A three-car train of Boeing Vertol SLRV's emerged from the new West Portal station in May 1981. — *William D. Middleton.*

The new West Portal station of the Twin Peaks Tunnel was rebuilt for platform loading and opened for service in 1980. The modernistic shed-like roof now hides the old concrete portal face. — *Harre W. Demoro.*

Inbound from the Municipal Railway's Judah Line, an articulated Boeing Vertol SLRV approached the entrance to the Market Street subway near Church Street and Duboce Avenue on the way to downtown San Francisco in 1984. — *William D. Middleton.*

Boston

Inbound from Riverside on the Massachusetts Bay Transportation Authority's Green Line light rail system, a Boeing Vertol SLRV approached Fenway Park station in the wake of a late November snowfall in 1985. — *William D. Middleton.*

Trolleys in Boston began operation through America's first subway in 1897. In this scene, a Boeing Vertol SLRV loads passengers at the Park Street subway station almost a century since the subway was opened. — *F.W. Schneider, III.*

185

Inbound to Boston from Cleveland Circle on the MBTA's Green Line light rail system, Boeing Vertol car No. 3516 headed down Beacon Street at Beaconsfield in Brookline in October 1982. — *F.W. Schneider, III.*

On a chilly, rainy December day in 1982 an inbound light rail vehicle loaded passengers at Coolidge Corner, on Beacon Street in suburban Brookline. — *F.W. Schneider, III.*

MBTA's Boeing Vertol SLRV No. 3463 sped west towards Cleveland Circle on a splendid October day in 1982. The car was running over well kept track near Beaconsfield in Brookline. — *F.W. Schneider, III.*

186

Toronto CLRV No. 4096 approached the High Park terminal of TTC's College-Carlton Street light rail line in August 1984. — *William D. Middleton.*

Toronto

During the mid-1970's, Canada's Urban Transportation Development Corporation developed a new Canadian Light Rail Vehicle (CLRV) design that proved much more successful than the Boeing Vertol SLRV effort. The Toronto Transit Commission installed nearly 200 single-unit versions of the CLRV during 1979-82, and a further 52 articulated versions were being delivered during 1986-87.

TTC No. 4040 turned into St. Clair Street to begin a westbound run to the Keele Loop in June 1980. The UTDC-designed Canadian Light Rail Vehicle had just picked up passengers at the St. Clair station junction with TTC's Yonge Street subway. — *William D. Middleton.*

The Toronto Transit Commission acquired nearly 200 of the Urban Transportation Development Corporation's new Canadian Light Rail Vehicles. CLRV No. 4049 is shown on TTC's Neville loop in July 1984. — *Edward A. Wickson.*

187

UTDC's prototype articulated CLRV was westbound on Howard Park Avenue in Toronto on July 1, 1984, while on an electric railway enthusiast charter. — *F.W. Schneider, III.*

UTDC articulated light rail vehicle prototype No. 4900 laid over at Toronto's Humber loop in February 1983. A fleet of 52 of the cars was being delivered to TTC during 1986-87, and another 50 were under construction for the new Santa Clara County light rail system in California. — *Edward A. Wickson.*

Paired for multiple-unit trials, two new Canadian Light Rail Vehicles operated through a January 1979 snowstorm on Toronto's Lake Shore Boulevard. The Urban Transportation Development Corporation built 196 of these modern cars for Toronto. — *Edward A. Wickson.*

Toronto's Long Branch Line was the first to get the new UTDC light rail cars. No. 4153 was eastbound on Lake Shore Boulevard at 27th Street in suburban Etobicoke in July 1984. — *F.W. Schneider, III.*

Marked for a westbound St. Clair Avenue trip to Keele Street, UTDC light rail car No. 4041 made a passenger stop at its St. Clair West junction with the Spadina subway on a September evening in 1980. — *Edward A. Wickson.*

During the early 1980's, the Southeastern Pennsylvania Transportation Authority at Philadelphia acquired 141 new light rail vehicles from Japan's Kawasaki Heavy Industries for operation on the city's West Side subway-surface lines, and Red Arrow suburban routes. Cleveland's Regional Transit Authority (RTA) outfitted its rebuilt Shaker Heights lines with 48 articulated light rail vehicles supplied by Breda of Italy, while Pittsburgh's Port Authority Transit was equipping its rebuilt system with a Siemens/Duewag articulated cars.

Philadelphia

Three generations of Philadelphia trolleys were lined up at SEPTA's Woodland Depot on November 11, 1980. No. 9000, at the left, was the prototype for a new fleet of 112 light rail vehicles for West Philadelphia subway-surface lines built by Kawasaki of Japan. At the center, repainted in Philadelphia's original PCC color scheme of silver and cream, with blue striping, is PCC car No. 2054, built by St. Louis Car in 1941. At the right, a Peter Witt car built by J.G. Brill in 1926. — *F.W. Schneider, III.*

The Southeastern Pennsylvania Transportation Authority's West Philadelphia subway-surface lines were outfitted with new Kawasaki light rail vehicles in the early 1980's. Trolley No. 9014 paused at 40th and Spruce to pick up passengers. — *F.W. Schneider, III.*

SEPTA No. 9069 rolls along Spruce Street between 40th and 41st streets on subway division trackage. — *F.W. Schneider, III.*

During the morning rush hour on December 9, 1985, an inbound car from the Angora Route turned off Baltimore Avenue to head into the West Philadelphia subway that gives SEPTA's subway-surface trolley passengers a fast trip to City Hall. (RIGHT) Two of the new Kawasaki cars, inbound from Darby and Angora, approached the 40th and Woodlawn portal of the trolley subway to City Hall in December 1985. — *Both William D. Middleton.*

Cleveland

A thorough modernization of their rail line by Cleveland's Regional Transit Authority during the early 1980's gave Shaker Heights commuters the latest in light rail technology. PCC cars were replaced by 48 new articulated light rail vehicles built by Italy's Breda Costruzioni Ferroviarie. (ABOVE) No. 803 paused at Parkland station along Van Aken Boulevard on a Blue Line trip to Warrensville Road in June 1984. (LEFT) No. 836 was outbound at Shaker Square on another Blue Line trip. — *Both F.W. Schneider, III.*

An inbound train for Public Square, top left, approaches the East 55th Street junction where Shaker Heights light rail trains commence joint operation with the RTA's Red Line rapid transit route. The joint light rail/rapid transit maintenance facility is beyond. (ABOVE) Breda articulated car No. 836 was ready to start an inbound Green Line trip from Green Road in 1984. — *Both F.W. Schneider, III.* (LEFT) One of the Italian-built articulated vehicles approached the line's East 79th Street station on an outbound trip to Shaker Heights in January 1986. — *William D. Middleton.*

Running east along Shaker Height's Van Aken Boulevard towards its Warrenville Road terminal, an RTA Blue Line train dipped under Lee Road in Shaker Heights in the summer of 1984. — *F.W. Schneider, III.*

Pittsburgh

Pittsburgh outfitted its rebuilt light rail system with a fleet of 55 Siemens/Duewag articulated cars, supplemented by rebuilt PCC's. One of the German-built cars emerged from the new Mt. Lebanon tunnel in April 1987, northbound in pre-opening test operations. — *William D. Middleton.*

Ready to begin an inbound subway local run, Siemens/Duewag light rail vehicle No. 4110 waited at South Hills Junction in a damp, early April snowfall in 1987. — *William D. Middleton.*

Running as a subway local to Station Square, Siemens/Duewag articulated light rail vehicle No. 4110 paused for passengers at Pittsburgh's Steel Plaza subway station in April 1987. — *William D. Middleton.*

The rebuilt Pennsylvania Railroad Panhandle Bridge over the Monongahela River provided Pittsburgh's Port Authority Transit with a link between its new downtown subway and the South Hills rail lines south of the city. Articulated light rail car No. 4102 headed south on a subway local run in April 1987. — *William D. Middleton.*

Pittsburgh's newly rebuilt South Hills light rail system was just about ready to go when Siemens/Duewag light rail car No. 4118 paused at Potomac station on a southbound test run early in April 1987. The line opened to regular service late the following month. — *William D. Middleton.*

Handsomely finished in SEPTA's bright red, white and blue livery, rebuilt PCC car No. 2147 headed down Philadelphia's Ogontz Avenue at 72nd Street on a southbound Route 6 trip in January 1986. — *F.W. Schneider, III.* (BELOW LEFT) In addition to acquiring new light rail vehicles for their rebuilt systems, several of the surviving eastern trolley lines rebuilt many of their durable PCC cars for extended service. Philadelphia PCC car No. 2732, built by St. Louis Car Company in 1947, was being rebuilt for continued service on North Philadelphia surface lines at SEPTA's Woodland Shops in December 1985. — *William D. Middleton.*

Toronto, Boston, and Philadelphia had all augmented their new car fleets with extensively rebuilt PCC cars, while Mexico City and the Newark Subway light rail line stayed out of the new equipment market altogether with rebuilding programs for their PCC car fleets. During the early 1980's, Pittsburgh initiated a rebuilding program for 45 PCC's that came close to being a complete remanufacturing of the cars that was expected to continue them in service through the end of the century. The most extensive PCC rebuilding of all was carried out at Mexico City in 1985, when a local manufacturer produced a prototype eight-axle, three-section articulated car from three old PCC cars. An order was placed early in 1986 for more of the rebuilt cars for the city's light rail system.

Rebuilt car No. 4001 was photographed at Station Square, inbound during the morning rush hour in January 1986. — *William D. Middleton.*

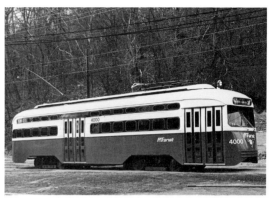

The most extensive of all PCC rebuilding programs was carried out by the shops of Pittsburgh's Port Authority Transit. No. 4000, completed in 1981, was the prototype for a fleet of 45 rebuilt PAT PCC's. — *F.W. Schneider, III.*

PCC's undergoing Pittsburgh's "from the frame up" rebuild are seen on the shop floor at Port Authority Transit's new Rail Maintenance Facility at South Hills Village in January 1986. — *William D. Middleton.*

Mexico City's Servicio de Transportes Electricos del D.F. initiated a rebuilding program in 1986 that will convert old PCC cars to three-section articulated "trens ligero" for operation on a rebuilt and expanded light rail system. This is the pilot set and numbered "000." — *John A. Kirchner.*

New Jersey Transit's Newark City Subway light
rail line was thoroughly rehabilitated during the
early 1980's, with its 24-car PCC fleet undergoing
a major overhaul that was expected to keep the
cars running well into the 1990's. Ex-Twin Cities
PCC No. 12 approached the Davenport Avenue
station on an outbound run in 1985, the line's 50th
anniversary year. — *William D. Middleton.*

Newark

Rush hour passengers boarded a PCC car
at the Newark City Subway's handsome
new Franklin Avenue terminal on a December morning in 1985. — *William D. Middleton.*

City Subway PCC car No. 19, a former Twin Cities Rapid Transit car built by St. Louis Car Company in 1946, approached the line's Davenport Avenue station on an inbound trip to Penn Station in December 1985. — *William D. Middleton.*

Westbound from Newark's Penn Station, New Jersey Transit PCC car No. 1 made a passenger stop at the City Subway's Washington Street station in December 1985, in the line's 50th anniversary year. The 4.3-mile line had just completed a thorough rehabilitation of its track and stations. — *William D. Middleton.*

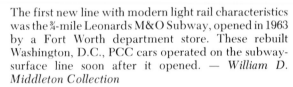

Before the end of the 1970's, major activity was underway on entirely new light rail systems in several of North America's growing cities. Technically, the first new light rail system dated from 1963, when Leonards, a Fort Worth department store, completed a ¾-mile long, part subway line of light rail characteristics that operated between the firm's downtown store and a parking lot on the banks of the Trinity River. Rebuilt and air-conditioned Washington (D.C.) PCC cars operated the service.

The first new line with modern light rail characteristics was the ¾-mile Leonards M&O Subway, opened in 1963 by a Fort Worth department store. These rebuilt Washington, D.C., PCC cars operated on the subway-surface line soon after it opened. — *William D. Middleton Collection*

More recently the Fort Worth cars have been rebuilt a second time by new owner Tandy Corporation to rectangular lines more comparable to contemporary light rail vehicles. — *LeRoy O. King, Jr.*

A Tandy light rail car waited for passengers at the company's Tandy Center in Fort Worth. The twice-rebuilt car bore little resemblance to its Washington (D.C.) PCC predecessor. — *LeRoy O. King, Jr.*

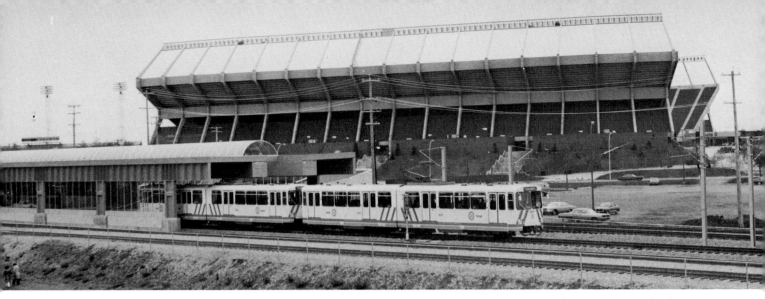

Edmonton, Alberta, opened the first really new North American light rail system in 1978. Here, an inbound train made up of two of the line's Siemens/Duewag articulated light rail vehicles leaves Stadium station in May 1978. — *Edward A. Wickson.*

Edmonton

The first really new systems, however, were built in Canada's western province of Alberta beginning in the late 1970's. Edmonton was the first to open, with a 4½-mile line into the northeastern sector of the city that operated on the surface in a Canadian National right-of-way, with a downtown subway. Two extensions have since opened, and a further extension across the Saskatchewan River to the south is under construction. Calgary opened a similar system in 1981 with an eight-mile South Corridor line. A Northeast extension opened in 1985, and a Northwest line is under construction.

Edmonton's Northeast light rail line used space in a Canadian National right-of-way for its 3.5 mile segment above ground. An outbound train ran parallel to CN diesels in this May 1978 photograph taken near Belvedere station. — *Edward A. Wickson*

Calgary

Headed by Siemens/Duewag articulated car No. 2026, a three-car Calgary light rail train emerged from the subway at 24th Street, Erlton, in October 1981. The train was northbound to the Calgary City Centre on the system's eight-mile South Corridor Line. — *John F. Bromley.*

Calgary followed Edmonton's lead with a similar light rail system that opened its first line in 1981. A three-car train for the new Northeast line loaded in the downtown 7th Avenue Mall in May 1985. (LEFT) An outbound Northeast line train has just crossed the Bow River in this May 1985 view. Beyond is the impressive skyline of booming downtown Calgary. — *Both Edward A. Wickson.*

A three-car train of Siemens/Duewag U2 articulated light rail vehicles crossed Deerfoot Trail on Calgary Transit's new Northeast light rail line in 1985. Beyond was the downtown skyline of the growing Alberta city. — *Edward A. Wickson.*

San Diego

In the U.S., San Diego was the first new system to open, with a 16-mile line to the Mexican border that operated through surface streets in downtown San Diego, and elsewhere on the right-of-way of the former San Diego & Arizona Eastern Railroad. The first section of a second line east to El Cajon opened early in 1986, and the city's Metropolitan Transit Development Board had plans in hand for still more extensions to the system.

Balloons lifted a striped parachute canopy to unveil San Diego's first new Siemens/Duewag light rail vehicle in an October 5, 1980, ceremony on downtown 12th Avenue. — *Metropolitan Transit Development Board.*

Southbound to San Ysidro in 1982, a San Diego Trolley train of Siemens/Duewag articulated light rail vehicles joined the old San Diego & Arizona Eastern right-of-way near 13th Avenue in downtown San Diego. Use of the old SD&AE line gave San Diego a low cost light rail route to the Mexican border. — *William D. Middleton.*

Popularly known as the "San Diego Trolley," the Metropolitan Transit Development Board's light rail line reaches its downtown terminal via surface trackage in C Street. Here, an inbound train from San Ysidro makes a stop at Gaslamp station on C Street in June 1984. — *William D. Middleton.*

At the San Ysidro terminal near the Mexican border in May 1982, a crowd of passengers wait to board a light rail train for the run to San Diego. — *William D. Middleton.*

A new East Line of the San Diego trolley system will extend light rail service 17.5 miles eastward to El Cajon over an old San Diego & Arizona Eastern branch by 1989. An initial section opened as far east as Euclid Avenue in March 1986. A two-car Euclid train headed east near 32nd and Commercial streets in June 1987. — *William D. Middleton.*

Running over rebuilt track on a line first laid down at the turn of the century as part of Portland's once-extensive electric interurban railway system, a two-car train of Bombardier LRV's ran westbound near Gresham in an early 1986 test operation of the Tri-County Metropolitan Transportation District's Banfield Line. — *Alfred L. Haij.*

Elsewhere on the West Coast, four additional new light rail systems had reached the construction stage by the mid-1980's. At Portland, a 15-mile Banfield light rail line extending east to Gresham from downtown Portland combined surface track, a right-of-way shared with a freeway, and private right-of-way. The line opened for service late in 1986. In California, the first section of a 19-mile system extending east and northeast from Sacramento opened early in 1987. In Santa Clara County, a 19-mile Guadalupe Corridor light rail system was underway that would link San Jose with residential areas to the south and the "Silicon Valley" high tech industrial area to the north, with the first section due to open late in 1987. In Los Angeles County, construction began late in 1985 for a 22-mile light rail route between downtown Los Angeles and Long Beach, with firm plans in hand for a second 17-mile, east-west route in the median of a new Century Freeway. All four of these new systems had plans for still further extensions and new routes.

Not far from the Gresham terminal of Portland's new Banfield light rail line, a Bombardier articulated light rail vehicle operated westbound in pre-opening test operation in March 1986. — *Alfred L. Haij.*

Portland

Portland's new Banfield light rail line reaches its downtown terminal over typical street railway trackage. No. 112 headed a two-car Gresham train approaching the Oak Street station in First Avenue just two months after the line's September 1986 opening. — *Harre W. Demoro.*

Bombardier articulated light rail vehicle No. 102 led an inbound train from Gresham down Morrison Street towards the Banfield Line's downtown Portland terminal on a rainy November day in 1986. On the right are the city's historic Pioneer Courthouse and the new Pioneer Courthouse Square. — *Harre W. Demoro.*

San Jose - Santa Clara

Santa Clara County Transportation Agency (California) light rail vehicle No. 804 was ready to begin a test run over the county's Guadalupe Corridor light rail system in June 1987. Canada's UTDC was building 50 of these big articulated cars for the agency. An initial section of the 19-mile line at San Jose was scheduled for opening in December 1987. — *William D. Middleton.*

The Santa Clara County Transportation Agency's new Guadalupe Corridor light rail line is expected to ease traffic congestion in one of California's fastest growing urban areas. South of San Jose the line shares a right-of-way with the new Guadalupe Expressway, while to the north the trains will operate in reserved center medians in principal streets. The line will operate through downtown San Jose in street trackage with the line's new UTDC articulated light rail vehicles. The full 19-mile system is expected to be open by 1990.

Sacramento

Sacramento's Regional Transit District employed federal funds transfered from a cancelled freeway project to build the new RT metro rail system. RT Metro's northeast line was built on an abandoned Western Pacific line and in a right-of-way originally acquired for the cancelled Interstate 80 Bypass freeway, while a line to the east was installed in a Southern Pacific right-of-way. Street trackage and a K Street transit mall carry trains through downtown Sacramento. The full system was expected to be in operation by the end of 1987. Long range plans for Sacramento rail transit contemplated extensions to Roseville and Folsom from the initial system, and new lines to the Sacramento airport and the city's south side.

On a bright June day in 1987, articulated light rail vehicle No. 113 headed an outbound train at Cathedral Square station in Sacramento's K Street Mall. Beyond the train is the city's Catholic cathedral. (BELOW) Articulated light rail vehicle No. 114 headed a rush hour train across Sacramento's Capitol Mall on a June afternoon in 1987. Beyond is the dome of the California State capitol. — *Both William D. Middleton.*

Inbound to downtown Sacramento from the northeast line's Watt/Interstate-80 terminal, a two-car Regional Transit District train headed by Siemens/Duewag light rail vehicle No. 104 passed Sacramento's Catholic cathedral in the K Street Mall in June 1987. — *William D. Middleton.*

Outbound from downtown Sacramento to the northeast line's Watt/Interstate-80 terminal, Sacramento RTD light rail vehicle No. 120 approached the Southern Pacific and Roseville Road overcrossing in June 1987. The rail line uses a bridge originally built for an aborted freeway project. —*William D. Middleton.*

Siemens/Duewag light rail vehicles were in for service at the Sacramento RTD's modern new light rail maintenance facility in June 1987. — *William D. Middleton.*

Sacramento's northeast light rail line terminates at this Watt/Interstate-80 station in the median of U.S. Interstate 80. Articulated car No. 112 waited to begin a downtown trip on a clear June afternoon, just a few months after the line's March 1987 opening. — *William D. Middleton.*

211

An artist's drawing of the planned Los Angeles-Long Beach rail line, developed before a car order had been placed, depicted Siemens/Duewag U2 articulated light rail vehicles northbound at Compton on former Pacific Electric Railway right-of-way. — *Los Angeles County Transportation Commission.*

Early in 1987 the Los Angeles County Transportation Commission ordered 54 of these articulated light rail vehicles from Japan's Sumitomo/Nippon Sharyo for its new Los Angeles-Long Beach and Century light rail lines. Deliveries were scheduled to begin in 1989. — *Los Angeles County Transportation Commission.*

Los Angeles

The most ambitious of all the new light rail projects that advanced into construction during the 1980's was initiated by Los Angeles County, which only two decades earlier had dismantled the last remnants of America's greatest network of street and interurban electric railways. Southern California's electric railway renaissance originated in a 1980 referendum that approved a 150-mile subway and light rail system plan for Los Angeles County, and a half cent sales tax that would help pay for it. By 1987 light rail vehicles were on order and construction had started on a 21.5-mile Los Angeles-Long Beach rail line, and a second 19.5-mile east-west Norwalk-El Segundo route that would be located largely in the median of a new Century Freeway.

> The county-wide rail transit system ratified by a 1980 referendum provided for a system of rapid transit and light rail routes for Los Angeles County that should eventually reach 150 miles. By 1987 construction of 4.5 miles of Metro Rail subway and 41 miles of light rail was underway. — *Los Angeles County Transportation Commission.*

TRANSIT DEVELOPMENT IN LOS ANGELES COUNTY

Metro Rail
Light Rail
Busway (Convertible to Rail)
Future Rail Transit Projects

Inbound on Buffalo's Main Street transit mall, Niagara Frontier Transportation Authority light rail car No. 107 passed the landmark Goldome Bank at Main and Huron in November 1984. — *William D. Middleton.*

The first, and thus far only, new light rail system in the eastern U.S. was opened at Buffalo in 1984. An unusual variation of light rail technology, the six-mile line, called light rail rapid transit, operates in a surface transit mall in downtown Buffalo and a rapid transit subway elsewhere. Planned branches and extensions will eventually enlarge the initial line into a regional system.

The closest thing to a standard car for these new North American systems proved to be the German-built Siemens/Duewag U2 articulated light rail vehicle originally developed for Frankfurt, Germany. With only slight variations, the U2 design was selected for Edmonton, Calgary, and San Diego, while an advanced U2 car was ordered for Sacramento. Portland acquired a Belgian articulated design produced by Canada's Bombardier, while the Santa Clara County project was acquiring a fleet of

the articulated cars developed by Canada's Urban Transportation Development Corporation. Buffalo's new light rail rapid transit line acquired a fleet of 27 unusually large double-end cars from the Tokyu Car Corporation of Japan.

Elsewhere in North America new light rail projects were planned or proposed for more than a dozen cities, with new ones being added to the list all the time. At Detroit preliminary engineering was completed for a 15-mile Woodward Avenue light rail corridor that was planned as the initial segment of a regional system. An 18-mile, bi-state line had reached the preliminary engineering stage at St. Louis, and Dallas was moving ahead on planning for an ambitious system that might eventually reach as many as 93 miles of line. In the east projects were being considered at Rochester, Washington (D.C.), and in the New York metropolitan area, where three different

Viewed from the atrium lobby of Buffalo's Hyatt Regency Hotel, Tokyu-built light rail vehicle No. 107 headed up the Main Street transit mall on NFTA's light rail rapid transit system soon after it opened for limited service in the fall of 1984. — *William D. Middleton.*

Former San Antonio Public Service car No. 300 ran past the city's art museum on West Jones Street in January 1986. The San Antonio Museum Association operates the tourist-oriented trolley on electric freight trackage of the Texas Transportation Company. (RIGHT) A refurbished Toronto Peter Witt No. 2424 loaded "Tour Tram" sightseeing passengers at York and Queen streets in June 1980. — *Both William D. Middleton.*

projects were proposed. In the south, projects had been proposed for Norfolk-Virginia Beach, Tampa, and New Orleans. At Houston, planning had been started for a 75-mile light rail system. In the midwest there were light rail proposals in various stages of planning at Dayton, Columbus and Milwaukee, while in the west there were projects being put forth at Denver, Phoenix and Seattle.

Quite apart from the robust growth of the trolley museum movement, there was a steadily increasing interest in the development of tourist-oriented "nostalgia trolley" projects. One of the first was at Detroit, where the city opened a mile-and-a-quarter line as part of its downtown revival efforts in 1976. Similar projects have since opened at Lowell (Mass.), Philadelphia, Orlando (Fla.), French Lick (Ind.), San Antonio, Ft. Collins (Colo.), Yakima (Wash.), and Seattle, while still more are underway at Tucson, Dallas and Galveston. Apart from its regular light rail operations, the San Francisco Municipal Railway operates an "Historic Trolley Festival" every summer, and the Toronto Transit Commission operates tourist season "Tour Tram" service. Similar operations in downtown historic districts are planned at Portland and San Jose in conjunction with their new light rail systems.

Typically, these nostalgia trolleys operate with either restored historic cars or imported antique trolleys from overseas systems. In at least one case, at Lowell, Massachusetts, old trucks from Australia were combined with brand new car bodies built to a 1902 Brill open car design.

In the century since it emerged as a major force in urban transportation at Richmond in 1888, the urban electric railway has passed through periods of both great growth and prosperity, and decline and failure. Indeed, a few decades ago it had all but vanished.

But now the enduring qualities of that remarkable and delightful invention from the genius of Van Depoele, Daft, Siemens, and Sprague are again recognized and back to work in the service of urban America. As the electric car began its second century of service, the time of the trolley is back!

Appendix

The technology of the trolley

PRINCIPAL CAR TYPES

CLOSED CAR: Throughout the history of electric traction the ordinary closed car, either single- or double-truck, was by far the most common type of trolley car. Although the most frequent arrangement for the closed car was with full front and rear platforms, this car was constructed in almost every conceivable entrance and exit arrangement, depending upon the method of fare collection employed and whether the car was built for single- or double-end operation.

OPEN CAR: Designed for summer trolley riding, the open car was enormously popular in the early years of electric traction. The usual pattern provided transverse benches extending the full width of the car, and longitudinal steps running the full length of the car to permit boarding and alighting at any point. On some lines, open cars were arranged with end platforms and center aisles, and were equipped with some sort of wire mesh along the lower section of the sides for a safer boarding and alighting arrangement.

SEMI-OPEN CAR: The semi-open car, an attempt to compromise between the closed and open car arrangements, was usually divided equally between open and closed sections. This type was most popular on the West Coast, where the climate was relatively mild and weather changes were frequent.

CALIFORNIA CAR: The original variety of semi-open car, the California car, was developed for the California Street Cable Railroad Company at San Francisco. This design placed the closed section in the center with an open section at either end.

CONVERTIBLE CAR: In order to obviate the high cost of duplicate sets of closed and open cars for winter and summer operation, the convertible car was developed during the 1890's. Side panels and windows which could be removed for storage, or slid into various types of roof pockets, were employed to enable conversion to an open car.

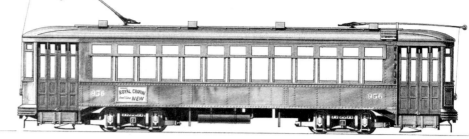

CLOSED CAR

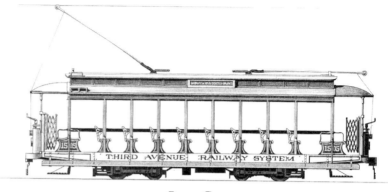

OPEN CAR

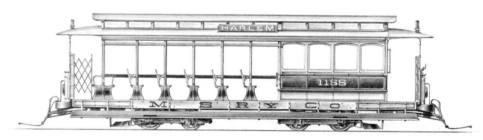

SEMI-OPEN CAR

CALIFORNIA CAR

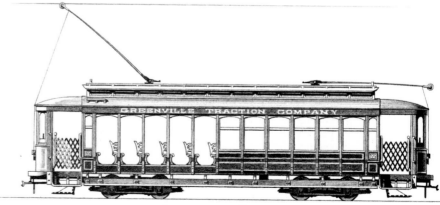

CONVERTIBLE CAR

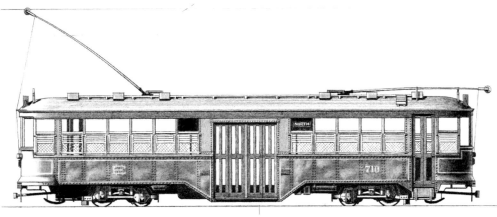

CENTER-ENTRANCE CAR

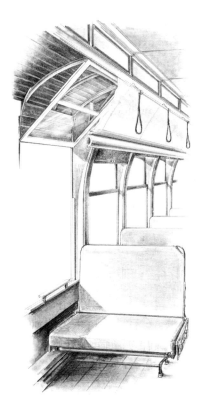

SEMI-CONVERTIBLE CAR

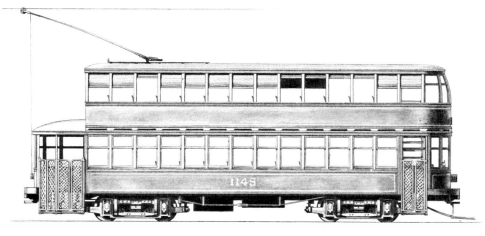

DOUBLE-DECK CAR

ARTICULATED CAR

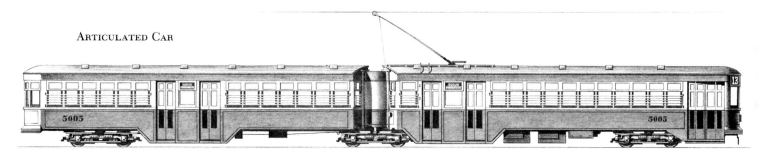

SEMI-CONVERTIBLE CAR: A far more practical and popular arrangement than the "full convertible" was the semi-convertible. It employed various types of window sash which could either be removed or slid into roof or wall pockets during mild weather. Side panels below the windows remained fixed in place.

CENTER-ENTRANCE CAR: Arranged for entrance and exit at the center of the body, rather than at the ends, the center-entrance car was most commonly used in a variety of "low floor" designs intended to speed boarding and alighting by reducing the number of steps.

PAY-AS-YOU-ENTER CAR

NEAR-SIDE CAR

PETER WITT CAR

DOUBLE-DECK CAR: Although the double-deck car was never a popular car type in North America, it was the subject of frequent experimentation by traction companies looking for equipment with a greater passenger capacity. A variety of configurations were tried; some of the most nearly successful placed a second story on what was essentially a "low floor" center-entrance car.

ARTICULATED CAR: Articulation, with either two carbodies resting on a common center truck or two independent carbodies permanently connected by an intermediate suspended conductor's platform, was employed by a number of systems to provide a car with a tremendous seating capacity that still was able to negotiate the restrictive curves common to street railways.

PAY-AS-YOU-ENTER CAR: The P.A.Y.E. car, a patented arrangement intended to improve fare collection, enjoyed wide application. Passengers boarded at the rear and paid their fare to a conductor stationed on the rear platform before passing into the car. Exit was normally at the front only, but sometimes was permitted at the rear as well by means of an arrangement that separated boarding from alighting passengers. In order to provide ample room for passengers waiting to pay their fares, most P.A.Y.E. cars had an unusually large rear platform.

NEAR-SIDE CAR: Another patented fare-collection design, the "Near-Side" car placed the conductor directly behind the motorman. Passengers boarded at the front and paid their fares as they passed the conductor. Exit was usually through the rearmost of two front doors. Another exit placed at the rear of the car was employed for emergencies or at terminals only.

PETER WITT CAR: Developed by a Cleveland street railway commissioner, the Peter Witt car had a front entrance and center exit, and passengers paid their fare to a conductor stationed at the center of the car as they either passed to the rear half or left the car. The same front-entrance center-exit arrangement was used in most one-man cars in which passengers paid their fares to the operator as they boarded the car at the front.

BIRNEY SAFETY CAR

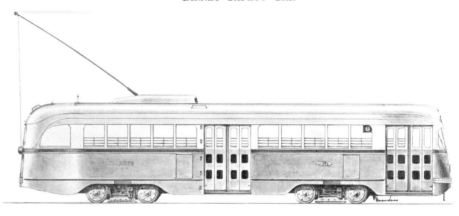

PCC STREAMLINED CAR

BIRNEY SAFETY CAR: The Birney, the first really successful standard car design, was a lightweight four-wheel car incorporating a number of patented features that permitted safe one-man operation. Minor variations were made in the thousands of Birneys produced by several builders between 1916 and 1930, and a number of double-truck cars incorporating the same safety features were turned out during the 1920's.

PCC STREAMLINED CAR: Developed by the Presidents' Conference Committee during the 1930's, the PCC car was a standardized streamlined streetcar design of radically improved performance. Although numerous improvements and modifications were made, the basic design concept and arrangement remained unchanged during the more than 15 years that PCC cars were in production. The "standard" PCC was a front-entrance center-exit single-end car, but it was also produced in several other arrangements to suit the requirements of individual systems.

CAR CONSTRUCTION

WOOD CONSTRUCTION: Until well into the current century, wood was almost universally employed as the basic construction material for street railway cars. Heavy timber sills beneath the floor were normally the basic structural element. Later, as longer double-truck cars came into use, metal truss rods were added beneath the carbody to help provide sufficient strength and rigidity. Platforms, usually lower than the car floor itself, were supported by wood or metal members suspended from beneath the car floor. Sides and roofs were framed in wood members and covered with wood sheathing or paneling.

SEMI-STEEL CONSTRUCTION: Shortly after the turn of the century, carbuilders began to use greater amounts of steel in carbody construction. Originally steel was used in place of timber for the main sills supporting the carbody, then was progressively adopted for other parts as well. When steel was employed for the main frame, as well as side plating, the construction was often called "semi-steel." Wood was still used for the side posts and roof.

STEEL CONSTRUCTION: Even before 1910 a number of cars had been built for several systems which were essentially all-steel in construction. Frames, side plating, side posts, and the "car lines" that supported the roof were all of steel. Side panels and the structural framing were riveted together to act as a girder which, together with the center sills, helped to support the car's weight. Although metal was sometimes used, wood was still frequently employed for roof sheathing, windows, flooring, and the interior finish.

Initially, steel cars were extremely heavy in construction, but beginning with the Birney car of 1915, increasing attention was given to weight reduction through better design and more extensive use of lighter metals and other materials. A number of cars of the 1920's and 1930's made wide use of aluminum and a few experimental cars were built almost exclusively of aluminum. The development of high-tensile alloy steels during the 1930's, together with the application of welding to carbody construction, permitted the production of lightweight carbodies of exceptional strength and rigidity for such modern cars as the PCC.

ROOF CONSTRUCTION: The most common type of roof construction in the early years of traction was what was generally referred to as the "monitor roof." A raised clerestory, or monitor, was provided in the central portion of the car roof. Operating sash in the sides and ends of the monitor helped to give better light and ventilation within the car. In the true monitor roof, properly called a "monitor deck" roof, or "deck roof," the raised clerestory was stopped off short of the platforms. A modification in which the raised section curved down at each end to join the main roof was widely used on steam railroad equipment and was consequently called a "railroad roof." It was sometimes used on street railway equipment as well. In later years the arch and "turtle-back" roofs became common. Both of these types curved from one side of the car to the other unbroken by a raised clerestory. Ventilators of some kind were usually installed to supply ventilation in place of that provided by the sash in the sides of a raised monitor.

TRUCKS

SINGLE TRUCK: Although double-truck equipment began to come into use during the early 1890's, the single-truck car remained the most common type until after 1900. On a very few early electric cars the horsecar practice of supporting the wheels directly in pedestals attached to the carbody was followed; but this method proved inadequate, and the separate metal truck on which the carbody rested was quickly adopted. Although a multitude of manufacturers were producing trucks of their own design, most of the more successful types were essentially similar in design. Journal boxes were free to move in the pedestal jaws of the metal truck frame, and were supported by several coil springs. The weight of the carbody was carried to the truck frames by means of coil springs, usually located at either side of the axles, and by elliptic springs mounted on extensions of the truck frame. The latter feature gave a single-truck car a longer "spring base," which was found to improve riding qualities. The single-truck car enjoyed a revival after World War I with the development of the Birney Safety Car. The Birney was mounted on a four-wheel truck that, although of improved design, was similar in its essential features to earlier types of trucks.

The single-truck car had several inherent limitations. As long as the axles remained fixed in a parallel position, the short-radius curves common on street railways limited the maximum practical wheelbase, which in turn restricted the over-all length of the car. Because of the short wheelbase, too, single-truck cars had a tendency to pitch and to "nose" from side to side. As a result, they were never particularly smooth riding, even under the best of conditions, and were entirely unsuited for high-speed operation.

Several attempts were made to develop a longer-wheelbase single truck to overcome these limitations. Almost all of these were some form of two- or three-axle "radial" truck in which the axles could rotate to nonparallel positions to accommodate short-radius curves. None enjoyed significant success in the U. S.

DOUBLE TRUCK: To permit greater carrying capacity than was possible with single-truck equipment, the double-truck car came into use during the early 1890's and by 1900 had become the most commonly built car type.

Trucks for double-truck cars were supplied by dozens of manufacturers in a wide variety of types. Generally the weight of the carbody was carried to each truck through a center bearing mounted on a transverse bolster beam. A king pin, or center pin, about which the truck rotated, connected the carbody and the truck at the center bearing. Usually side bearing plates mounted on the carbody and truck bolster prevented the carbody from rocking on the center bearing. On some types of trucks the entire weight of the carbody was carried by side bearings. From the bolster beam the weight of the car was carried through varying arrangements of coil or elliptic springs to the truck frame and then through coil springs to the journal boxes, which carried the axle bearings. The equalizer bars employed in trucks designed for rapid transit or interurban railway service were seldom found on street railway trucks.

Generally the wheelbase of street railway trucks was considerably shorter—around 4½ to 5 feet—than that of trucks designed for high-speed service. In the most widely used kinds of two-motor streetcar trucks the motors were "outside hung" (carried outside the axles) in contrast with the "inside hung" (suspended between the axles) mounting customary in long-wheelbase, high-speed trucks for interurban or rapid transit service.

Another common truck was the "maximum traction" truck designed for single-motor applications. By means of an off-center bolster, as much as three quarters of the weight was carried to the single-powered axle. Large-diameter wheels were provided on the powered axle, while the unpowered axle was fitted with small-diameter wheels. Several other designs for single-motor trucks obtained maximum traction by means of locomotive-type side rods which connected wheels on the powered axle with those on the unpowered axle. None of the latter were particularly successful, however.

During the late 1920's a number of attempts were made to create an improved type of truck that would offer a smoother ride and quieter operation. These efforts culminated in the radically improved truck used on the PCC car. Among its many innovations were a longer wheelbase (6' 3"), inside-mounted roller bearings, hydraulic shock absorbers, extensive use of rubber springing and insulation, and rubber-cushioned "resilient" wheels.

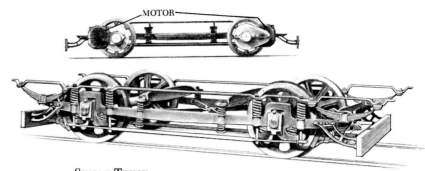

SINGLE TRUCK

MOTORS

Almost without exception, motors for street railway service were designed for direct current operation at 500 to 600 volts, with horsepower ratings ranging from about 25 to 60. The customary method of installation employed the "wheelbarrow" mounting originally developed by Frank Sprague, which permitted the motor to be directly geared to the axle. One side of the motor frame contained bearings mounted on the axle. This permitted the motor to rotate slightly about the axle as a center, thus maintaining perfect alignment between the gearing on the axle and the armature shaft no matter how irregular the track or the motion of the axle. The other side of the motor was hung from the truck frame on a spring mounting.

Radical improvements were made in both motors and gearing during the various experimental efforts of the 1920's and the PCC car development program. The 55 h.p. motors developed for the PCC car weighed only 700 pounds, less than half as much as motors of similar power of a decade and more earlier. One of the principal sources of streetcar noise had been the gearing that connected the motor to the axle, and the PCC car developers came up with a hypoid gearing and worm drive that virtually eliminated noise from this source.

CONTROLS

The earliest type of controller for streetcars was little more than a simple rheostat operated by the motorman. This made use of a series of diminishing resistance steps in series with the motors to gradually bring the motor up to speed. During the 1890's the series-parallel controller was developed which greatly reduced the loss of electric energy involved in the use of a simple rheostatic controller. Initially, two or more motors were placed in series position together with a

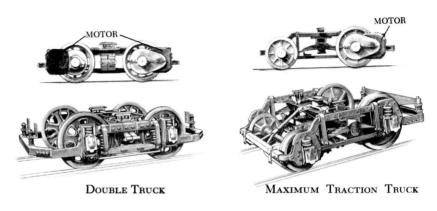

DOUBLE TRUCK

MAXIMUM TRACTION TRUCK

PCC TRUCK

resistance. The resistance was gradually reduced until "full series" position was reached, when the motors were switched to a parallel position, again with a resistance in the circuit. The resistance was once more gradually reduced until "full parallel," the normal running position, was reached. The resistance was gradually reduced by means of a hand-operated drum-type controller in which fingers on the controller made contact with copper segments of the drum as each position, or "point," of the controller was reached. Arcing between the points as the drum was rotated was a common weakness of this type of controller, and most were equipped with a magnetic "blowout" coil, which created a strong magnetic field that served to quench an arc.

Another weakness of the conventional type of controller was the limited number of positions, or "points," available, preventing smooth acceleration of a car. During the 1920's extensive development work was done on controllers that supplied a greater number of control points and some form of au-

tomatic operation in order to provide a smooth rate of acceleration. In the development program for the PCC car it was found that surprisingly high rates of acceleration were acceptable as long as they were smooth and uniform. As a result, the controller perfected for the PCC car employed automatic motor operation and more than a hundred control points in place of the hand-operated controller with a dozen or so points typical of those applied on older equipment.

BRAKES

The earliest electric cars used only brakes that were hand operated by the motorman. Although such braking had been reasonably adequate for horsecars, it quickly proved insufficient for the faster, heavier electrics. By the late 1890's air brakes were being widely applied to electric cars. The most common type was a simple straight air system in which the brake shoes were applied against the wheels through a linkage operated by a compressed air brake cylinder and

220

piston. The usual source of compressed air for the braking system was a motor-driven compressor, but many cars employed high-pressure storage tanks which had to be recharged at stationary charging stations along the line. Axle-driven compressors were also frequently used.

Maximum braking effectiveness in a streetcar depended upon applying the greatest possible pressure through the brake shoes short of causing the wheels to slide. As a consequence, a braking system that provided the proper amount of pressure to a car that was empty would apply insufficient pressure when the car was heavily loaded, or brake pressure that was adequate for a loaded car would prove too great for an empty car. This problem was sometimes solved by the application of a "variable load valve," a device which employed mechanical measurement of truck spring deflection to vary the brake pressure setting.

Another early type of brake was the magnetic brake. To brake a car equipped with this system, the traction motors were reversed to act as generators; and the current generated was passed through electromagnetic track shoes suspended above the rails. The shoes were drawn against the rails, creating a braking force, and at the same time conventional wheel tread brakes were applied through a leverage attached to the streetcar's magnetic shoes.

A variation of the magnetic brake was the "traction increaser," in which a magnetic device similar to the track brake was mounted on the truck in such a manner that it did not actually touch the rail. The magnetic pull between the electromagnet and the rail had the effect of increasing the weight on the wheels, thus permitting a greater braking force without causing wheel slip.

To provide the greater braking force required for the high-performance PCC car, its designers used a combination of three braking systems working automatically in sequence. Initially, a dynamic braking system came into play, employing the motors as generators. Next, a magnetic track brake was applied; and finally, as the car slowed to a stop, air-operated drum brakes were applied. In later all-electric models of the PCC car, a spring-applied, electrically

released driveshaft brake replaced the air-operated drum brake.

CURRENT COLLECTION

OVERHEAD SYSTEM: Almost universally used for street railway systems, the overhead system employed a trolley pole which was held against an overhead wire by means of spring tension in a swiveling trolley base. Originally a large trolley wheel, held by a trolley "harp," was used for current collection. Later, a sliding shoe was developed which eventually became the preferred means of current collection on almost all trolley lines. To prevent damage to the overhead wire system in the event a trolley left the wire, many companies used a spring-operated retriever which automatically pulled the pole down if a dewirement occurred. Pantographs and bow trolleys, while common on overseas lines, were only rarely employed in North America for overhead current collection on street railway systems. The pantograph, which employed one or two flat collectors that slid along the overhead wire, was widely used, however, on rapid transit systems using overhead current distribution. The pantograph was raised and held against the wire by spring tension and lowered by compressed-air pressure.

UNDERGROUND CONDUIT SYSTEM: Aside from a few short-lived experimental installations, the underground conduit system was used only on the street railway systems of Washington, D. C., and New York City. Sliding shoes on a truck-mounted "plow," which projected through a slot between the rails, collected current from the underground power rails. Two shoes, one each for the positive and return rails, were required. In a few early experimental installations, various types of surface contact systems were tried in which current collection devices mounted beneath the car drew current from an underground power supply by means of surface contacts that were energized only when a car passed over them.

THIRD RAIL: Although third-rail current collection was obviously unsuited for street railway service, it nevertheless was employed by the majority of rapid transit systems in North America. Truck-mounted iron

collection shoes, held against the top of the rail by their own weight, were employed for current collection. In a few protected third-rail installations in which the power rail was inverted, current collection was by means of an "underrunning" shoe held against the bottom side of the rail by spring tension.

FENDERS AND LIFEGUARDS: A variety of devices intended to prevent an unfortunate pedestrian from being run over by the wheels were applied to streetcars. Fenders, usually resembling a bed spring or a wire net, were mounted on the front of a car. Lifeguards were similar pedestrian catchers suspended beneath the carbody just ahead of the front truck. A lifeguard, normally held in a raised position, was dropped to the pavement by means of a linkage attached to a guard at the front of the car, which was actuated by striking an object on the track. Although fenders were eventually discarded by most street railway companies, some form of lifeguard was employed by almost every system throughout the street railway era.

WARNING DEVICES: Whistles or horns were seldom applied to cars designed solely for street railway operation. The most common type of streetcar warning signal was some kind of gong, usually foot-operated and mounted beneath the motorman's platform, but sometimes mounted on the roof and sounded by means of a hanging cord. Occasionally, pneumatically operated gongs were used, and on the PCC car an electrically operated gong was provided.

HEADLIGHTS: The earliest electric cars were equipped with oil-burning headlights, but soon afterward various types of incandescent lights were introduced. In recent years the automotive-type "sealed beam" headlight was applied to the PCC car. In some experimental cars of the 1920's, double headlights, much like those on an automotive vehicle, were used; and in at least one North American city — Montreal — streetcars carried no headlights at all but relied instead on a hooded indirect lighting arrangement on the front dash. Sometimes streetcar headlights were mounted on the roof, but the usual location was a flush mounting in the front dash below the windows.

221

CONDUIT PLOW

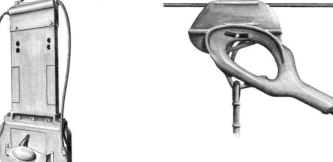

TROLLEY SHOE

THIRD-RAIL SHOE

RETRIEVER

TROLLEY BASE

TROLLEY WHEEL AND HARP

HEATING SYSTEMS: The earliest streetcar heating systems employed coal-burning cast-iron stoves installed within the carbody, a method that provided either too much or too little heat, depending upon the distance of a passenger from the heater. Several manufacturers developed improved car heaters which burned coal or oil and employed either forced hot air or circulating hot water to obtain more even heat distribution. Sometimes such heaters were installed beneath the car floor and were tended by employees at car line terminals, but more often they were located on the front or rear platform where they could be tended by the conductor or motorman.

In later years most street railway systems converted to the use of electric resistance heaters located either under the seats or on the floor along the walls. Although electric heaters were somewhat more costly to operate, they provided clean, even heat and needed little attention on the part of the operating crew. An unusual feature of the modern PCC car was the use of current generated during dynamic braking to help heat the car.

FARE REGISTERS AND BOXES: The earliest type of fare register was a large unit usually mounted above the door on the bulkhead at one end of the car, where it could readi-

ly be seen. By means of a rod arrangement and a pull cord the conductor could set the register and ring up a fare from anywhere in the car. Later, as new interior arrangements were developed that provided a stationary location for the conductor, various types of registering fare boxes, into which a passenger dropped his fare, were evolved. The same type of fare box was used for one-man car operation.

SANDERS: To avoid wheel slipping on wet, dirty rail, streetcars were equipped with sanders, which applied dry sand from a protected sandbox onto the rails by gravity or pneumatic feed.

DESTINATION SIGNS: In the early years of electric traction, cars were commonly lettered with the name of the route over which they ran. This obviously made it difficult to assign equipment to another route, and the street railways soon changed to some form of wood or metal destination sign which could be quickly replaced with another when the occasion required. These were hung on the side or front dash of the car, or were mounted on the roof at the front and sides. Signs illuminated from behind were frequently placed in the sash of the monitor deck at the front and on each side. Sometimes revolving signs, mounted on the roof above

the platforms or on each side, were used. Later, printed fabric roller signs were introduced.

SEATS: Trolley car seats were generally designed with durability, rather than comfort, foremost in mind. Often seats were simply made of wood slats. When upholstery was provided, it was more than likely some durable material such as rattan. In some cars designed for heavy loading, all or part of the car was given over to longitudinal seating along the sides, with the remainder of the space devoted to standing room. Most often, however, most of the seating was of the transverse type. Double-end cars were usually fitted with the "walkover" seat, on which the back could be flipped over when the car's direction of operation was changed. During the 1920's car designers began to take greater interest in passenger comfort, and innovations such as individual leather-upholstered seating were provided. By the time the PCC car was introduced, such features as fabric upholstery, contoured seats, and spring and rubber cushions had become common.

DOORS: Many early cars were without doors to the platforms, or had only folding gates to prevent boarding or alighting when the car was in motion. When doors came

222

into use, the most common was the folding type, manually operated by the conductor or motorman. Sliding doors were also common. Later, air-operated door mechanisms were developed which permitted doors to be operated from a distance. When one-man operation became common, exit doors were frequently provided with a treadle device in the step well, which, when a passenger stepped on it, automatically opened the door. Electric door motors were developed for later models of the PCC car.

SIGNAL SYSTEMS: As long as two-man car operation continued, trolley cars were provided with some type of bell signal, usually operated by a simple pull cord, with which the conductor could signal starts and stops to the motorman. An electric buzzer system, operated either by a pull cord or push buttons, was supplied to permit passengers to signal their desire to alight at the next stop.

TRACK AND CURRENT DISTRIBUTION SYSTEMS

TRACK: The earliest street railways usually employed some form of wrought-iron bars or flat strips attached to wood stringers for rails. Quite often the iron bars were bent or formed in such a way as to provide a path for the wheel flange. Wrought iron or steel T-rail of the sort used by steam railroads was often used for street railway track, although it was usually lighter in weight. Paving close to the rail with standard paving blocks was difficult, however; and the protruding head of the rail presented a danger to vehicular traffic and brought frequent objections by city officials. In 1877 the Cambria Iron Company of Johnstown, Pa., developed the first rolled steel "girder" rail for street railway use, and this type soon became by far the most frequently used. Girder rail was rolled with various types of protruding lips or grooves which acted as a flangeway for the car wheels. Generally a rather deep rail section — usually 7 or 9 inches — was employed. The 9-inch section was preferred for ease in paving adjacent to the rails. Although continuously welded rail sections did not come into general use on steam railroads until recent years, various forms of welded or cast joints were in common use on street railways

before the end of the 19th century. The earliest method of this type was the cast-welded joint introduced in 1894. In this process a mold was placed around the rail ends and molten iron was poured into it. A similar type of joint was produced by the Thermit process. A mold was placed about the rail ends and the thermit, a mixture of powdered aluminum and iron oxide, was ignited. The aluminum burned with sufficient heat to melt the iron, which then flowed into the mold to make the joint. Electrically welded joints were also used in street railway track, although the joint was usually made by welding iron bars on either side of the rail rather than by the butt-welding common in modern practice.

Street railway rails were often supported on conventional wooden ties, but the requirement for great rigidity and the heavy loads imposed by street traffic also led to the extensive use of various types of steel ties or a concrete supporting structure. Street railway companies were customarily required to maintain the pavement between the rails and for a distance of 2 feet or more on either side. Stone paving blocks or bricks were commonly employed for this purpose, although ordinary concrete or asphalt paving was frequently used as well. One early text on street railway construction suggested that track and paving be designed so as not to attract vehicular traffic, thereby reducing wear on the paving and permitting faster schedule speeds by keeping the tracks clear of traffic.

CURRENT DISTRIBUTION: In the early years of electric railway operation, the streetcar companies quite frequently generated their own power. Initially, power was generated at the direct current voltage — usually 500 to 600 volts — required for car operation. Because of the excessive voltage drop and line loss involved in transmitting low-voltage direct current over any distance, high-voltage alternating current generation and distribution came into general use. Substations, which used transformers to reduce the voltage and motor-generators or synchronous converters to convert the alternating current to direct current, were located at intervals along the streetcar lines. The spacing and capacity of substations were governed by the anticipated density of car operation.

OVERHEAD CURRENT COLLECTION: Current collection by trolley pole from a simply suspended overhead trolley wire was almost universally employed by street railway systems. A hard drawn copper wire, supported at intervals of 80 to 125 feet, was normally used. Initially, soldered "ears" were employed to attach the wire to its supports, but later a grooved wire was developed to which a mechanical clamping ear could be attached. The principal types of supporting systems for trolley wires were span wire construction, in which the trolley wire was suspended from transverse wires extending between poles on either side of the track, and bracket construction, in which the wire was suspended from a metal bracket mounted on a pole. When bracket construction was used on double-

FRONT EQUIPMENT

CAB INTERIOR

track lines, the poles were usually placed between the tracks with brackets on both sides. Wood poles were most frequently used; but in areas where appearance was important, ornamental cast-iron or steel poles were employed. Sometimes in downtown areas no poles at all were used; the trolley wire was suspended from span wires attached to the fronts of buildings on opposite sides of the street.

Ordinarily, the overhead trolley wire was used for the positive circuit, with the return circuit to substation or powerhouse being made through the rails, thus requiring rail joints to be carefully bonded. On a few systems — most notably in Cincinnati and Havana — the return circuit was made by means of a second overhead wire, which of course required double trolley poles.

UNDERGROUND CONDUIT CURRENT COLLECTION: In Washington, D. C., and New York City, current collection was from power rails mounted in a conduit beneath the track. Shoes mounted on a "plow," which projected through a slot in the pavement, slid along separate positive and return rails. Construction of conduit systems was essentially the same as that for cable lines; and in fact, a substantial part of the conduit mileage in both New York and Washington represented a conversion of what had originally been cable lines. Rigid cast-iron yokes set in concrete at intervals furnished support for the running rails, power rails, and the continuous steel sections that formed the slot between the rails through which the plow extended. At points where a transition was made from conduit current collection to the normal overhead wire collection, a pit was placed between the rails where an employee removed the plow. Although the unsightly overhead wire was eliminated, conduit current collection systems were substantially more costly and required the installation of exceedingly complicated and troublesome specialwork at crossings or junctions.

Principal carbuilders and suppliers

THIS DIRECTORY of some of the principal carbuilders and equipment suppliers to the street railway industry is derived largely from Interurbans Special No. 24, "Railway Car Builders of the United States & Canada," by the late E. Harper Charlton, with the author's kind permission.

Adams & Westlake Company, Chicago, Ill.

Adams & Westlake, one of the most prominent among the dozens of suppliers of miscellaneous equipment for street railway cars, produced a wide variety of lighting fixtures, signal lamps and lanterns, headlights, and miscellaneous hardware and fittings for streetcar use.

Allis-Chalmers Company, Milwaukee, Wis.

Although Allis-Chalmers was overshadowed by the two giants of the electric industry — General Electric and Westinghouse — it was an important supplier of motors and controllers for electric railway equipment and also produced a complete line of air-braking equipment for the traction industry.

American Car Company, St. Louis, Mo. (1891-1931)

One of the leading street railway carbuilders, American built streetcars of every description for systems all over the U. S. The firm was purchased by J. G. Brill in 1902, but continued to operate under the American name until it was reorganized as J. G. Brill of Missouri in 1931, only four months before the plant closed permanently. The first of the famous Birney Safety Cars was constructed in 1915 by American, which subsequently turned out hundreds of them in both single- and double-truck designs.

American Car & Foundry Company (1899-)

ACF was organized in 1899 through the merger of 13 predecessor companies in the East and Midwest and remains today as one of the major railway carbuilders. Although ACF has been predominantly a common-carrier carbuilder, it also manufactured a number of street and interurban railway cars and has been one of the major producers of rolling stock for rapid transit systems.

Barber Car Company, York, Pa. (1908-1914)

Although Barber was not a major carbuilding firm, it is noteworthy for its distinctive streetcar design. Developed by Edward A. Barber, superintendent of the Black River Traction Company at Watertown, N. Y., the first Barber cars were constructed in the Watertown company's shops 2 years before formation of the car company itself. Featuring an improved four-wheel truck design, the Barber cars were rectangular in shape, with a flat front end intended to force air into the carbody for ventilation. Perhaps because of their awkward appearance, Barber cars never attained any appreciable popularity.

Barney & Smith Car Company, Dayton, O. (1849-1923)

One of the leading carbuilders of its time, Barney & Smith produced all types of street railway, interurban, and steam railroad cars which operated throughout the U. S. and in foreign countries. Unlike many carbuilders, Barney & Smith designed and produced its own line of trucks.

Boeing Vertrol Company, Philadelphia, Pa.

A helicopter-building division of the Seattle-based Boeing Company, Boeing Vertol entered the light rail field in 1973 with a successful bid for a combined Boston and San Francisco order for 230 U.S. Standard Light Rail Vehicles. The problem-plagued SLRV was not a successful design, and the car finally entered regular service only after extensive modifications. Boeing Vertol supplied one further order, for Chicago rapid transit cars, and then left the transit field in 1978.

Bombardier Inc., Montreal, Que. (1942-)

Originally established as a tracked snow vehicle manufacturer, Bombardier later developed the popular individual snowmobile. The company entered the mass transit field in 1974 when it won a large order for Montreal subway cars, and has since expanded into locomotives and rail passenger cars. In 1979 the company acquired a North American license for light rail vehicles developed by BN of Belgium, and has supplied 26 articulated light rail vehicles for Portland's Banfield light rail project. Bombardier became a principal shareholder in the Belgian company in 1986 and continues to market light rail vehicles and other rail equipment.

J. G. Brill Company, Philadelphia, Pa. (1868-1956)

The greatest of all the electric railway carbuilders was the Philadelphia firm founded in 1868 by John G. Brill and his son, G. Martin Brill. At first, of course, Brill produced horse and cable cars. With the development of electric traction in the 1890's, the company quickly achieved a dominant position in the carbuilding industry which it retained throughout almost the entire traction era. In addition to possessing its home plant in Philadelphia, Brill acquired control of carbuilding firms at St. Louis, Mo.; Cleveland, O.; Elizabeth, N. J.; Springfield, Mass.; and Danville, Ill., between 1902 and 1908 and constructed a plant at Paris, France, in 1912. Brill cars were sold in great numbers throughout North America and could be found in almost every country in the world.

In addition to producing basic carbodies, Brill turned out virtually every component of trolley cars short of motors, controls, and other electrical equipment. Brill trucks in particular were among the finest in the industry. Cars of every description rolled out of the Brill plant. One of the most popular of all car types was the semi-convertible design developed by Brill early in the century.

During the 1920's Brill was among the leaders in the development of more modern cars to meet the competitive threats of buses and private automobiles, and Brill's Master Unit car was easily the most successful of the improved car designs that preceded the PCC streamliner. When the PCC appeared on the market in 1936, Brill, rather than join in its production, elected instead to proceed independently with the development of its similar "Brilliner" streamlined car. The Brilliner's greatest shortcoming was a truck design inferior

to that of the PCC car. Brill's last trolley cars were produced by the Philadelphia plant in 1941; and the carbuilder retired from the field, leaving only Pullman-Standard and St. Louis Car in the trolley-building business.

Briggs Car Company, Amesbury, Mass. (1890-1903)

Briggs, an old New England carriage and wagon builder, constructed a plant at Amesbury in 1890 and entered the carbuilding field, producing electric cars for systems in almost every city and town in New England. Production ended in 1903, when Briggs was succeeded by the Southern Car Company of High Point, N. C.

Brownell Car Company, St. Louis, Mo. (1875-1902)

Brownell was formed in 1875 as the successor to the Brownell & Wight Car Company originally organized in 1857. Brownell was an important builder of horse and cable as well as electric cars. Among the distinctive designs produced by the company were "Low's adjustable car," a convertible design, and the patented Brownell "Accelerator Car," an arrangement that permitted more rapid passenger flow. Brownell cars enjoyed wide distribution until the firm was purchased by American Car Company in 1902.

Canadian Car & Foundry Company, Ltd., Montreal, Que. (1909-1964)

Canadian Car, formed from the acquired Canada Car Company and Dominion Car Company in 1909, was the leading Canadian streetcar and interurban builder throughout the era of electric traction. The company's extensive electric car production, which included the only Canadian-built PCC cars, ended in 1948, although the firm continued to produce steam railroad equipment until 1964, when Hawker Siddeley Canada, Ltd. (q.v.) acquired its facilities.

Carter Brothers, Newark, Calif. (1872-1903)

Carter was originally located at Sausalito, Calif., and moved to Newark in 1879. The Carter shops produced a wide variety of equipment for both steam railroads and street railways. Both horse and cable cars were included in the company's early production, and some of the earliest electric cars to operate in Oakland, Sacramento, and

San Francisco were built in the Carter shops.

Casebolt & Van Gulpin, San Francisco, Calif. (1857-1876)

Henry Casebolt, originally a blacksmith, built the first horsecars for San Francisco's Market Street line — the first streetcar line in California. Later the firm built cable cars, and Casebolt invented a cable grip that was widely used on several San Francisco lines. Casebolt's best known invention, however, was the "balloon car," a type of horsecar that pivoted on its truck, permitting the car to change direction at the end of the line without having to unhitch the mule.

Cincinnati Car Company, Cincinnati, O. (1902-1938)

Cincinnati Car was an outgrowth of the Cincinnati Street Railway Company. Its production was devoted exclusively to street, rapid transit, and interurban railway equipment. Cincinnati cars were unusually well designed, and one of the firm's most successful cars was its distinctive curved-side light-weight car of the 1920's, which was produced in volume for both street and interurban railways. Cincinnati cars were found principally on electric railways in the Midwest, but the firm occasionally built equipment for systems in almost every part of the U. S. Production ceased about 1931.

Clark Equipment Company, Battle Creek, Mich.

Although Clark was not an important carbuilder, the company developed and built the B-2 type truck widely used under the PCC streamlined streetcar. Clark car production was confined to a single experimental "standee" window PCC car built for Brooklyn in 1936, six three-unit articulated rapid transit trains for Brooklyn subway-elevated lines, and the "Autotram," a streamlined railway gas car built in 1930.

Danville Car Company, Danville, Ill. (circa 1900-1913)

A general carbuilding firm, Danville built a modest number of street railway and interurban cars for lines throughout the central states. J. G. Brill acquired the Danville firm in 1908 as part of its expansion program but closed the plant only 5 years later.

Duplex Car Company, New York, N.Y. (1896-1902)

The Duplex company was not actually a carbuilder, but it developed an unusual type of convertible car that was produced under franchise by several builders, principally Briggs and Jackson & Sharp. The Duplex design incorporated curved windows and side panels constructed much like the top of a roll-top desk which slid upward into the roof on curved tracks. The intricate arrangement proved costly to build and relatively few were ever constructed.

Federal Storage Battery Car Company, Silver Lake, N.J. (1909-1920's)

The firm, known as the Railway Storage Battery Car Company after 1912, was organized by Thomas Edison to exploit his alkaline nickel-iron storage battery and a battery car developed by Ralph U. Beach. Built in both single- and double-truck models, the Edison-Beach storage battery car enjoyed a modest popularity on street railways during the relatively brief period of interest in this type of equipment. Both the Edison-Beach car and the rival lead-acid storage battery type, built principally by Brill, suffered from the great weight of the necessary batteries, docile performance characteristics, and a tendency to frequent battery failure.

General Electric Company, (1892-)

Organized in 1892 through merger of the Edison General Electric Company and the Thomson-Houston Electric Company, GE was one of the two giants of the North American electrical industry. Although GE was never a carbuilder, from the time of its formation to the present it has been a major supplier of motors, controls, and other electrical equipment, as well as air-brake equipment, to the electric railway industry. During the early part of the century GE developed a line of gas-electric cars for railway service, and built a few experimental gas-electrics for street railway service.

Gilbert Car Manufacturing Company, Troy, N.Y. (1820-1895)

The firm was organized in 1820 by Orasmus Eaton and was initially a builder of stage coaches and other horse-drawn vehicles. It was operated under various names until reorganization under the Gilbert name in 1882. Railway carbuilding began in 1841 and Gilbert production ultimately included horse and electric cars for street railways. Gilbert cars enjoyed wide distribution throughout the U. S., as well as a considerable export market. About 1890 an employee of the firm, John Taylor, developed a highly successful truck design and within a few years manufacture of the Taylor truck dominated the company's production. In 1895 Gilbert was succeeded by the Taylor Electric Truck Company (*q.v.*).

Hale & Kilburn Manufacturing Company, Philadelphia, Pa.

Hale & Kilburn, a specialist in seating equipment, was one of the largest suppliers of seats of every description for use in street railway equipment.

J. Hammond & Company, San Francisco, Calif. (1883-1907)

Often known as the "California Car Works," Hammond was a leading supplier of horse, cable, and electric cars—many of them mounted on trucks of the company's own design — to street railways in California and elsewhere on the Pacific Coast. The firm claimed to have originated the design for the "California"-type combination open and closed cars, which featured a closed center section and open sections at each end. This car was first built for San Francisco's California Street Cable Railroad Company. Unable to recover from the devastation of the 1906 San Francisco earthquake and fire, the firm ceased operation in 1907.

Harlan & Hollingsworth Corporation, Wilmington, Del. (1836-1944)

Outstanding both as a car manufacturing firm and as a shipbuilder, Harlan & Hollingsworth built a wide variety of rolling stock for steam railroads, street and interurban railways, and elevated lines. Prominent among Harlan & Hollingsworth cars of the 19th century were many of the early passenger cars operated on the New York elevated system. The firm's plant was absorbed by Bethlehem Steel Company in 1905 and continued to produce railway cars until 1944. Notable among the cars produced under Bethlehem management were the all-steel articulateds constructed in 1935 for the Key System transbay lines at San Francisco-Oakland.

Hawker-Siddeley Canada, Ltd., Montreal, Que.

An English firm originally established by A.V. Roe Company, Hawker-Siddeley acquired a Canadian Car automotive plant at Thunder Bay, Ont., in 1964 and became active in the production of a variety of passenger rolling stock. Electric railway production included a large fleet of Canadian Light Rail Vehicles for Toronto and a prototype Articulated Light Rail Vehicle, which were built for the Urban Transportation Development Corporation. UTDC (q.v.) acquired a majority interest in the plant in 1984 and now operates it as its Can-Car Rail subsidiary.

Heywood Brothers & Wakefield Company, Wakefield Mass.

Another specialist in seating equipment, Heywood-Wakefield was a principal supplier of seats for street railway cars throughout the traction era, and remains active today as a supplier of seating for railway equipment.

Holman Car Company, San Francisco, Calif. (1883-1913)

A general carbuilder, Holman produced a modest number of street and interurban railway cars which saw service in the San Francisco and Central California area, among them a batch of cars for the California Street Cable Railroad Company in 1907-1908. In 1913 the firm undertook construction of the first 20 cars for the new Municipal Railway of San Francisco and went bankrupt in the process.

Jackson & Sharp, Wilmington, Del. (1863-1901)

Eminent as both a shipbuilder and a carbuilder for steam railroads, Jackson & Sharp, popularly known as the "Delaware Car Works," also produced a full range of horse and electric cars for street railway service, many of which were mounted on the firm's own trucks. The Jackson & Sharp plant was purchased by American Car & Foundry in 1901 and continued to produce railway equipment through the Second World War. It is still a part of the ACF organization.

Jewett Car Company, Newark, O. (1894-1918)

Although Jewett was principally noted for the manufacture of exceptionally well built and handsomely proportioned cars for Midwestern interurban railways, the firm's initial production was devoted to horsecars, most of which were built for Pittsburgh, Pa. Shortly after 1900 Jewett built several large orders of elevated cars for New York, Brooklyn, and Chicago, as well as a large volume of streetcars for systems as divergent in locality as Chicago and San Francisco. Jewett went bankrupt and ceased operation in 1918.

Jones' Sons Car Company, Watervliet, N.Y. (1839-1922)

Jones' Sons was originally established as a Schenectady wagon builder under the name of Witbeck & Jones in 1839 and began the manufacture of street railway cars in 1864, producing thousands of cars that were sold throughout the world. An early entrant into electric car production, the firm was active as a carbuilder until about 1912.

G.C. Kuhlman Car Company, Cleveland, O. (1892-1932)

One of the leading streetcar builders, Kuhlman produced street and interurban railway equipment of every description. J. G. Brill absorbed the Kuhlman firm in 1904 as part of a vast expansion program, although production continued under the Kuhlman name. Notable among Kuhlman-built cars were the first "two rooms and a bath" articulated cars produced for Cleveland in 1893, the first "Peter Witt"-type cars, and several lightweight streetcars of advanced design produced during the 1920's. The plant was reorganized as J. G. Brill of Ohio in 1931, but production ceased only a year or so later.

Laclede Car Company, Laconia, N.H. (1881-1928)

Laclede, a prominent early builder of street railway equipment, built a large volume of both trucks and cars for horse, cable, and electric railways until the firm was purchased by the rival St. Louis Car Company in 1903.

Laconia Car Company, Laconia, N. H. (1881-1928)

Laconia was organized in 1881 from the predecessor Ranlett Manufacturing Company, a carriage and railroad-car building concern established in 1844. The company produced a large volume of horse and electric cars, as well as trucks of its own design, for street railways throughout New England, plus a modest number of cars for more distant systems. After about 1915 the firm also turned out a number of cars for steam railroads. The decline of electric railways, particularly rapid in the New England states, brought an end to Laconia operation in 1928.

Light Weight Noiseless Electric Street Car Company, St. Paul, Minn. (1924-1927)

Organized to exploit a truck designed by W. J. Smith of the Twin City Rapid Transit Company, the Light Weight Noiseless firm manufactured its cars in the Snelling Shops of the Twin City Lines. During the firm's brief period of activity it produced a large order of cars for Chicago, as well as lesser numbers for such cities as Nashville, Chattanooga, and Evansville, Ind. Although the firm's designs were not particularly successful, they were significant efforts toward the development of a modern lightweight car.

McGuire Manufacturing Company, Chicago and Paris, Ill. (1888-1943)

The McGuire Company was later known as McGuire-Cummings Manufacturing Company and finally as Cummings Car & Coach Company. It was initially active as a builder of car trucks, later produced snowplows and sweepers, and finally manufactured a general line of steam and electric railway equipment. McGuire trucks were highly regarded and were widely used, and the company's rugged snow sweeper was popular with traction systems throughout the world. Although its last cars were produced in 1930, the firm remained in business until 1943.

Motores Y Adapciones Automotrices (Moyada), Mexico City, D.F., Mexico

This automotive manufacturer completed a prototype three-section articulated light rail vehicle for Mexico City Transit (STE) in 1985, utilizing components from PCC cars, and subsequently received an order for 16 more of the rebuilt cars. The firm was licensed in 1986 to build the Canadian UTDC articulated light rail vehicle.

National Brake & Electric Company, Milwaukee, Wis.

Although less well known than some of the leaders in the field, National supplied a complete line of air-braking equipment for electric railway service.

Newburyport Car Manufacturing Company, Newburyport, Mass. (1887-1905)

Notable among a proliferation of early New England carbuilders, the Newburyport firm produced a large volume of horse and electric cars for New England street railways. After delivery of a final order to the Boston Elevated in 1903, the company was liquidated in 1905.

Niles Car & Manufacturing Company, Niles, O. (1901-1917)

Despite its short life, the Niles firm achieved a deserved reputation for the quality and handsome proportions of its electric cars. Although the greater part of its production was devoted to the interurban railway equipment from which it derived its reputation, Niles also did a substantial business in street and elevated railway equipment produced for a variety of systems.

Osgood Bradley Car Company, Worcester, Mass (1820-1930)

Osgood Bradley, originally established as a carriage builder, turned out its first railway cars in 1833. Producing steam railroad and street railway equipment of every description, the Osgood Bradley plant by 1910 was second in size only to the great Pullman works at Chicago. The Osgood Bradley plant was absorbed by Pullman in 1930 and remains in operation as a principal carbuilding facility of the Pullman-Standard organization.

Ottawa Car Manufacturing Company, Ottawa, Canada (1891-1948)

A leading Canadian streetcar builder, Ottawa Car produced a wide variety of street railway equipment that saw service in all parts of Canada. One of the firm's notable cars was the elegant special car Duchess of Cornwall and York, produced for the Ottawa street railway system in 1900 to transport the future King George and Queen Mary during a visit to the Canadian capital. The firm was reorganized as a car and aircraft builder in 1939 and went out of business in 1948 shortly after completing a final order of cars for the Ottawa Transportation Commission.

Pressed Steel Car Company, Pittsburgh, Pa. (1896-1954)

Pressed Steel, originally known as the Schoen Steel Company, initially concentrated on the production of steel freight cars. In 1906 the company began to produce steel passenger cars and soon afterward was outshopping a large number of rapid transit, street, and interurban railway cars. Among these was the first steel trolley cars ever built, which were produced for the Montreal street railway system in 1907. The company continued in the carbuilding business until 1954, when the Pittsburgh plant was closed.

Preston Car & Coach Company, Preston, Ont. (1908-1921)

A carbuilder of modest size, Preston built a distinctive line of street and interurban cars that saw service in many parts of Canada. In order to compete for a Toronto Peter Witt car order, J. G. Brill of Philadelphia bought the Preston plant in 1921 and organized the Canadian Brill Company, Ltd., which subsequently built 50 cars for Toronto. Only 2 years later, however, Brill gave up the operation and the Preston plant passed from the scene.

Pullman Car & Manufacturing Company, Chicago, Ill. (1867-   )

Pullman was organized by sleeping car pioneer George Pullman in 1867 as Pullman's Palace Car Company, and the firm has retained a place among America's greatest builders of railroad cars for nearly a century. In 1899, when it merged with the Wagner Palace Car Company, the firm was reorganized as the Pullman Company. In 1927 Pullman carbuilding activities were consolidated under the Pullman Car & Manufacturing Company which became the Pullman-Standard Car & Manufacturing Company in 1934 a few years after Pullman's acquisition of the Standard Steel and Osgood Bradley car companies. Pullman plunged into the streetcar business in a big way in 1891 with the formation of its Streetcar Department, which produced electric railway equipment of almost every description. Prominent among earlier Pullman streetcars were several experimental double-deck cars of the 1890's and the hundreds of roomy "big red Pullmans" that operated into recent years on the Chicago street railway system. In 1933 Pullman produced the first experimental PCC car, and afterward became one of the principal builders of the streamlined streetcars.

St. Louis Car Company, St. Louis, Mo. (1887-1972)

Second only to J. G. Brill in volume, St. Louis Car was one of the great carbuilders of the electric traction era. The thousands of cars constructed by St. Louis included cable and horsecars, electric streetcars of every description, and a substantial volume of rapid transit cars. St. Louis was active as a steam railroad carbuilder as well, and produced carbodies for many of the famous Electro-Motive gas electrics and diesel-electric cars of the 1920's, as well as the bodies for some of the earliest EMD diesel-electric locomotives. St. Louis, like Brill, manufactured a complete line of trucks and trolley car appurtenances of every description. In 1936 St. Louis turned out the first production-model PCC cars and remained the leading PCC carbuilder until the last domestic order was completed for San Francisco in 1951. The firm is presently a division of General Steel Industries and is still active as a principal manufacturer of rapid-transit equipment.

John Stephenson Car Company, New York, N.Y. (1831-1917)

The Stephenson shops were organized as a carriage-building firm in 1831 and only a year later produced the world's first streetcar, the famous *John Mason* for the pioneer New York & Harlem Railroad. Stage coach and omnibus production dominated Stephenson's output for another two decades, however, and not until the great New York street railway boom of the 1850's did the firm come into its own as a carbuilder. Throughout the remainder of the 19th century the company was one of the major builders of horse, cable, and — finally — electric cars. Between 1876 and 1891 alone, Stephenson produced some 25,000 streetcars for companies in the U. S. and abroad. Along with its cars, Stephenson built a full line of single and double trucks for street railway service. J. G. Brill, in its expansion program of the early 1900's, acquired the Stephenson firm in 1904, although production continued under the Stephenson name. The Stephenson plant, located at Elizabeth, N. J., after 1898, was never tooled up for the manufacture of steel cars, and Brill discontinued carbuilding at Elizabeth in 1917.

Stockton Combine Harvester & Agricultural Works, Stockton, Calif.

Despite its unlikely title, the Stockton Works produced some of the earliest street railway equipment operated on the West Coast. Beginning about 1888 the firm built some of the first cable cars operated in Seattle, Portland, and San Diego, and the first electric cars run in Salem, Oregon, and Oakland, Calif. During the early 1890's the company was one of the largest western carbuilders, and Stockton cars were to be found on almost every street railway system in the Far West. Carbuilding ceased around 1896 when the company turned its energies to agricultural equipment more in keeping with its title.

Southern Car Company, High Point, N.C. (1904-1917)

An outgrowth of the Briggs Car Company of Amesbury, Mass., Southern built a complete line of street and interurban railway cars for systems throughout the South and points as far distant as New York City and Puerto Rico. The car company went out of business in 1917.

Standard Steel Car Company, Pittsburgh, Pa. (1902-1930)

The celebrated railway equipment salesman "Diamond Jim" Brady and Chief Engineer John M. Hansen of Pressed Steel, dissatisfied with their opportunities at Pressed Steel Car Company, formed the Standard Steel Car Company in 1902 with a plant at Butler, Pa. Although Standard was mainly a steam railroad carbuilder, the company built a number of cars for street and interurban railways. Far more important than Standard's electric car production, however, was the extensive volume of electric car trucks of all types produced by the Standard Motor Truck Company, an outgrowth of the carbuilding firm organized in 1906. In 1930 the Standard Steel Car Company was absorbed by Pullman Car & Manufacturing Company.

Taylor Electric Truck Company, Troy, N.Y. (1895-   )

Successor to the Gilbert Car Manufacturing Company, the Taylor firm produced a wide range of trucks for both single- and double-truck street railway equipment.

Taylor trucks were well designed and enjoyed a high degree of popularity among traction systems.

Perley A. Thomas Car Works, High Point, N.C. (1917-   )

The Thomas works, although it was not a direct successor to the Southern Car Company, was organized by a former Southern employee who within a month after Southern went out of business took over its carbuilding plant at High Point. Thomas produced a line of extremely well-built cars which were ordered by street railway systems in almost every part of the U. S. and points as far removed as Cuba, Puerto Rico, and Central and South America. After electric car production ceased in 1930 the company turned to the fabrication of steel bus bodies and continues to produce these today.

Twin City Rapid Transit Company, Minneapolis-St. Paul, Minn.

Dissatisfied with the standard products of commercial carbuilding firms, the Twin City system designed and built its own distinctive rolling stock from just after the turn of the century until the advent of PCC car operation after World War II. Many larger systems built substantial numbers of cars for their own use, but none depended so completely on its own shops for car manufacture, and none manufactured cars for other systems as extensively as did Twin City's shops. In addition to manufacturing hundreds of cars for its own lines, the Twin City Rapid Transit's Snelling Shops produced a majority of the cars operated on the Duluth-Superior street railway system, and Twin City cars were found in Winnipeg and Seattle as well. For a brief period during the 1920's the Light Weight Noiseless Electric Street Car Company (q.v.) employed the facilities of the Snelling Shops to produce several orders of cars for other street railway systems.

Urban Transportation Development Corporation, Ltd., Toronto, Ont. (1973-   )

UTDC was formed by the Ontario government in 1973 to design, develop and market new transit equipment and systems, and has since developed a wide range of transportation products and services. One of UTDC's first projects was the development of a new Canadian Light Rail Vehicle for the Toronto Transit Commission, and a total of 196 of these CLRVs was supplied to TTC during 1977-1981. These CLRVs, and a subsequent Articulated Light Rail Vehicle prototype were manufactured for UTDC in Hawker-Siddeley Canada's Canadian Car Division plant at Thunder Bay, Ont. In 1984, UTDC assumed a majority interest in the plant and began operating it as a subsidiary corporation, Can-Car Rail. A total of 102 ALRVs is currently being manufactured there for TTC and the new light rail system at San Jose, California.

Wason Manufacturing Company, Springfield, Mass. (1845-1931)

Wason, another of the New England wagon and coach builders that turned to carbuilding, constructed a substantial volume of cars for street and interurban railways as well as trucks of its own design. Although the company's production went largely to New England systems, Wason cars could be found almost everywhere in the U. S. After acquisition of the Springfield plant by J. G. Brill in 1906, production continued under the Wason name until 1931, when the name was changed to J. G. Brill of Massachusetts. Less than a year later, the new company was out of the carbuilding business.

Westinghouse Electric & Manufacturing Company, Pittsburgh, Pa.

Westinghouse, together with General Electric, dominated the electrical manufacturing field throughout the era of electric traction. Westinghouse produced a complete line of motors, controls, and other electrical equipment in activities that paralleled those of the rival General Electric organization.

Westinghouse Traction Brake Company, Pittsburgh, Pa.

Founded by air-brake pioneer George Westinghouse, the Westinghouse Traction Brake Company was the leading supplier of air-braking equipment throughout the history of the street railway organization. Still a leader in the field, the firm is currently active in the development of automatic braking and control systems for automation of rapid transit systems.

Woeber Brothers Carriage Company, Denver, Colo. (1880-1920)

Despite its misleading name, the Woeber works was an important builder of street railway equipment. With the exception of a single group of company-built cars, virtually every car ever operated by the Denver Tramways was constructed by Woeber Brothers, and the company also produced equipment for a number of other cities in the western states.

Where the cars still run

A DIRECTORY of the electric street railways or light rail systems, operating or under construction, and operating trolley museums in North America. For a much more detailed guide to North American trolley museums, the reader is referred to Interurbans Special 85, Trolley to the Past, *by Andrew D. Young, published in 1983.*

NEW ENGLAND STATES

MAINE

SEASHORE TROLLEY MUSEUM, Kennebunkport, represents both the largest and the oldest of all the electric railway museum projects. The musuem's collection of more than 120 items of electric railway rolling stock includes examples of virtually every important type of street railway equipment. Cars operate through the Maine countryside over a 1½-mile line.

MASSACHUSETTS

MASSACHUSETTS BAY TRANSPORTATION AUTHORITY, Boston, operates a five-route, 35-mile light rail system. A 122-car operational fleet of Boeing Vertol articulated SLRVs is supplemented by some 57 PCC cars, while 100 articulated No. 7 Surface Rail Cars were being delivered by Kinki Sharyo during 1986-87.

LOWELL NATIONAL HISTORIC PARK, Lowell, operates two 15-bench open car replicas over a mile-long tourist line.

CONNECTICUT

BRANFORD ELECTRIC RAILWAY ASSOCIATION, East Haven, conducts the second largest trolley museum project in the U.S. The Branford collection comprises some 90 items of electric railway equipment including examples of every major type of streetcar from a Toronto horsecar replica to the first production-model PCC streamliner built for Brooklyn in 1936. Cars are operated over a mile-and-a-half of former Connecticut Company track through coastal meadows and marshes to Short Beach.

CONNECTICUT ELECTRIC RAILWAY ASSOCIATION, Warehouse Point, operates over a mile-and-a-half of track in the roadbed of a long-abandoned Hartford & Springfield Street Railway branch. While originally confined to New England equipment, the museum's 40-car collection now includes a wide variety of equipment from many parts of the U.S. and Canada.

MIDDLE ATLANTIC STATES

NEW YORK

NIAGARA FRONTIER TRANSPORTATION AUTHORITY, Buffalo, operates a 6.4-mile light rail rapid transit line to the northeast from downtown Buffalo. A fleet of 27 Tokyu light rail cars operates in the line's subway and a mile-long downtown transit mall.

NEW JERSEY

NEW JERSEY TRANSIT, Newark, operates 24 PCC cars over its 4.3-mile Newark City Subway.

PENNSYLVANIA

ARDEN ELECTRIC RAILWAY, near Washington, maintains a collection of 26 items of electric railway equipment, most of them from Pennsylvania properties. The museum's mile-long line is laid to the 5 feet 2½-inch broad-gauge used by most Pennsylvania trolley systems.

PENN'S LANDING TROLLEY operates a mile-long tourist trolley over freight track on Delaware Street on the Philadelphia waterfront. A fleet of seven cars came largely from the Philadelphia Suburban Transportation Company.

PORT AUTHORITY TRANSIT, Pittsburgh, operates 26 miles of trolley lines to the South Hills suburbs. A downtown subway and light rail upgrade for 10.5 miles opened early in 1987. A fleet of aging PCC cars was being replaced by 55 Siemens/Duewag articulated light rail cars and the planned remanufacture of 45 PCC cars.

SHADE GAP ELECTRIC RAILWAY, Rockhill Furnace, runs trolleys that meet the narrow-gauge trains of the East Broad Top Railroad. Nearly half of the line's 16-car roster came from Pennsylvania lines; the remainder are from as far afield as Portugal and Brazil.

SOUTHEASTERN PENNSYLVANIA TRANSPORTATION AUTHORITY, Philadelphia, operates a 61-mile trolley system that includes five surface routes in North Philadelphia, five subway-surface lines in West Philadelphia, and two suburban routes from the 69th Street Terminal at Upper Darby. A total of 141 Kawasaki light rail vehicles operates on the subway-surface and suburban lines, while SEPTA is completing the rebuilding of 122 PCC cars for the remaining surface routes.

SOUTH ATLANTIC STATES

MARYLAND

BALTIMORE STREETCAR MUSEUM has a representative collection of 12 cars from the broad-gauge Baltimore system ranging from an 1859 horsecar to PCC cars. Cars are operated over a half-mile line in Jones Falls Valley.

NATIONAL CAPITAL TROLLEY MUSEUM, Wheaton, maintains a 16-car collection that includes a Washington, D.C., historic collection. Cars are operated on a 1¼-mile line.

FLORIDA

GRAND CYPRESS RESORT TROLLEY LINE, Orlando, operates four former Brussels, Belgium, trams on a 3½-mile line within the resort grounds.

NORTH CENTRAL STATES

OHIO

Greater Cleveland Regional Transit Authority operates a two-route, 13.2-mile light rail system between downtown Cleveland and Shaker Heights. Service is provided by 49 Breda articulated LRVs, supplemented by 16 PCC cars.

Ohio Railway Museum, Worthington, maintains a collection of 16 items of electric railway equipment from the Midwest and operates a two-mile line.

Trolleyville U.S.A., Olmstead Falls, maintains a collection of some 27 cars, a number of them from Ohio properties. Cars operate over a 1½-mile line.

INDIANA

Indiana Transportation Museum, Noblesville, has a former Indianapolis horsecar and streetcar in its collection of 17 pieces of electric equipment. A half-mile track is operated.

Springs Valley Electric Railway, French Lick, operates a single car on a two-mile tourist line to West Baden Springs.

MICHIGAN

Detroit Citizens Railway operates tourist trolley service on a 1¼-mile narrow-gauge (2 feet 11½ inches) line in downtown Detroit. Seven former Lisbon, Portugal, cars and a British double-decker are operated.

ILLINOIS

Illinois Railway Museum, Union, operates on two miles of line and displays some 68 items of electric railway equipment which include a number of representative Chicago cars.

Relic, South Elgin, includes three streetcars in an 11-car collection that operates over a mile of former Aurora, Elgin & Fox River Railroad track.

WISCONSIN

East Troy Trolley Museum includes a former Milwaukee horse car in a 28-car collection made up largely of interurban equipment. Cars operate on five miles of track.

MINNESOTA

Lake Superior Museum of Transportation, Duluth, operates two former Lisbon, Portugal, single-truck trolleys on 1,200 feet of narrow-gauge (2 feet 11½ inches) track at The Depot, the St. Louis County Heritage and Arts Center in the former Duluth Union Depot.

Minnesota Transportation Museum, Minneapolis, operates four former Duluth and Minneapolis streetcars on a mile of line installed on the old roadbed of the Twin Cities Rapid Transit Como-Harriet line.

IOWA

Midwest Electric Railway, Mount Pleasant, operates a one-mile line on the grounds of the Midwest Old Settlers' and Threshers' Association reunion. A seven-car collection includes four streetcars.

SOUTH CENTRAL STATES

LOUISIANA

Regional Transit Authority, New Orleans, operates a single 6.5-mile trolley line on St. Charles Avenue with 35 standard Perley A. Thomas cars of 1923 and 1924 vintage. Both line and cars are on the National Register of Historic Places.

TENNESSEE

Chatanooga Choo Choo and Terminal Station runs three streetcars on a short line that is part of redevelopment of Chatanooga's old Southern Railway terminal.

TEXAS

San Antonio Museum Association runs a former San Antonio car over several blocks of electric freight trackage operated by the Pearl Brewery.

Tandy Center Subway, Fort Worth, operates eight rebodied PCC cars on a 1.3-mile subway-surface line.

MOUNTAIN AND PACIFIC STATES

COLORADO

Fort Collins Municipal Railway Society has restored one of the city's old Birney trolleys and operates it on track rebuilt in the city's original Mountain Avenue route.

CALIFORNIA

California Railway Museum, Rio Vista Jct., displays a fleet of nearly 50 electric cars and locomotives, most of them from the western U.S. Cars are operated on a 1½-mile track.

Los Angeles County Transportation Commission is building a 22-mile light rail line between Los Angeles and Long Beach which should open in 1989, and a 20-mile, east-west line that will open between Norwalk and El Segundo in the median of the Century Freeway in 1993.

Orange Empire Trolley Museum, Perris, maintains a collection of more than 60 items of electric railway equipment, most of them from the Los Angeles area. Cars operate on a 1½-mile main line as well as a loop that is laid for both standard gauge and the 3-foot 6-inch gauge used by Los Angeles trolleys.

Sacramento Regional Transit District is building an 18-mile light rail system that will operate lines east to Folsom and northeast from downtown Sacramento. A fleet of 26 advanced U2 articulated cars is being delivered by Siemens-Duewag. Service on an initial section began early in 1987.

San Diego Metropolitan Transit Development Board operates a 16-mile light rail line between Centre City San Diego and San Ysidro, on the Mexican border. A second 17-mile East Urban Corridor line is under construction, with an initial 4.5-mile section already in service. MTDB operates 30 Siemens/Duewag U2 articulated light rail vehicles.

San Francisco Municipal Railway operates 130 Boeing SLRVs on a five-route, 21-mile light rail system which reaches downtown San Francisco through the 3.2-mile Market Street subway. Muni also operates 40 cable cars on a three-route, 4.4-mile system that is the world's only surviving cable railway system.

Santa Clara County Transportation Agency, San Jose, is building a 19-mile Guadalupe Corridor light rail line north and south from San Jose that should begin operation on an initial section late in 1987. Canada's UTDC is supplying 50 articulated cars.

OREGON

Tri—County Metropolitan Transportation District of Oregon completed the 15-mile Banfield light rail line east from downtown Portland late in 1986. A fleet of 26 Bombardier articulated cars operate on the line.

The Trolley Park, Glenwood, has a collection of eight cars, half of them from Portland. Cars are operated on a ¼-mile track.

WASHINGTON

The Waterfront Streetcar, Seattle, operates four Australian trams on a 1½-mile tourist trolley line along Alaskan Way on the waterfront.

Yakima Interurban Trolley Lines operates two former Oporto, Portugal, trolleys on electrified track of the former Yakima Valley Transportation Company.

CANADA

ALBERTA

Calgary Transit operates a new 17.2-mile light rail system with a fleet of 83 Siemens/Duewag articulated cars. Cars operate on lines to the south and west of downtown Calgary, with a new route to the northeast under construction.

Edmonton Transit operates 37 Siemens/Duewag articulated light rail vehicles over a new 6.4-mile light rail line to northeast Edmonton. A 1.5-mile South Edmonton extension is under construction.

Fort Edmonton Park operates a restored Edmonton streetcar in this historic park at Edmonton.

Heritage Park Pioneer Village, Calgary, operates a restored Calgary trolley, an open observation car from Montreal, and a Winnipeg horse car replica in this 60-acre historic park.

ONTARIO

Halton County Radial Railway near Rockwood has a collection of more than 30 city, interurban and service cars, most of them from Toronto. The museum runs cars over a 1¼-mile line.

Toronto Transit Commission owns one of the largest trolley car fleets in North America. A fleet of 196 new Canadian Light Rail Vehicles was supplemented (in 1986) by 81 still-active rebuilt PCC cars, with 52 articulated versions of the CLRV due for delivery during 1986-87. Cars operate over a nine-route, 46-mile street railway system. A new Harbourfront light rail line will operate with PCC cars.

MEXICO

Servicio de Transportes Electricos del D.F., Mexico City, operates a fleet of about 50 PCC cars on two lines that are currently being rebuilt to light rail standards. Many PCCs were rebuilt during the 1970's, and more are undergoing major rebuilding during the 1980's.

Bibliography

The literature of the street railway is far too encompassing to cover in more than the briefest summary in the space available here. Following are some of the principal sources consulted in the preparation of this volume which should be of some help to the reader with an interest in further, or more specific information.

BIBLIOGRAPHIES: Much more extensive references to the literature of the street railway can be found in an article by Foster M. Palmer, "The Literature of the Street Railway," published in the *Harvard Library Bulletin*, Vol. 12, No. 1 (Winter 1958), and *Street, Interurban and Rapid Transit Railways of the United States — A Selective Historical Bibliography*, by Thomas R. Bullard (Forty Fort, Pa., Harold E. Cox, 1984).

TEXTS, CATALOGS AND MANUALS: Throughout the period of their growth and maturity as a great industry the design, construction, operation, and equipment of electric railways was the subject of an enormous variety of published texts, manuals, catalogs, reports, and other publications. Those listed here are little more than a sampling of the many that are available.

C.B. Fairchild's, *Street Railways: Their Construction, Operation and Maintenance* (New York, Street Railway Publishing Co., 1892), is an exceptionally complete guide to the technology of the street railway in its early years. Other volumes representative of the many texts covering the electric railway field are *Electric Railways*, by Sydney W. Ashe and J.D. Keiley (New York, D. Van Nostrand Co., 1907, 2 vols.); A. Morris Buck's, *The Electric Railway* (New York, McGraw-Hill Book Co., 1915); *Electric Traction for Railway Trains*, Edward P. Burch (New York, McGraw-Hill Book Co., 1911); *The Electric Railway in Theory and Practice*, by Oscar T. Crosby and Louis Bell, Ph.D. (New York, the W.J. Johnston Co., 1893); and C. Francis Harding's, *Electric Railway Engineering* (New York, McGraw-Hill Book Co., 1911).

"The Electric Railway Number," of *Cassier's Magazine*, Vol. 16, No. 4 (August 1899) contained an exceptionally valuable series of articles describing both the history and then-current technology of the electric railway. The entire issue was republished in recent years by The Light Railway Transport League (London, 1960).

Electric Railway Dictionary, edited by Rodney Hitt (New York, McGraw Publishing Co., 1911) is a comprehensive encyclopedia of the electric railway rolling stock and components of its time, which was near the peak of the industry. Catalogs published regularly by the car builders provide details of representative rolling stock throughout the life of the industry. *City and Interurban Cars*, a catalog of Philadelphia car builder J.G. Brill Co. dating from about 1911, has been republished by Pacific Railway Journal (San Marino, Calif., 1961). *Modern Types of City and Interurban Cars and Trucks*, was published by pioneer car builder John Stephenson Co. (Elizabeth, N.J., 1905); a reprint appeared as *Electric Railway Cars and Trucks* (Fulton, Calif., Glenwood Publishers, 1972). *Niles Cars*, a catalog of the Niles Car & Manufacturing Co. (Niles, Ohio, ca. 1910) has been reprinted by Caxton Printers, Ltd. (Caldwell, Idaho, 1982). *St. Louis Car Co. Electric Cars, Coaches & Trucks* (St. Louis, ca. 1908) is a typical catalog from this major builder.

McGraw Electric Railway Directory, is a directory of electric railway companies, officials and other basic information published annually by McGraw-Hill Co., New York.

Poor's Manual of the Railroads of the United States from 1868 to 1913 and *Poor's Manual of Public Utilities* from 1913 to 1918 contain electric railway corporate and financial information. *Moody's Manual* includes similar information from 1901 until 1924, when it was succeeded by *Poor's*, which was merged in 1940 with the *Standard Corporation Records*. *Moody's Analysis of Investments*, which became *Moody's Manual of Investments* in 1926, is still another source of such information.

Special Reports: Street and Electric Railways, 1902, issued by the Bureau of the Census in 1905, and subsequent reports under the same or different titles at five-year intervals through 1937 are an excellent source of economic and statistical information concerning electric railways.

PERIODICALS: Throughout the history of the industry, developments in the electric railways have been well covered by a variety of trade and technical journals.

Electric Railway Journal was the leader among the industry's trade journals. It began in 1884 as *Street Railway Journal*, became *Electric Railway Journal* in 1908, and was finally known as *Transit Journal* from 1932 until publication ceased in 1942. The *Journal* is a voluminous source of technical and historical information about the industry. Of particular value are its annual issues published on the occasion of the convention of the American Street Railway Association, which typically contained detailed articles devoted to the electric railways of the host city or region or special reports on electric railway practices. Second only to the *Journal* was *Electric Traction*, which was first published in 1905 as the *Interurban Railway Journal*, became *Electric Traction Weekly* in 1906, and finally just *Electric Traction* in 1912. The journal is still being published as *Mass Transportation*.

Brill Magazine was a promotional journal published by car builder J.G. Brill from 1907 to 1927 that is an excellent source of information about leading electric railway systems, as well as Brill cars and equipment. The full run of *Brill Magazine* has been reprinted in recent years by Dr. Harold E. Cox (80 Virginia Terrace, Forty Fort, Pa.).

Although primarily devoted to main line railroads in North America, the trade journal *Railway Age*, which traces its origins to the *American Railroad Journal* founded in 1832, provides regular coverage of contemporary rail transit.

Proceedings and other publications of the American Street Railway Association are a valuable source of technical information about the industry. Founded in 1882, the association later became the American Electric Railway Association and, in 1933, the American Transit Association. Beginning in 1923, a committee of the Association chose the recipient of the Charles A. Coffin prize, awarded annually to a leading electric railway. Exhibits submitted by candidates for the prize formed the basis for *Electric Railway Practices* (1923-30/31), which provide a valuable source of information about modern electric railway practices of the period.

HISTORIES: A number of general histories of the street railway industry have appeared in recent years.

George W. Hilton's, *The Cable Car in America* (Berkeley, Calif., Howell-North, 1971) is the definitive work on the cable propulsion era in street railway history. John A. Miller's, *Fares, Please!* (New York, D. Appleton-Century Co., 1941) is a good general history of all forms of urban transit. A reprint was published by Dover Publications in 1960. *Trolley Car Treasury*, by Frank Rowsome, Jr., and Stephen D. Maguire (New York, McGraw-Hill Book Co., 1956) is a well-illustrated popular history of street and interurban electric railways.

ENTHUSIAST LITERATURE: Over the past half century, a number of railway enthusiast organizations have been organzied which have helped to record the history of the electric railways through their many periodicals, monographs and books.

The Electric Railroaders' Association (89 East 42nd Street, New York, NY 10017), founded in 1934, has published the monthly *Headlights* since 1939. This excellent illustrated journal provides both a variety of historical material and comprehensive coverage of current developments in the electric railway field.

The Central Electric Railfans' Association (P.O. Box 503, Chicago, Ill. 60690) was organized in 1938. Since then, C.E.R.A. has published some 125 numbered Bulletins, initially under the general title *Trolley Sparks*, devoted to the history of electric railways in the Midwestern states and elsewhere.

Interurbans, established by the late Ira L. Swett in 1943, was published as a periodical devoted to electric railways until 1948, and published a series of numbered *Specials* beginning in 1944 which were typically devoted to the history of the electric railways of a particular area, or to a specific property. *Interurbans Special* publication continues today as the book program of Interurban Press (P.O. Box 6444, Glendale, Calif. 91205), which includes titles

devoted to both electric railways and main line railroads.

While the National Railway Historical Society, founded in 1935, is largely devoted to main line railroading, the Society's monthly journal, *National Railway Bulletin*, includes regular electric railway news, and two chapters of the Society have conducted extensive electric railway history publication programs. The NRHS Connecticut Valley Chapter at Warehouse Point, Conn., published *Transportation*, a series of publications devoted to the electric railways of New England, from 1946 through 1981. The North Jersey Chapter published *The Marker*, a series of monographs about the electric railways of New Jersey, New York, and Pennsylvania from the early 1940's through the mid-1950's.

A great many more individuals, regional enthusiast groups, and other organizations have produced occasional publications devoted to the history of individual electric railway companies. For specific references to both these and the publications of the organizations noted above, the reader is referred to the Bullard and Palmer bibliographies cited at the beginning of this brief summary.

Index

236

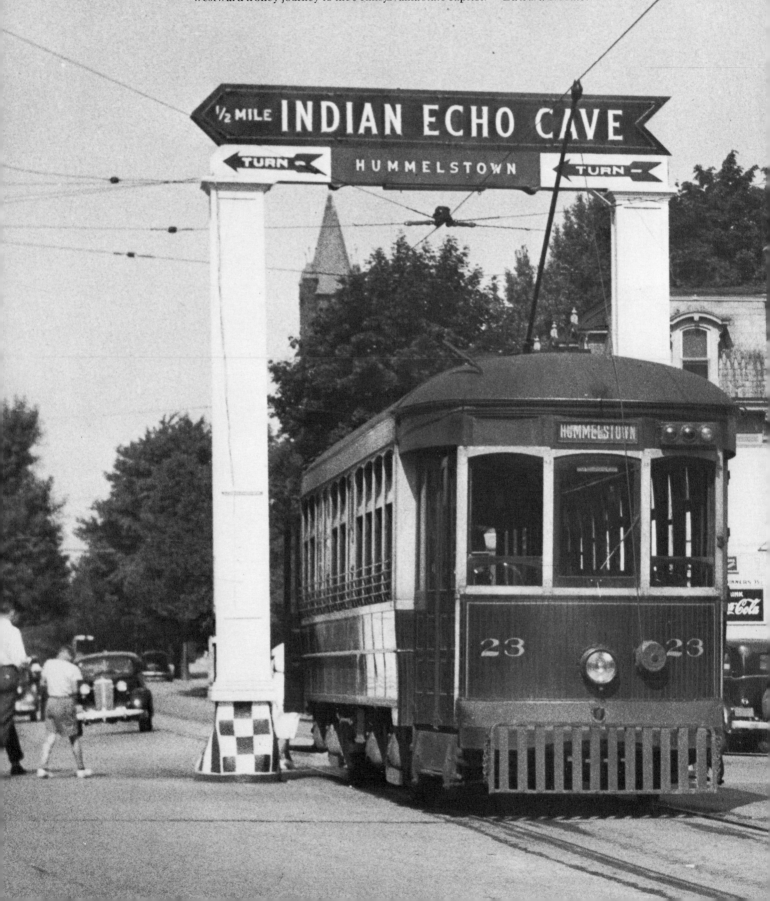

Hershey Transit No. 23, a sturdy wood semi-convertible car built by J.G. Brill in 1916, waited at the end of the line at East Main and Hanover streets in Hummelstown, Pennsylvania, to begin a return trip to Hershey in the summer of 1938. Until a connecting line of the Harrisburg Railways had been abandoned two years previous, Hershey passengers could transfer here to continue a westward trolley journey to the Pennsylvania state capitol. — *Edward S. Miller.*